ALWAYS A BULLDOG

Players, Coaches, and Fans Share Their Passion for Georgia Football

Tony Barnhart

Library of Congress Cataloging-in-Publication Data
Barnhart, Tony.
Always a Bulldog / by Tony Barnhart.
p. cm.
Includes bibliographical references.
ISBN 978-1-60078-406-4 (alk. paper)
1. University of Georgia—Football—History—Anecdotes. 2. Georgia Bulldogs (Football team)—History—Anecdotes. I. Title.
GV958.G44B37 2011
796.332'630975818—dc23
2011023786

This book is available in quantity at special discounts for your group or organization. For further information, contact:

Triumph Books
542 South Dearborn Street, Suite 750
Chicago, Illinois 60605
(312) 939-3330 | Fax (312) 663-3557
www.triumphbooks.com

Printed in U.S.A.
ISBN: 978-1-60078-406-4
Design and page production by Prologue Publishing Services, LLC
All photos courtesy of the University of Georgia unless otherwise specified
The 1980 Georgia-Florida game prayer reprinted by permission of Dan Magill

To Georgia Bulldogs everywhere
who know that the University of Georgia
is not a location on a map,
but a place in the Heart

Contents

FOREWORD

NOT VERY LONG AGO, about 700 people turned out for a big party at the Classic Center in Athens. The invitations said that we were going to celebrate my 90th birthday. But to me, even though I was the guest of honor, it was a celebration of our love for the University of Georgia.

This book is titled *Always a Bulldog*, and as far back as my memory will let me go (and some days that is better than others), I have always been a Bulldog. I cannot remember a time when Georgia was not a part of my life.

They say I was the first baby born in Athens General Hospital on January 25, 1921. Most babies were born at home back then. But my father went to the University of Georgia and was a senior in 1917 when war broke out with Germany. He returned to Athens after the war but did not graduate. He later became editor of the *Athens Banner-Herald* newspaper.

My mother was in the first women's class ever at the University of Georgia, but she quit school when I was born.

I was eight years old on October 12, 1929, the day that our beautiful Sanford Stadium was dedicated in a game against Yale, which was one of the nation's great college football powers at the time. I had received a football uniform for Christmas, and I was dressed out and ready to play. But when I got to the stadium, the game had already started. I went and found my daddy—the first Daniel Hamilton Magill—who was sitting in the press box.

I said, "Daddy! Daddy! They've already started. They've already chosen up sides."

Later on, I was a ballboy for the Georgia baseball team that was coached by John White. My job was to chase foul balls and bring them back, and then after the game I would clean up under the grandstands. Coach White couldn't pay me, but any money I found I got to keep. One day I found a silver dollar. I had never seen a silver dollar in my life and had no idea what it was. But Coach White let me keep it, and my daddy, always the frugal one, insisted that I open a bank account.

When I got to high school, they let me run the Georgia tennis courts. My job was to collect 10¢ from anybody who wanted to play there. I would keep a ledger, and at the end of the month people would come by and settle up with me. Some did. Some didn't.

When the time came for college, I went to Georgia. I could not imagine going to school anywhere else. But as my father felt called to duty in 1917, I joined the Marine Corps on the day after Pearl Harbor, December 8, 1941. They told me they wanted me to finish college before I enlisted, and in 1942 Georgia was nice enough to give me a degree. I joined the service and did my boot camp at Parris Island. In early August 1945 I learned that I was going to be sent to Okinawa to be part of the Marine division scheduled to make the first landing in Japan.

But on August 15 we learned that the Japanese had surrendered and that the war was over. I dropped to my knees and thanked God because I knew I was going to see my wife and little baby again. And then all of us got drunk for two days. It would have been longer, but 48 hours, I learned, was about as long as a man can drink and still stand up.

Dan Magill in his football uniform in 1929 before the Georgia-Yale game that dedicated Sanford Stadium. *Photo courtesy of Dan Magill*

When I got back after the war, I lived in Atlanta and worked for the *Atlanta Journal* covering high school sports. But in 1949 Coach Wallace Butts, who was also the athletics director, asked me to come back to Georgia as his assistant. I never left Georgia again. And I have never wanted to leave.

I think I am one of the luckiest people in the world because I have spent most of my life working for a place I love. In 1949 Coach Butts asked me to fill in for our sports information director, who had left. So I filled in…until the late '70s, when I handed the job over to Claude Felton, who is the best sports information director in America. He's still there and is still the best.

In 1955 Coach Butts asked me to hire a new tennis coach. I really couldn't find anybody to do the job, so I decided just to do it myself. [Magill went on to be the most successful men's tennis coach of all time, with 706 match victories, 13 SEC championships, and two national championships.]

We have enjoyed moments of great glory at the University of Georgia. I was privileged to see Charley Trippi, who finished second in the Heisman Trophy race in 1946 (he should have won it). Georgia Tech's legendary coach Bobby Dodd called Trippi the best football player he ever saw. I saw Francis Tarkenton, the son of a preacher from Athens, draw up a play in the dirt and beat Auburn in 1959. We had a downturn in the early '60s, but then came Vince Dooley—I called him St. Vincent the Merciful—as our coach in 1964. He stayed for 41 years as our coach and our athletics director and gave us the glory years of the 1980s with Herschel Walker the Goal Line Stalker.

We went 20 years without an SEC championship (1982 to 2002) but then Georgia came back—we always do—when we won the SEC title under coach Mark Richt in 2002. That is the great thing about Georgia. Like all schools, we have our down moments. We have our moments of despair. But Georgia *always* fights back.

When all those people turned out for that celebration back in February, I was reminded how strong the Bulldog family really is. Back in the 1940s and '50s we lost eight straight games to Georgia Tech, something that would be unthinkable now. I remember Coach Butts lamenting the fact that we didn't have as much money as Tech with all of their engineers and the like.

So then we were a part of starting Georgia Bulldog clubs in all 159 counties in this state. The Georgia Bulldogs are, and will always be, the Majority Party of the Empire State of the South. When the Bulldog Nation is united, it is hard to stop us.

So I have given a big portion of my life to Georgia. I hope I have made a contribution to its success on some level. But no matter what I have given to Georgia, it is just a fraction of what the university has meant to me and my family. There is no way we can ever repay the debt that we all owe our alma mater.

We came to Georgia as high school kids with no direction. We grew up here. A lot of us fell in love here. We made friends here that will last the rest of our lives.

No matter where we travel or where we live or what we accomplish, our hearts will always be in Athens at the University of Georgia.

They were the very best years of our lives. Trust me on this. I'm 90, and every day I'm at Georgia is another great day.

Daniel Hamilton Magill Jr.
Athens, Georgia
February 23, 2011

DAN MAGILL'S PRAYER AT THE 1980 GEORGIA-FLORIDA GAME

Among his many duties at Georgia, Dan Magill was called upon to deliver the invocation at the annual Jacksonville Bulldog Club breakfast on the morning of the Georgia-Florida game. On November 8, 1980, Magill delivered this prayer. On the morning of this breakfast, Georgia was undefeated and ranked No. 2 as it prepared to meet Florida at the Gator Bowl.

Lord, your Georgia Bulldog People are hunkered down on the banks of the St. John's [River] here in Jacksonville on the morn of the ninth battle of the campaign of 1980.

In case you've overlooked it, Lord, we've won all the other battles, and please don't think us greedy in wanting to win them all. We covet only what every other school covets: the national collegiate football championship! You let us come close to it in 1927, 1942, 1946, and 1971. You may not remember it, but we do.

Lord, we wish to call your attention to a couple of facts. Your devoted disciple, St. Vincent the Merciful [Georgia Coach Vince Dooley], has never had us on NCAA probation. He has been a good boy. He has sacrificed part of his hair. He has even sacrificed his wife Barbara's spleen to our noble cause, and I believe he would sacrifice even more—perhaps *her* hair—if need be.

Lord, we know you move in mysterious ways. We know that after Coach Dooley banged his head against the windshield in his car wreck that our offensive strategy greatly improved the very next game. [During the 1980 season coach Vince Dooley and his wife, Barbara, were involved in an automobile wreck. Barbara Dooley went to the hospital where her spleen was removed. Vince Dooley suffered a concussion.]

Lord, we pray that you don't let these Florida Philistines do unto us today what we have done unto them so many times. Let us "do it unto them" just one more time.

Lord, you have stripped us of the presidency [Georgia native Jimmy Carter] when you won a "big one" for the Gipper [Ronald Reagan]. Now your Georgia Bulldog People have a Dream—a Dream of being No. 1 in the land.

We want you with us today as you were last week in the fourth quarter when you gave Scott Woerner the strength to smite loose the ball and Tim Parks the vision to find it. [The week before this game Georgia led South Carolina 13–10 late in the fourth quarter. South Carolina drove deep into Georgia territory, but eventual Heisman Trophy winner George Rogers fumbled, and the Bulldogs recovered to preserve the victory.]

Oh, Lord, let our Dream come true. Free our people. Let "No. 1" ring throughout our land. From Ludowici westward to Tallapoosa....from Hiawasee down to Hahira, let No. 1 Ring!

And, Lord, if you let all these good things come to pass, we promise to be as humble as Herschel.

Amen.

Just hours after Coach Magill delivered this prayer, Georgia beat Florida 26–21 on a 93-yard pass play from Buck Belue to Lindsay Scott in the final minute of play. Georgia went on to post a 12–0 record and win the national championship.

ACKNOWLEDGMENTS

I FOUND OUT A LONG TIME AGO that the only way I could write a book was to ask for help from people who were a lot smarter than I. For this book, that list is pretty long:

• Any book involving Georgia always begins with Claude Felton, who is the best damn sports information director at any university in America. As I have said so many times, it is simply my good fortune that he happens to work at the University of Georgia. Whenever I sent him an email that started: "Claude, I need to contact..." he got right back to me with a phone number, an email address, or both. At the 11th hour of his book, I threw him a curveball and told him I wanted to talk to famed PBS broadcaster Charlayne Hunter-Gault, one of two students who broke the color barrier at Georgia in 1961. Complicating matters slightly was the fact that Ms. Hunter-Gault lives in South Africa. He was back to me in less than an hour with a contact email, and before lunchtime I had a commitment for an interview from Ms. Hunter-Gault. Claude Felton is amazing.

• I was 11 years old when Vince Dooley became Georgia's head coach in 1964. After admiring his work from afar as a student and a fan, I finally got the chance to work with him professionally as a sportswriter at the *Atlanta Journal-Constitution* starting in 1984. Later in life I had a chance to write his autobiography, and today I consider Coach Dooley and Barbara to be friends. They have helped me in ways they will never know, and for that I am lucky and extremely grateful.

• Both Greg McGarity and I graduated in 1976 from Georgia's Henry W. Grady School of Journalism. I went into newspapers. Greg went into athletics administration, which is yet another reason why Greg is smarter than I. Last August, after 18 years of working at the University of Florida, Greg McGarity came home as the new athletics director at Georgia. He was very supportive of this project, and I appreciate it.

• All of us who try to write books about Georgia and its incredible football history stand on the shoulders of Loran Smith. He blazed the path and set the standard. He has always been an incredible resource and was again so very helpful when I needed him for this project. Loran is one of those special people who will do anything he can to support and help Georgia. I truly appreciate his help and friendship over the years.

• I must again thank the one, the only Dan Magill. He agreed to write the foreword to this book, which also includes an essay about him by Greg McGarity. It is still not enough to honor the man who is, and will always be, the greatest Bulldog of them all. He just turned 90 years old, but his spirit, the Bulldog spirit, is forever young.

• The Georgia football lettermen, as always, were generous with their time and gracious in their spirit. One of the goals with this book was to get as many different "voices" into the storytelling as possible. I remember calling Hugh Nall and asking him to retell the story of the infamous "Seagraves Party" of 1980. We laughed nonstop for 45 minutes. You will laugh, too, when you read it in chapter 4.

• I owe a special debt of gratitude to my classmates and fellow staff members of the *Red & Black*, the student newspaper at the University of Georgia. From 1974 to 1976 I can promise you that nobody—but nobody—enjoyed their college experience more than we did. Their friendship made me want to include chapter 1, "Memories of Athens," in the book. Here is just a partial list of the *R&B* crowd: Mary Kay Andrews (aka, Kathy Hogan Trochek), Deborah Blum, Steve Burns, Bill Durrence, Melita Easters, Bill Eichenberger, Rick Franzman, Lynn Plankenhorn Hood, Jimmy Johnson, Dan Kibler, Miriam Pace, Bob Longino, Nancy Rogers, Minla Shields, Patricia Templeton. Thanks for the memories, guys.

• None of this would be possible without the three most important people in my life: my wife, Maria; my daughter, Sara Barnhart Fletcher; and my mother, Sara Lord. Never has one man been so blessed with the support of three incredibly strong and intelligent women. On August 14, 2011, Maria and I will celebrate 34 years of marriage, which proves that when it comes to wives, all of us in the sports business have definitely outkicked our coverage.

And finally, I want to thank all of the Georgia alumni who were so willing to share their memories with me: Lee Epting, Swann Seiler, Sonny Seiler, Walter Corish, and Derek Dooley (UGA law school) are just a few who gave of their time to make this book the best it could be.

At the end of the day, *Always a Bulldog* is a celebration of a special place and some collective memories of what, for most of us, were some of the best years of our lives.

Thank you all for making this celebration possible.

INTRODUCTION: ONCE *a* BULLDOG

I WAS 10 YEARS OLD WHEN MY MOTHER received a mail-order package from Rich's department store in Atlanta. Inside the package were two sweatshirts. One had the familiar face of UGA, the mascot of the University of Georgia. The other had the gold "T" of Georgia Tech.

I was 15 months older than my brother, David, so I got to choose first.

I chose Georgia.

I certainly didn't know it at the time, but it was a choice that would impact the rest of my life. Because from that moment on, Georgia was my school and the Bulldogs were my team. The die had been cast. There was no going back. I might change political parties. I might change professions. I might change churches or my favorite music or my style of clothes. But, by God, I was not going to change schools. No sir. I was locked in for life.

As the late, great Lewis Grizzard once told me, you really don't choose to be a Georgia Bulldog any more than you choose your parents or what color eyes you have. We are Americans by birth and southerners by the grace of God. But we become Bulldogs only through divine intervention. Lewis believed that to be a Bulldog was to be one of God's Chosen People.

He wasn't kidding.

Somebody was sure looking out for me when it came to being a Bulldog. This stuff doesn't just happen by accident.

I grew up in Union Point, Georgia (population about 1,500), which is located just a half-hour away from Athens in Greene County. Because of that proximity, a lot of time was spent in the Classic City. After the theaters went out of business in Union Point and Greensboro, Athens became the closest place we could take a date to see a movie.

Thanks to Mrs. Lois Cheves, mother of Becky (one of my early heartthrobs), I was able to attend my first Georgia football game on September 25, 1965. I watched the Bulldogs beat Vanderbilt 24–10, and I remember that Preston Ridlehuber returned a punt for a touchdown. I remember the bands, the pretty girls, the colors, the pretty girls, and the energy in that stadium. And did I mention the pretty girls?

There was a big reason for the excitement in Sanford Stadium that day. The week before, Georgia had upset Alabama, the defending national champions, 18–17 in what was only the 12th game as head coach for Vince Dooley, who would go on to win 201 games at Georgia and be inducted into the College Football Hall of Fame.

The week after the Vanderbilt game, Georgia went on the road and beat Michigan 15–7 in a huge upset. When the team returned home, the tiny airport in Athens was jammed with more than 10,000 fans.

"It was one of the most incredible sights I had ever seen," Coach Dooley said. "They considered us to be conquering heroes. We had gone up North and conquered Michigan. And now we were returning home to the South. It was really remarkable."

"I was sitting up front with the pilots when we returned to Athens that night," said quarterback Kirby Moore. "We couldn't believe it. It was over 40 years ago, and I still get chills thinking about it."

It was, in retrospect, the perfect time to become a Bulldog.

Thanks to Billy and Mary Jean Ashley, the parents of my best friend, Eric, I spent a lot of Saturdays at Sanford Stadium watching the Bulldogs. They would invite me along to keep Eric company and to share their tailgate and enjoy a beautiful fall afternoon. And there are no fall afternoons quite as beautiful as the ones in Athens.

The Ashleys were very good to me, to the point where I began calling Mary Jean Ashley my Momma Jean. When we lost Momma Jean in June of 2009, I spent a lot of time thinking about those trips to Athens and the impact they had on my life.

I learned that being a Georgia Bulldog was not just about where you choose to go to college. It is so much bigger than that. It ultimately defines who you are and who you want to be.

Here is what I mean: in high school and later as a student at Georgia, I went to a lot of football games in Sanford Stadium. But on June 10, 1976, I made the most important visit of all as I walked into Sanford Stadium to receive my degree in journalism from the University of Georgia.

I became the first member of my family to ever graduate from college. My mother was there. My future wife, Maria, was there. It was a proud day. Whatever success I have had in my life and my career began at Georgia. It gave me a chance to grow up (and, Lord knows, I needed all the help I could get in that area) and to develop a vision of what I wanted to do with my life.

Almost 30 years later, in May of 2005, Maria and I were back in Sanford Stadium to watch our daughter, Sara Catherine, graduate summa cum laude with highest honors (obviously she has her mother's looks and her mother's brains) from Georgia. Three years later we returned to campus as Sara Catherine received her degree from the University of Georgia School of Law. She was the president of the Double Dawg Society, a group of UGA law students who also received their undergraduate degrees at Georgia. She is a Bulldog through and through.

How cool is that?

I've lost track of the number of relatives who either went to Georgia or have some ties to the university. My late father-in-law, Jaime Villegas, taught at the University of Georgia.

I tell you my personal story knowing that I represent just one of thousands upon thousands of people who have an emotional bond with the University of Georgia that transcends football—although football is a very important part of it—and is lifelong. It is for those people that I wanted to write *Always a Bulldog.*

I wanted to put together a list of the people, places, and things that all of us need to know in order to truly call ourselves Bulldogs. It is a shared history of great games, great moments, great coaches and players, and just plain folks who have made the Georgia Bulldogs, as the great Dan Magill still says, "The Majority Party of the Empire State of the South."

So many memories, so little time:

• Onion rings from the Varsity, an ice cream cone from Hodgson's Pharmacy, and a cheeseburger wrapped in waxed paper from Allen's World Famous Hamburgers. Now that was some good eatin'. In chapter 1, "Memories of Athens," we look at those places and others where we gathered with friends and dared to dream about the future.

• Sitting on the tracks on the east end of Sanford Stadium. That great tradition ended in 1980. I can't believe we've had an entire generation that did not get a chance to sit on the tracks. In chapter 3, "The Traditions," former radio legend Larry Munson tells of his experience with the "Track People."

• Georgia received a visit from Prince Charles on October 22, 1977. Of course, Georgia lost the game to Kentucky, aka, the best team money could buy, 33–0.

• Listening to the Redcoat Band's postgame concert at Sanford Stadium. I still get chills when the Redcoats play "Tara's Theme" from *Gone with the Wind* as the shadows begin to creep into the stadium on a cool autumn day.

• The "Blackout" game with Auburn in 2007. It was one of two games where I *know* the energy in Sanford Stadium literally overwhelmed Georgia's opponent. The other was Georgia's 21–0 win over Alabama in 1976.

Is this book a definitive list of everything you need to know to call yourself a Bulldog? Of course not. The history and tradition at Georgia is so wide and so deep that this effort barely scratches the surface. Just call it one man's attempt to say thank you to a place that changed his life and the lives of so many others.

Let's just say that what we have here is a sliver of information to spark your memory and to hopefully bring a smile to your face. I encourage you to mentally add your own personal memories to this list.

For, at the end of the day, it is our memories of Georgia that matter most. It is why, no matter what we do or where we go, in our hearts we are always a Bulldog.

I hope you enjoy it.

chapter 1

MEMORIES *of* ATHENS

GET A GROUP OF UNIVERSITY OF GEORGIA alumni together and sooner or later—regardless of their age or when they graduated—the subject will turn to Athens and how, without question, it is the best damn college town in America.

Every generation of Georgia graduates has its own set of special memories. For my generation it was Zoo Night on the deck of T.K. Harty's, hanging out on the deck at O'Malley's, or watching a sporting event on the big-screen TV at the Fifth Quarter Lounge.

A lot of my time at Georgia was spent with my fellow staff members of the *Red & Black*, the student newspaper. There was many a night, after we had put the paper to bed in our little office the corner of Milledge and Springdale (where we kept cold beer in the Coke machine), the production staff would adjourn to a nearby apartment (Myrna Court) I shared with Bill Durrence, and, for lack of a better term, we would enthusiastically celebrate life.

I am proud to say that more than 35 years later, Bill Durrence and a number of those folks from the *Red & Black* are still my friends. I wish I could mention every one of them here, but among that group of very talented people, we have a Pulitzer Prize winner (Deborah Blum), a best-selling author (Kathy Hogan Trocheck, aka Mary Kay Andrews), and an Episcopal priest (Patricia Templeton). I've been working with photographers all my life, and Durrence is still the best one I've ever met.

The author with his Georgia classmates at a *Red & Black* reunion in 2010. Seated (from left): Nancy Rogers, Kathy Hogan Trocheck (aka Mary Kay Andrews), Deborah Blum. Standing (from left): Steve Burns, Minla Shields, Tony Barnhart, Rick Franzman, Jimmy Johnson, Rev. Patricia Templeton, Lynn Plankenhorn Hood, Bill Durrence. *Photo courtesy of Steve Burns*

Yes, we all went to Georgia to get an education. Most of us did get our formal education and the degree that comes with it. But we also got another education when it comes to making friends that will last a lifetime. Many of the most lasting memories we have of our time at Georgia were gatherings with friends at restaurants, clubs, and other assorted watering holes when all of us were blissfully naïve and ridiculously poor.

Here are just a few of those places where we made those memories. A lot of them—most of them, in fact—no longer exist in Athens, which only adds to their charm. And for every one that I list here, there are 100 more that could have been in this chapter. It is not a definitive list and does not pretend to be.

Yes, there is a common theme here of eating and drinking (usually both). But it is *who* we did the eating and drinking with that was so important at the time and gives us memories we still enjoy today.

This is just one man's trip down Memory Lane in Athens. Feel free to add your own stops.

Allen's World Famous Hamburgers

by Zell Miller

Every college town has a favorite place to get a hot cheeseburger and a cold beer. But very few towns have a place like Allen's World Famous Hamburgers.

The year was 1956, and I had just enrolled at Georgia after serving in the Marine Corps. I had a wife and two babies. So I needed to make some money while I was going to school, and jobs were pretty hard to come by.

Allen Saine was the owner, and he was willing to give me a job. He gave me $7 a night and all the hamburgers I could eat and all the milk I could drink.

The great thing about Allen's was it was like that bar in the TV show *Cheers*. It was a place where everybody knew your name. There were folks who came in there every day. It was their place to hang out.

There were no frills with Allen's. We served the hamburgers in waxed paper and put some pickles and onions in there in case you wanted them. The place just never changed, and there was a certain comfort in that.

When I got into politics, I decided I would go back to Allen's where I got started to launch some of my campaigns. Putting on that white robe again reminded me where I had come from. I was fortunate to become the lieutenant governor of Georgia for 16 years, was governor of the state for eight years [1991 to 1999], and then a United States senator. But I can promise you that I never forgot where I came from. I will always have great memories about Allen's for as long as I live.

Zell Miller, who retired as a United States senator in 2005, lives in his beloved Young Harris, Georgia.

NOTES ON ALLEN'S

Allen's opened in 1955 on Prince Avenue in the Normaltown section of Athens and served as a popular watering hole for students and locals alike. It was also a good place to hear live music. Allen's was a beer joint and damned proud of it.

Allen's was thought to be lost when the doors closed in 2003, a victim to the burgeoning restaurant and club scene in downtown Athens. But two Georgia graduates, Mike Hammond and Hilt Moree, brought it back with the original sign and a lot of the memorabilia. They moved it to Hawthorne Avenue about a mile from the original location.

"We get a lot of former students who want to sit at the bar, drink a cold one, and go down memory lane," said Moree. "It is a tough business, but it is a labor of love."

For more on Allen's, go to www.allensbarandgrill.com.

BARNETT'S NEWS STAND

For 65 years Barnett's News Stand was located at 147 College Avenue, just a few steps away from the university's arch. And for all that time Barnett's served as *the* place where students and locals alike could go to get the real pulse of what was going on in Athens.

There was nothing fancy about Barnett's. It was a throwback to another time and sold a little bit of everything. If you wanted an out-of-town newspaper like the Sunday *New York Times*, Barnett's had it. If you wanted a magazine about snowboarding in Utah, the only place in Athens you were going to find it was at Barnett's News Stand. If you wanted to the latest best-selling book, Barnett's would have it first. And if you wanted the latest gossip about Athens and the university or local politics, somebody at Barnett's would know the inside skinny.

Barnett's first opened its doors in 1942, and in 1978 Midge Gray and her husband, Tommy Easterling, bought the business. Gray operated the business until May 18, 2008. By then, such mom-and-pop operations simply could not compete in an Internet world where the larger bookstores could sell for significantly lower prices.

It also hurt Midge when the soul of Barnett's News Stand, long-time manager Carl Smith, passed away in 2006.

Gray tried find a buyer to keep the business alive but eventually leased the space to the owner of a women's apparel shop, The Red Dress Boutique, which is still located there.

"He [Carl Smith] was my right-hand man; we worked side by side for 20 years," Gray told the *Athens Banner-Herald* in 2008 just before she closed the doors. "And we were pretty good friends."

Hodgson's Pharmacy

by Harold B. Hodgson III

My dad, Harold B. "Doc" Hodgson Jr., opened Hodgson's Pharmacy in 1956 on a simple premise: take care of your customers and your employees. Treat them like family, and they will take care of you.

He believed in personal service. He believed our customers were our friends. He began the business by selling ice cream cones for a nickel. He didn't make any money doing that, but he did it in order to get the kids in here. And once the kids were in the store, he believed that the parents would stay and have their prescriptions filled. He was right, of course.

I could tell you so many stories about how Dad would get out of bed in the middle of the night if a customer really needed a prescription. Some of our older customers could not get out of their homes right away. He would make sure that the medicine got to them, even if we had to take it right up to their door.

When we had candy left over from Valentine's Day, he made sure it got to the firemen and the policemen. He believed in taking care of them and making sure they were customers for life.

I can't tell you how many young people he helped. But people helped him when he was coming along, and he felt he was supposed to return that favor.

In June of 2009 we moved from our original location in Five Points to another building just a few steps away. The old place was huge, and the way our business is changing, we just didn't need all that space. There is no question that the big boys in the drug store business are making it tough for us to compete. There are times when I feel like our days are numbered.

But we have so many good memories here. The Georgia cheerleaders still come by on game days. We have some special things on the wall to honor them, and coach Mike Castronis, who worked with the cheerleaders, was one of the finest men I've ever met.

We have pictures of every one of the national championship teams in women's gymnastics. This was a home for them.

We are still here, and today we sell ice cream cones for $1. It's still a pretty good value. The kids who were so much a part of this place as students have left Georgia, but many of them still come back with their children and in some cases their grandchildren. That is the most gratifying thing of all. There is something about Athens that keeps pulling people back.

"Doc" Hodgson died on February 28, 2008. The store is still managed by his son, Harold B. Hodgson III.

R.E.M., The B-52s, and the Classic City Music Scene

April 6, 1980, was Easter Sunday and one of the biggest days in the history of the University of Georgia.

It was the day that a highly recruited football player from Wrightsville, Georgia, decided he was going to sign to play for the Georgia Bulldogs. His name was Herschel Walker. That fall, the Georgia football team would go 12–0 and win the 1980 national championship. With Walker as its star player, Georgia would win three straight SEC championships. So April 6, 1980, is a big day on the historical calendar for Georgia.

But April 5, 1980, is also huge day in the history of Athens. That night, at an old church on Oconee Street, a bunch guys who thought they had a pretty decent band played their first gig for the birthday party of a friend, Kathleen O'Brien. She lived in a renovated part of the building. In fact, to get to the old sanctuary where the music was being played, you had to go through O'Brien's closet.

That band became R.E.M.

Every university town has some kind of music scene. But in the 1970s and 1980s Athens became the launching pad for some of the best music ever produced.

The B-52s played their first-ever gig in Athens on Valentine's Day 1977 at a house party on North Milledge Avenue. Not long after that they became one of the hottest bands to play the club circuit in New York.

And from the success of The B-52s and R.E.M. came one great band after another that called Athens home. It was a creative atmosphere that spawned bands like Love Tractor, Pylon, and Widespread Panic. And they performed in venues that became legendary, like the 40 Watt Club, the Uptown Lounge, the B&L Warehouse, and the Rockfish Palace.

In 2003 *Rolling Stone* magazine called Athens the No. 1 college music scene in the country.

During his time at Georgia, George Fontaine, class of 1976, was the social chairman of Phi Delta Theta fraternity and was thus charged with booking bands for parties. He had a lot of good ones to choose from.

"There was just something about Athens that drew creative people who wanted to show what they could do through music," said Fontaine, who later helped transform the old Georgia Theatre into a music venue. He went on to establish his own record label, New West Records. "People talk about Austin [Texas] as a great music town, but Athens is different in the way the campus melts into downtown. It's just different.

"It was the happiest time of my life, and if I could, I would move back to Athens tomorrow."

Neil Williamson, now the sports marketing director of WSB Radio in Atlanta, was the general manager of WUOG, the campus FM station, in the late '70s. He saw a lot of great musical acts come through Athens.

"I remember standing outside and looking at the marquee on the Georgia Theatre one day," said Williamson. "The upcoming acts were Taj Mahal, a great blues singer; the Art Ensemble of Chicago, a wonderful avant-garde jazz band; David Allan Coe;

and The Police. They were all coming to Athens in the space of just a few days!

"I was on the concert committee at Georgia for four years, and we got vilified by the *Red & Black* for bringing in acts that weren't big enough stars. We brought in Jimmy Buffett, Boston, Jackson Browne, Hall & Oates, Kenny Rogers, Dottie West, and Dolly Parton. Not bad."

The Murder of T.K. Harty

T.K. Harty's was one of the most popular student hangouts in Athens during the 1970s. The bar was known for its huge outdoor deck and a very narrow corridor where the ladies had to walk to get to the powder room. It was also known for "Zoo Night" when, for $10, students got a plastic cup and all the beer they could drink.

T.K. Harty's was located in The Station, a former railroad depot on Hoyt Street that became the closest thing Athens had to an entertainment district in the 1970s.

The owner, Ted "T.K." Harty, was only 29 years old but was a classic entrepreneur who had a vision. He was the first bar owner in Athens to build a deck, and he believed he could recreate his success in college towns around the country.

"Your first impression of Ted was that he was a Yankee. He was abrupt," said Athens caterer Lee Epting, who owned The Station complex back in the 1970s. "But we got along okay and later became friends. I wanted him to fashion the bar after one I saw in Heidelberg [Germany]. It would be a place for the students to hang out and meet their professors for a cold beer. Plus, I thought he had the perfect name for a bar."

With an agreement from Harty, Epting began to build the rest of The Station complex. He started an upscale restaurant, the

Valdosta Dining Car. Then he entered into an agreement with John Mooney, who wanted to start a pizza place called "Somebody's Pizza."

"What we found out later was that John had worked for Everybody's Pizza near Emory [University in Atlanta] and worked there just long enough to learn their business and their recipes," Epting said. "That turned out to be a sign."

Epting laid out the ground rules on how everybody in the complex would work together.

"T.K. would anchor one end and sell draft beer," said Epting. "John would sell beer in cans and be anchored in the other end of the complex. I would have the upscale restaurant in the middle. There was enough business for everybody, and we would all serve our specific clientele."

But Mooney, said Epting, did not stick with the plan.

"He would go down to T.K.'s and start giving away tokens for nickel beers and soliciting T.K.'s customers," said Epting. "Every day I was getting a call from one of them complaining about the other."

Epting ultimately decided that he wanted to get out of The Station complex and, because Harty was an original investor in the project, Epting sold the lease to Harty. And it wasn't long before Harty served Mooney with an eviction notice.

On August 30, 1977, Harty was found slumped over his desk in his Athens home. He had been shot in the back of the head, execution style.

Mooney was charged with hiring Elmo Florence, a local electrician, to execute Harty. Florence was convicted of Harty's murder and served 30 years in prison before being granted parole in December 2007. Mooney was also convicted and sentenced to life in prison.

Mooney escaped from a minimum security prison in 1980, and there were rumors that he was dead. But in April 1989 the television series *Unsolved Mysteries* aired a program on the T.K. Harty murder and publicized the fact that Mooney was still at large. He was recaptured several months later and still remains in prison.

The Fifth Quarter Lounge

Okay, this one is personal.

Located out on the Atlanta Highway, the Fifth Quarter Lounge was one of the first places in Athens to buy a big-screen projection television and draw huge crowds for sporting events. In 1975 I watched two of the biggest sporting moments in my young life while at the Fifth Quarter.

The first came on October 21, 1975, in the sixth game of the World Series between the Boston Red Sox and the Cincinnati Reds. The game went into extra innings tied at 6–6. It was a Tuesday night, and part of my brain said I needed to get back to my apartment because of class the next day. But as the game went into the 10th, the 11th, and finally the bottom of the 12th inning, it became clear that I had to stay. No one left the Fifth Quarter because they knew there was going to be a dramatic ending to the game.

The place was packed, and so we could not hear the play-by-play call from Dick Stockton on NBC. All we could see was Carlton Fisk of the Red Sox as he dipped his shoulder to hit a low pitch from the Reds' Pat Darcy. The NBC cameraman had the presence of mind to keep the lens on Fisk (although later he would say he was distracted by a rat at his location so he didn't move the camera) as he waved his arms and implored the ball to stay fair as it hugged the left-field line of Fenway Park. When the ball went out of the park for a home run, the Fifth Quarter went nuts as Fisk happily ran around the bases.

We didn't know it at the time, but Fisk's home run would become one of the defining moments in the history of major league baseball. It tied the 1975 World Series at three games each. The next night, however, Cincinnati won 4–3 to win the championship.

The next big moment at the Fifth Quarter came just 17 days later, on November 8, 1975. It was the annual Georgia-Florida game in Jacksonville, and I was stuck back in Athens. But instead of watching the game on TV at my apartment, I went down to the Fifth Quarter with a bunch of friends from the *Red & Black*. Again, the place was packed. We couldn't hear the TV, but it didn't matter. We could see it and we could *feel* it.

Georgia trailed in the game 7–3 with only 3:24 left. The Bulldogs had the ball but were 80 yards away from the Florida goal line. It looked like a long, fun day at the Fifth Quarter would end in disappointment for our Bulldogs.

But miracles do happen. All season long Georgia had been running a play where tight end Richard Appleby was given the ball to run around the right end. In fact, Georgia had run the play earlier in the game. This time, Appleby took a handoff from quarterback Matt Robinson, but instead of running the ball, Appleby stopped and threw an 80-yard touchdown pass to Gene Washington. The roof almost came off the place. Georgia won the game 10–7 and eventually went to the Cotton Bowl.

The Fifth Quarter was eventually purchased by Craig Hertwig, who was an All-America tackle for Georgia in 1974. Sadly, it is no longer with us.

THE LAST RESORT

Somewhere out there, perhaps hanging on the wall of a fraternity house in Athens, is a contract between Steve Martin and the Last Resort.

"It was framed and hanging in the restaurant over the cash register, and one night, I am told, somebody just took it off the wall," said Jaamy Zarnegar, the manager of the Last Resort for the past 19 years. "I'm sure they didn't know what they had. It's probably somewhere in Athens, or they may have thrown it out not knowing what it was."

"My wife was there the night Steve Martin played," said Jimmy Nivens, who was the manager of the Last Resort in 1977 and 1978. "He led the crowd out into the street and kept performing with an arrow though his head."

Martin was among the many talented young performers who played the Last Resort in Athens in the late 1960s and '70s. The club opened in 1966 on 184 Clayton Street, strictly as a music venue. Legend has it the club got its name because it was down the street from three different finance companies. If you got turned down by all three, the bar was your "last resort."

The Last Resort was owned for a while by legendary Athens musician Terry "Mad Dog" Melton.

Among the performers who worked there were Tom Waits, Greg Allman, David Allan Coe, The B-52s (who made their first public appearance there), John Lee Hooker, Doc and Merle Watson, Loudon Wainwright III, Randall Bramlett, and Jimmy Buffett.

"I saw the contract we had for Jimmy Buffett," Zarnegar said. "He got $200 for three nights—in cash, up front."

Before the Last Resort, the music venues in Athens consisted mostly of local bands playing at fraternity and sorority houses. But the Last Resort provided a home for a bunch of talented people as the Athens music scene began to take off in the 1970s and '80s.

"We signed a lot of artists, like Tom Waits and David Allan Coe (who would arrive on a Harley with a couple of tattooed bikers),

The Last Resort, whose signature mural is an Athens landmark, was a music venue in the '60s and '70s. Today it is one of the most popular restaurants in the Classic City. *Photo courtesy of The Last Resort*

who were also working in Atlanta and just liked the Last Resort," said Nivens. "The place had an incredible run, but nothing lasts forever."

Nivens worked for Lynn Miller, who bought the club and expanded it. Unfortunately, the crowds did not come to fill the larger venue on a regular basis.

The club closed as a music venue in the mid-1980s, and then new owner Melissa Clegg reopened the doors in August of 1992 as an upscale restaurant. Today it remains one of the favorite spots for students, former students, and locals. Clegg brought in Zarnegar as a partner/manager and turned the restaurant over to him in 1999.

"We have groups of sorority sisters who come back to Athens with the intention of going to the football games but never leave the restaurant," said Zarnegar. "They are having too good of a time. I know parents who came here as students and then come back with their children who are now students. They say that this will always be their favorite place. We now have several generations who love the Last Resort. We love what we do here. You hit on a restaurant like this once in a lifetime."

Steve Martin would be proud. And he would also get the crab cakes, which are the best in Athens.

The Iron Horse

In 1954 Abbott Pattison was the artist in residence at the University of Georgia and felt the UGA campus, so steeped in traditional art, could use a piece of modern sculpture. So he created *The Iron Horse*, a two-ton, 12-foot piece of iron that had been formed (loosely) in the shape of a horse.

The horse was placed in front of Reed Hall and, to put it mildly, the reaction was instantly and overwhelmingly negative.

Students would put hay in the horse's mouth and pile manure behind it. They would spray paint it and tip it over on a regular basis. Finally campus officials had to put the horse's feet in concrete. But the students simply would not embrace *The Iron Horse*.

Finally the school gave up and moved the horse to a secret location. In 1958 L.C. Curtis, a professor of horticulture, offered to give the horse a home in one of the fields on his farm located in Greene County, about 18 miles from Athens. It has remained there ever since.

Today *The Iron Horse* is located on Highway 15 between Greensboro and Athens. For Georgia fans traveling to the football games on Saturday, it is an indicator that Athens—The Promised Land—is not far away.

"*The Iron Horse* is so important to me. It was so much a part of my life and my childhood. We would drive from Savannah to the games in Athens, and daddy liked to go the back way. And when we got close to Athens, the children would try to be the first to say that they saw *The Iron Horse*. Daddy [Frank "Sonny" Seiler] would tell us that it was the horse's job to guard Athens. Today I drive with Daddy to the games early on Friday because I have things to do with the university. And I still get excited to see the horse because it means that I'm almost there." —Swann Seiler, former president, UGA Alumni Association.

The Downtown Varsity

Once upon a time there were two locations of the Varsity in Athens. The big location at the intersection of Milledge and Broad still proudly stands as a testament to gastronomic bliss. There is still no better way to get a real taste of Athens and game day at Georgia than to get a chili dog, an order of onion rings, and a PC (plain chocolate) at the Varsity.

But there once was a smaller, more intimate Varsity downtown, right on the corner of Broad and College Avenue, just across from the arch that serves as the entrance to the University of Georgia. It was there for 46 years and would serve several generations of UGA students before it closed in December 1978.

Georgia's North Campus is now mostly administration buildings and classrooms, but back in the day there were a bunch of dormitories on that end of the campus, and the Downtown Varsity would stay open late to satisfy the insatiable hunger of the students.

The original Varsity was on the corner of Broad and College Avenue, but closed in December 1978.

When the dormitories were moved to the south side of campus, it became easier for the students to eat along the fast food places on Baxter Street. At the time, owner Frank Gordy told reporters that "it broke my heart" to have to close what had become an Athens landmark.

To his credit, Gordy held off closing the Downtown Varsity as long as he could. He announced it on December 1, 1978, the day before the last game of the season against Georgia Tech. The restaurant finally closed its doors on December 20.

"What I will never forget is that there was a room off to the side of the main eating area where they had put a TV," said Walter Corish, a 1965 graduate from Savannah. "I was walking past the Downtown Varsity on November 22, 1963. I saw people gathering around the TV inside. I stepped in and learned that President [John F. Kennedy] had been shot."

OTHER GREAT MEMORIES OF ATHENS

Here are just 20 favorite memories gathered from UGA alumni. It could have been more than 100.

1—DIRK AND TONY AT THE FROG POND LOUNGE, RAMADA INN, AND THE ACROPOLIS LOUNGE AT THE HOLIDAY INN. Dirk Howell and Tony Brown were two UGA students who began singing together in 1973. The two split in 1976, and Dirk still resides in Athens and plays with his own Dirk Howell Band. Tony Brown went to Nashville to chase his dreams in country music and became a success as T. Graham Brown.

2—BUBBER'S BAIT SHOP. No bait was sold at Bubber's. "Bubber didn't sell beer on credit, but he would hold a check for as long as you needed him to," said George Fontaine. "That's my definition of an optimist."

3—O'MALLEY'S. A great bar with a great multilevel deck. It became famous for its Drink N' Drown Nights.

4—STEVERINO'S ON FIVE POINTS. Many a Thursday and Friday class was skipped to enjoy sitting outside at Steverino's.

5—THE DEARLY DEPARTED HARRY BISSETT'S ON BROAD STREET.

6—SHRIMP BOATS ON BAXTER. Nice folks who really catered to students.

7—Harry's Tavern on Five Points. This was the favorite hangout of Georgia tennis coach Dan Magill.

8—The Western Sizzlin' on Baxter. When you had a date but not a lot of money, you could take her to get a decent steak at Western Sizzlin'.

9—The largest streak in history. For a few unforgettable weeks in 1973 and 1974, streaking—running through campus with no clothes, no I'm not kidding—was the craze on college campuses. Of course, the largest collective streak in history belongs to the students at the University of Georgia. On March 7, 1974, a total of 1,543 people streaked through campus.

10—Effie's. One of the most famous houses of ill repute in the world was finally shut down (along with other similar establishments) by the city of Athens in 1972. Effie's was finally burned to the ground by the Athens Fire Department in 1977.

11—The Swamp Guinea. A wonderful eatery for fried fish and barbecue located about 10 miles east of Athens in Madison County. Their motto: "Come pick a bone with us!"

12—The Mayflower Restaurant. It opened in 1948 and has been operated by the Vaughn family since 1963. It is going strong and remains a favorite of students and locals for breakfast.

13—The B&L Warehouse. A lot of brain cells were lost at the B&L. There were always great bands and great Thursday night parties. Fittingly, the building on Oconee Street now houses the University of Georgia campus police.

14—Charlie Williams' "Pinecrest Lodge." This was *the* place to go on the Friday night before a UGA home game. It began serving in 1929 on Whitehall Road and remained there until it closed in 2004.

15—Gigi's Restaurant on Baxter Street. This was basically the first real Italian sit-down place in Athens. For those who came

The Swamp Guinea provided a lot of food for just a little money. These advertisements, taken from the *Red & Black* student newspaper, ran in 1967 and 1978.

from smaller towns close to Athens, it was a real treat. The architect was Robert Green, who was an apprentice of Frank Lloyd Wright. Today it is a Chinese restaurant.

16—THE DAVIS HOUSE. They had an all-you-could-eat southern buffet for $2.95. For students on a budget (and who wasn't?) it was a life-saver.

17—POSS'S BARBEQUE. This place was located on the Atlanta Highway at Timothy Road. Big Bob Poss was one of the funniest people I ever met. Big Bob and his son, Little Bobby, both played for Georgia and made it a hangout for football players.

18—THE PEDDLER STEAK HOUSE. They would bring the meat to your table and cut it the thickness that you wanted.

19—THE GRILL. A downtown staple for over 20 years, this '50s-style diner stays open 24 hours. After a night at the clubs, I'm told that the homemade fries sure do taste good.

20—BETWEEN THE HEDGES. A downstairs club located below Allen's in Normaltown.

chapter 2

THE 100 MOST IMPORTANT MOMENTS *in* GEORGIA FOOTBALL HISTORY

WHENEVER YOU ATTEMPT TO PUT TOGETHER a list like this, it is inevitable that you are going to leave out some moments that were special. So if there is a moment that is special to you that is missing from this list, I beg your forgiveness. But here are 100 moments that you should know.

January 30, 1892
Georgia plays its first-ever football game against Mercer. The game took place on a field behind New College on campus. Georgia won 50–0. It is worth noting that back then touchdowns only counted for four points. Legend has it that Georgia actually scored 60 points in the game, but that the scorekeeper had left his post for a while to buy a bottle of booze and did not record the additional points.

February 20, 1892
Georgia and Auburn meet in football for the first time at Atlanta's Piedmont Park. The game was organized by professors Charles

Herty of Georgia and George Petrie of Auburn, who had learned about football when the two were students together at Johns Hopkins. The game, won by Auburn 10–0, started the oldest continuous football rivalry in the South.

November 26, 1896

Georgia, coached by a future Hall of Famer in Pop Warner, defeats Auburn, coached by another future Hall of Famer, John Heisman, 12–6, in Atlanta. It gave Georgia its first-ever undefeated season (4–0). Warner coached Georgia for two seasons, 1895 and 1896.

October 30, 1897

Georgia player Richard Vonalbade "Von" Gammon suffers serious injuries in a game against Virginia that was played in Atlanta. He died the next morning at Grady Memorial Hospital. In response to the tragic death, the Georgia state legislature passed a bill making it illegal to play football at state institutions of higher learning. But Gammon's mother, Rosalind, implored Governor W.Y. Atkinson not to sign the bill because her son loved football so much and would not want to see it end because of his death. Atkinson did not sign the bill, and football continued at Georgia and the rest of the schools in the state. Today a plaque honoring Gammon's death hangs in Georgia's Butts-Mehre Heritage Hall.

1913

Bob McWhorter, who scored 61 touchdowns in four seasons, becomes the first Georgia player to be named All-America.

November 14, 1925

Georgia plays state rival Georgia Tech for the first time since 1916. Georgia did not field a team in 1917–1918 because of World War

II. The series was supposed to resume in 1919, but a dispute between the schools severed athletics relations between the two. Georgia Tech won the 1925 game 3–0 in Atlanta.

December 3, 1927

Georgia's undefeated (9–0) and No. 1–ranked team, led by ends Tom Nash and Chick Shiver, needed just one more win over Georgia Tech in Atlanta to claim a spot in the Rose Bowl. It had rained all night before the game, and Georgia Tech officials (allegedly) further watered the field to slow down the talented Georgia team. In a sea of mud, Georgia Tech won 12–0. Georgia was still declared national champions by two polls—Boand and Poling—but did not go to a bowl game. The team, coached by George "Kid" Woodruff, became known as the "Dream and Wonder" team. This event was important because it became the impetus for the building of Georgia's Sanford Stadium in 1929.

October 12, 1929

Sanford Stadium is dedicated with a 15–0 victory over Yale.

November 21, 1936

Georgia travels to the Polo Grounds in New York and pulls an upset with a 7–7 tie with Fordham. That Fordham team included the famed "Seven Blocks of Granite." One of those blocks was future Hall of Fame coach Vince Lombardi. The tie knocked Fordham out of a chance to go to the Rose Bowl, and the following week it lost to NYU 7–6.

1939

After only one season, Joel Hunt leaves Georgia to become the head coach at Wyoming. His top assistant, Wally Butts, was elevated to head coach. Butts, "the Little Round Man" from Milledgeville, won 140 games and four SEC championships in 22 seasons as head coach.

November 1, 1941

Auburn and Georgia were tied 0–0 in Columbus, Georgia, and it looked like the Bulldogs were headed to their second tie of the season (Georgia and Ole Miss had battled to a 14–14 draw on October 10). There were only three seconds left, and Georgia had the ball at its own 35-yard line. There was time for only one play. Georgia's Frank Sinkwich threw the ball as far as he could, hoping to find Lamar "Racehorse" Davis open in the Auburn secondary. The game's final gun fired with the ball in the air. Davis outjumped at least two Auburn defenders for the ball and raced into the end zone for the touchdown and a 7–0 victory.

January 1, 1942

Sinkwich runs and passes for 382 yards of total offense, an Orange Bowl record that still stands, as Georgia beats TCU 40–26 in Miami. It was Georgia's first-ever bowl appearance.

November 21, 1942

Georgia was 9–0, ranked No. 1, and everybody's favorite to win the national championship when the Bulldogs went to Columbus, Georgia, to play Auburn, which was struggling at 4–4–1. Two weeks before, Georgia had beaten Florida 75–0, and Florida had actually beaten Auburn earlier in the season 6–0. But in what would go down as one of the biggest upsets in SEC history, Auburn defeated Georgia 27–13.

November 28, 1942

The Bulldogs thought the loss to Auburn the week before would cost them a trip to the Rose Bowl. But the Rose Bowl committee announced that it would take the winner of the Georgia–Georgia Tech game (Tech was ranked No. 2 at 9–0) in Athens. It was never a contest. Charley Trippi ran 86 yards for a touchdown right before halftime as the Bulldogs coasted to a 34–0 win and clinched their first-ever SEC championship.

December 8, 1942

Wearing his Marine uniform (he had enlisted earlier in the year), Frank Sinkwich accepts the Heisman Trophy in ceremonies held in New York. He became the first player in school history to win college football's most prestigious award.

Joseph R. Taylor, President of the Downtown Athletic Club, awards Frank Sinkwich (center) the Heisman Trophy in New York on December 8, 1942, while runner-up Paul Governali (right) from Columbia looks on. *Photo courtesy of AP Images*

January 1, 1943
Georgia makes its first and only trip to the Rose Bowl. Heisman Trophy winner Frank Sinkwich was slowed by ankle injuries and so most of the carries went to sophomore Charley Trippi, who ran for 130 yards and was the game's most outstanding player. Georgia beat UCLA 9–0. Georgia finished 11–1 and was declared national champion in several polls.

October 20, 1945
After spending the 1943 and 1944 seasons in the military, Charley Trippi returns to Georgia for the fifth game of the 1945 season, a home meeting with LSU. Georgia lost that game (32–0) and again the following week against Alabama (28–14). But then Trippi hit his stride, and Georgia won its last four games to finish 8–2. The Bulldogs went on to beat Tulsa in the Oil Bowl 20–6.

November 30, 1946
Georgia beats Georgia Tech 35–7 to end an undefeated regular season and clinches another SEC championship. That team would go on to beat North Carolina (and Charlie Justice) 20–10 in the Sugar Bowl to finish 11–0. Notre Dame, which had a tie to Army on its record, was declared national champion in the major polls while Georgia was voted No. 1 in the Williamson Poll.

November 27, 1948
Behind senior quarterback Johnny Rauch, Georgia beats Georgia Tech 21–13 in Athens. The Bulldogs went 9–1 and 6–0 in the SEC to win their third SEC championship since 1942. Georgia went on to lose to Texas in the Orange Bowl.

November 30, 1957

Theron Sapp scores on a one-yard run for a touchdown to give Georgia a 7–0 win over Georgia Tech at Grant Field in Atlanta. The victory broke Georgia's eight-game losing streak to the hated in-state rival. Because of this one run, Sapp became immortal and has forevermore been known as "the Drought Breaker." His No. 40 jersey is one of only four that have been retired at Georgia.

November 7, 1959

Charlie Britt, a great two-way player at quarterback and defensive back, throws a 34-yard touchdown pass and then returns an interception 100 yards for a touchdown as Georgia beats Florida 21–10 in Jacksonville.

November 14, 1959

Trailing 13–7, quarterback Fran Tarkenton draws up a play in the dirt and then throws a 13-yard touchdown pass to Bill Herron with less than a minute left to give Georgia a 14–13 victory over Auburn and its first SEC championship since 1946.

November 26, 1960

Georgia defeats Georgia Tech 7–6 in Athens to finish 6–4. Despite the fact that the Bulldogs had won the SEC championship the season before, a powerful alumni group forced Butts to resign. Butts, who remained on campus as athletics director, was replaced by popular assistant Johnny Griffith.

November 22, 1963

On the same day that President John F. Kennedy is assassinated in Dallas, Joel Eaves of Auburn agrees to replace Wally Butts as the new athletics director at Georgia.

December 4, 1963
Vince Dooley, a 31-year-old assistant coach at Auburn, is hired as the head coach at Georgia for a salary of $12,500 a year.

November 7, 1964
With the scored tied at 7–7 in the annual Georgia-Florida game, Georgia coach Vince Dooley sends sophomore kicker Bobby Etter in to kick a go-ahead field goal. The snap was bobbled, and Etter picked up the ball and ran for the score, giving the Bulldogs a 14–7 victory over the Gators. It was Georgia's first win over a ranked opponent under Dooley.

September 18, 1965
Alabama was the defending national champions when it visited Georgia. The Crimson Tide led the game 17–10 late in the fourth quarter. Georgia ran what became known as the "flea-flicker" play as quarterback Kirby Moore threw to tight end Pat Hodgson, who flipped the ball back to running back Bob Taylor, who was trailing the play. Taylor ran untouched into the end zone for a touchdown. Dooley elected to go for the two-point conversion and the win. Moore found Hodgson in the back of the end zone, and Georgia shocked Alabama 18–17.

October 2, 1965
Georgia was given no chance of winning at Michigan, which had won the Rose Bowl the season before. But Georgia, led by quarterbacks Preston Ridlehuber and Kirby Moore, was the quicker team and beat the Wolverines 15–7. More than 10,000 people turned out at the Athens airport to welcome the team back home.

October 16, 1965

Georgia was 4–0 and appeared headed to an SEC championship when the Bulldogs went to Florida State. Georgia running back Bob Taylor suffered a broken leg, and the Bulldogs lost 10–3. Georgia stumbled down the stretch with many more injuries and finished 6–4. Taylor would never play football again.

November 5, 1966

Georgia was 7–1 with a nonconference loss to Miami. Florida was 7–0, ranked No. 7, and could win its first SEC championship ever by beating Georgia in Jacksonville. Florida had the best quarterback in the conference in Steve Spurrier, who was on his way to winning the Heisman Trophy. Florida led 10–3 at halftime, but in the second half Spurrier was overwhelmed by the pressure of George Patton and Bill Stanfill, two Georgia All-Americans. Georgia won 27–10 and stayed alive for the SEC championship. The next week Georgia rallied from a 13–0 halftime deficit to beat Auburn 21–13 and clinch its first SEC championship since 1959. It was the first of six SEC championships Dooley would win as head coach.

December 16, 1967

Georgia loses to N.C. State 14–7 in the Liberty Bowl in Memphis. The starting quarterback for N.C. State that day was Jim Donnan, who would eventually become Georgia's head coach from 1996 to 2000.

September 14, 1968

Georgia plays Tennessee at Knoxville in the first SEC game ever contested on an artificial surface. Tennessee's Bubba Wyche threw what would become a controversial 20-yard touchdown pass with no time left to bring the Vols to within two points. That was before instant replay, and after the game a review of the film showed that Tennessee's touchdown pass bounced off the turf before being caught. Tennessee was successful on a two-point conversion to tie the game 17–17.

November 16, 1968
Georgia defeats Auburn 17–3 at Jordan-Hare Stadium to give the Bulldogs their second SEC championship in three seasons.

December 1968
Bill Stanfill becomes the first player—and the only player—in Georgia history to win the Outland Trophy (for outstanding interior lineman).

November 14, 1970
Georgia was 4–4 and given no chance of winning at Auburn, which was 7–1, ranked No. 8, and had quarterback Pat Sullivan and wide receiver Terry Beasley. But Georgia got 96 yards rushing from running back Ricky Lake to win 31–17.

November 13, 1971
Both Georgia (9–0) and Auburn (8–0) were undefeated and ranked in the top 10 when they met in Athens. But the Bulldogs were no match for Auburn's Sullivan, who completed 14 of 24 passes for 248 yards and four touchdowns. Auburn won the game 35–20. Sullivan was awarded the Heisman Trophy.

November 25, 1971
"Poulos over the Top!" It was Thanksgiving night, and a national television audience watched while Georgia and Georgia Tech did

battle at Grant Field. Georgia trailed 24–21 and had the ball at its own 35-yard line with only 1:29 to go. Sophomore quarterback Andy Johnson led the Bulldogs down the field and kept the drive alive with a fourth-down pass to tight end Mike Greene with only 48 seconds left. Johnson completed a pass to the Georgia Tech 1-yard line, and with only 14 seconds left running back Jimmy Poulos jumped over the Georgia Tech defense to give the Bulldogs a 28–24 victory.

November 3, 1973

After a 12–7 loss to Kentucky the week before in Athens, there was not a whole lot of optimism when Georgia went to Knoxville to play Tennessee. But with his team holding on to a 31–28 lead, Tennessee coach Bill Battle elected to fake a punt at his own 28-yard line. Georgia stopped the attempt and took possession of the ball. Five plays later Andy Johnson picked up the ball on a botched handoff attempt and ran for the touchdown to give Georgia a 35–31 victory.

November 8, 1975

"Appleby to Washington—80 yards!" Georgia already had two losses and was an underdog in Jacksonville when it played Florida. Georgia's "Junkyard Dawg" defense gave up a lot of yardage between the 20s but allowed only one score. As a result, Georgia trailed by only four, 7–3, in the final four minutes. In one of the most notable trick plays in Georgia history, tight end and Athens native Richard Appleby took the ball on an end around. Instead of running the ball, as he had done earlier in the game, Appleby stopped and threw an 80-yard pass to Gene Washington to give Georgia a stunning 10–7 victory over the Gators. The replay of Larry Munson's call of the play would be reaired constantly the next week throughout the state. Georgia would go on to finish 9–2 and earn a spot in the Cotton Bowl.

October 2, 1976

In one of the most anticipated home games in years, Georgia defeats Alabama 21–0 at Sanford Stadium, touching off one of the biggest postgame celebrations Athens has ever seen.

November 6, 1976

"Fourth and Dumb." Trailing 27–13 at halftime, Georgia rallied behind quarterback Ray Goff to dominate the second half and post a 41–27 victory over Florida in Jacksonville. With Florida still holding a 27–20 lead, Gators coach Doug Dickey elected to go for a first down deep in his own territory. Georgia's Johnny Henderson made the tackle behind the line of scrimmage. The Bulldogs tied the game 27–27 and never looked back. Dickey was criticized for the call, which became known as "Fourth and Dumb." The following week Georgia would beat Auburn 28–0 to clinch the SEC championship.

October 22, 1977

Prince Charles of England visits Sanford Stadium for the Georgia-Kentucky game. Kentucky won 33–0.

October 28, 1978

"Yeah, Yeah, Yeah, Yeah!" After trailing Kentucky 16–0, Georgia fought back and trailed 16–14 in the final moments of a game at Kentucky. Behind the running of Willie McClendon, Georgia drove the length of the field, and Rex Robinson kicked a 29-yard field goal with only three seconds left to give Georgia a dramatic 17–16 victory. Larry Munson, the Voice of the Bulldogs, never said the field goal was good. He just screamed, "Yeah! Yeah! Yeah! Yeah!"

December 2, 1978

Georgia won so many close games in 1978 that the team became known as the "Wonder Dawgs." Never was this truer than on the first Saturday in December 1978, when freshman quarterback Buck Belue brought the Bulldogs back from a 20–0 deficit to beat Georgia Tech 29–28 in Athens. With Georgia Tech leading 28–21, Belue threw a touchdown pass to Amp Arnold on fourth down with only 2:24 left. Then Arnold ran for a two-point conversion for the victory. Georgia won four games by a total of six points during the 1978 season.

October 13, 1979

Georgia celebrates the 50th anniversary of Sanford Stadium with a 21–14 win over LSU in Athens.

April 6, 1980

On Easter Sunday, running back Herschel Walked ends one of the most intense recruiting battles in the history of college football by finally signing with the University of Georgia. In three years with Walker in the lineup, Georgia posted a record of 33–3 with three SEC championships and one national championship.

September 6, 1980

After a 6–5 season in 1979, Georgia opens the 1980 season in Knoxville against Tennessee. Georgia fell behind 15–2 and then inserted freshman running back Herschel Walker into the game. Walker scored two touchdowns, including a 16-yard scamper where he ran over Tennessee safety Bill Bates, and Georgia

Coach Vince Dooley is carried off the field after Georgia defeated Notre Dame 17–10 in the Sugar Bowl, January 1, 1981. *Photo courtesy of AP Images*

stormed back to win 16–15. It set the stage for Georgia's run to the national championship and Walker's remarkable career.

November 8, 1980

"Run, Lindsay!" It remains the single biggest play in Georgia history. Trailing 21–20 with 1:03 left and with the ball at the Georgia

7-yard line, quarterback Buck Belue threw over the middle to Lindsay Scott in an attempt to get a first down and keep the drive alive. A Florida defender slipped down, and Scott raced down the Georgia sideline for the score and a dramatic 26–21 victory. The next day Georgia was ranked No. 1 in the polls.

January 1, 1981

Behind 150 yards rushing from Herschel Walker (who dislocated his shoulder early but returned to the game), Georgia defeated Notre Dame 17–10 in the Sugar Bowl to win the national championship. All-America safety Scott Woerner intercepted two passes, and freshman Terry Hoage blocked a field goal attempt. All 17 of Georgia's points were set up by turnovers.

November 7, 1981

For the second straight year Georgia found itself trailing Florida 21–20 in the fourth quarter and deep in its own territory. It wasn't as dramatic as the year before, but the Bulldogs drove 95 yards on 17 plays to score on Herschel Walker's touchdown run with 2:31 left. Georgia won 26–21 to go 8–1. The following week Georgia beat Auburn 24–13 in Athens to clinch its second straight SEC championship.

September 6, 1982

It was Labor Day night, and Sanford Stadium hosted a meeting under the (portable) lights between the last two national champions, Georgia and Clemson. Herschel Walker was limited because of an injured thumb. But Stan Dooley blocked a punt and recovered it for a touchdown, and sophomore kicker Kevin Butler made two field goals as Georgia won 13–7.

November 13, 1982

"Look at the Sugar Falling out of the Sky!" Herschel Walker scored a touchdown to give Georgia a 19–14 lead in the fourth quarter, but Auburn threatened to come back and steal the game. With radio legend Larry Munson imploring Georgia's defense to "hunker down, you guys!" Georgia finally stopped the Auburn's potential winning drive with only 42 seconds left. The win gave Georgia its third straight SEC championship. As the final seconds ticked down, Munson screamed, "Look at the sugar falling out of the sky!" That was Munson's way of saying that Georgia was going back to the Sugar Bowl for the third straight year. This time the Bulldogs would play Penn State for the national championship.

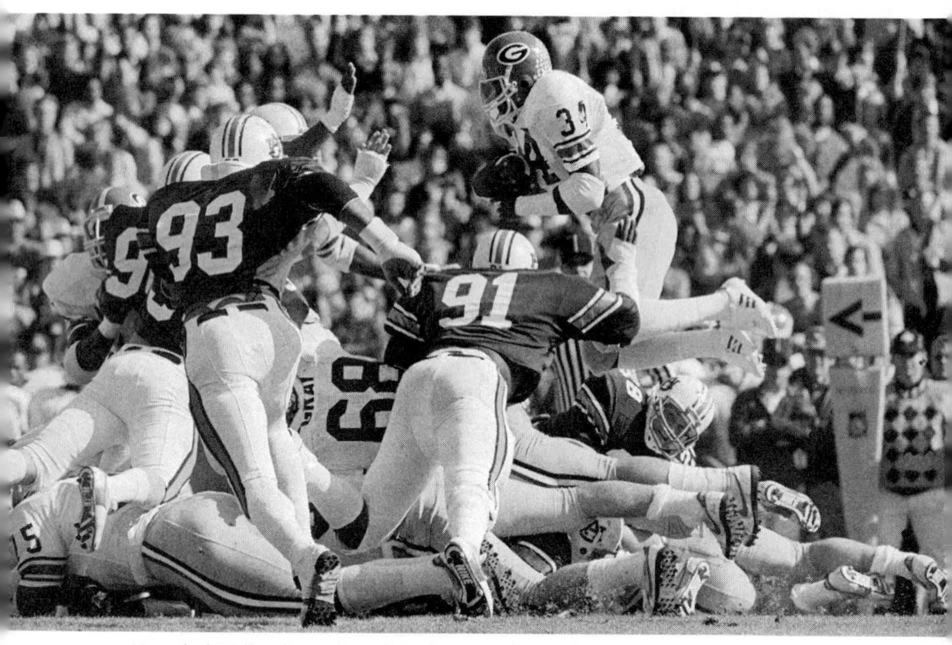

Herschel Walker leaps for a first down against Auburn on November 13, 1982. Georgia won 19–14 and was on its way to its third consecutive Sugar Bowl. *Photo courtesy of AP Images*

December 4, 1982

After leading Georgia to an 11–0 regular season and a No. 1 national ranking, Herschel Walker wins the Heisman Trophy in ceremonies at the Downtown Athletic Club in New York City. Walker became only the second player in Georgia history (Frank Sinkwich was the first in 1942) to win college football's highest honor.

January 1, 1983

Georgia had a chance to win its second national championship in three years, but Penn State's Todd Blackledge threw a 47-yard touchdown pass to Greg Garrity to give the Nittany Lions a 27–23 victory. It was the first national championship for Penn State coach Joe Paterno.

February 22, 1983

Herschel Walker is declared ineligible for his senior season after it is revealed that he signed a multimillion-dollar contract with the New Jersey Generals of the USFL.

November 5, 1983

"First and 99!" Georgia trailed Florida 9–3 when it took possession at its own 1-yard line in the third quarter in a game played in Jacksonville. Led by quarterback John Lastinger, the Bulldogs drove 99 yards in 16 plays to take the lead. Barry Young scored the touchdown on a one-yard run, and the defense made the lead hold up for a 10–9 victory.

January 2, 1984

"What Time Is It? In Texas it's 10 to 9!" Georgia (9–1–1) was given little chance of beating No. 2 Texas in the Cotton Bowl. But the Bulldogs, who trailed 9–3 for most of the game, got a chance to win when Texas muffed a punt and Gary Moss recovered for Georgia. On third down, John Lastinger ran 17 yards for the winning touchdown. Georgia finished 10–1–1 and knocked Texas out of the chance to win a national championship. Georgia completed the most successful four-year run in school history with a record of 43–4–1.

September 22, 1984

"Oh, My God! Oh, My God!" Clemson was ranked No. 2 in the nation after winning its first two games by a combined score of 95–7. Georgia fell behind 20–6 but stormed back to take a 23–20 lead at Sanford Stadium. The score was tied at 23–23 when Georgia took possession with 2:10 remaining. Georgia could get no closer than the Clemson 44-yard line with only 11 seconds left. Kevin Butler's 60-yard field goal was good with room to spare. Larry Munson never said that the field goal was good. He just screamed, "Oh, my God! Oh, my God!"

November 9, 1985

Florida was ranked No. 1 in the AP poll despite being on NCAA probation. Georgia was 6–1–1 and had been tied on the road at Vanderbilt (13–13) just three weeks before. But the Bulldogs got long touchdown runs from Keith Henderson and Tim Worley to upset the Gators 24–3.

November 15, 1986

"The War between the Hoses." Georgia was 6–3 when it went on the road to play an Auburn team that was ranked No. 8 and right in the middle of the SEC race. It didn't help the Bulldogs when they learned that starting quarterback James Jackson would not make it to the game after attending his grandmother's funeral.

But backup quarterback Wayne Johnson played the game of his life, and Georgia upset the Tigers 20–16 at Jordan-Hare Stadium. After the game, Georgia fans stormed the field, and Auburn officials turned the stadium's water cannons on them in an effort to break up the celebration.

December 29, 1987

Freshman place-kicker John Kasay makes a 39-yard field goal on the last play of the game as Georgia beats Arkansas 20–17 at the Liberty Bowl in Memphis. Georgia finished 9–3.

November 26, 1988

Georgia defeats Georgia Tech 24–3 to give coach Vince Dooley his 200th career win.

December 14, 1988

Vince Dooley announces that he will be retiring as head coach after 25 seasons with Georgia. Early indications were that Erk Russell, who served as Dooley's defensive coordinator from 1964 to 1980 before leaving to become the head coach at Georgia Southern, was the leading candidate to be Georgia's new head coach.

December 20, 1988

At a news conference in Montgomery, Alabama, where he was a coach in the Blue-Gray All-Star game, Georgia Southern coach Erk Russell announced that he would not be leaving to become the next head coach at Georgia. On that same day, N.C. State coach Dick Sheridan met with the Georgia search committee at the Holiday Inn in Commerce, Georgia.

December 23, 1988

Sheridan, who had agreed to become Georgia's head coach after meeting with the school's search committee, announces that he will remain in his current job. The search for Vince Dooley's replacement continued.

January 1, 1989

Dooley wins his final game 34–27 over Michigan State in the Gator Bowl in Jacksonville. His final record: 201–77–10 with six SEC championships and one national championship.

January 2, 1989

Former quarterback and current assistant Ray Goff, 33, is named Georgia's head coach at a press conference at the Omni Hotel in Jacksonville.

October 5, 1991

In the afternoon, the Atlanta Braves clinch the first of 14 consecutive division championships, and that night, Georgia upsets No. 6 Clemson 27–12 behind freshman quarterback Eric Zeier.

April 18, 1992

At its annual spring game, Georgia celebrates the 100th anniversary of its football program.

October 30, 1993

It was one of the toughest losses Georgia has had to Florida. In the mud and the rain of Jacksonville, junior quarterback Eric Zeier threw 65 passes against the Gators. With only five seconds left and his team trailing 33–26, Zeier had apparently tied the game on a 12-yard touchdown pass to Jerry Jerman. But officials ruled that Florida's Anthone Lott had called timeout just before the snap, and the score came off the board. Zeier's 65th attempt fell incomplete, and Florida beat Georgia for the fourth consecutive year. Zeier's 65 passing attempts in a game is still the Georgia record.

November 23, 1993
On Thanksgiving Day, the last Georgia–Georgia Tech freshman/JV game takes place. For 60 years the game was played to benefit the Scottish Rite Children's Hospital with the tagline: "Strong legs run so weak legs can walk." Interest in the game began to wane as freshmen became eligible to play and scholarship reductions made it difficult to field junior varsity teams. Georgia won the last JV game 21–14 and had a record of 28–30–1 in the series.

December 6, 1994
Vince Dooley becomes the first coach in Georgia history to be inducted into the College Football Hall of Fame.

November 17, 1995
Ray Goff, who was an All-SEC quarterback at Georgia in 1976, is fired by athletics director Vince Dooley after seven seasons as head coach. Goff agreed to coach the team for the rest of the season.

November 23, 1995
Georgia's players send Goff out as a winner in his final regular season game as the Bulldogs' head coach. Kanon Parkman kicked a 34-yard field goal with 47 seconds left to give Georgia an 18–17 victory in Atlanta.

Receiver Hines Ward (19) outruns Georgia Tech linebacker Delaunta Cameron as he scores on a 54-yard pass from quarterback Mike Bobo in the first half of what would be a 27–24 Bulldogs victory, November 29, 1997. *Photo courtesy of AP Images*

December 18, 1995

Glen Mason, who had led Kansas to a 10–2 season, is introduced as the new head coach at Georgia during a press conference in Athens.

December 25, 1995
After taking the job at Georgia, Mason was allowed to coach his Kansas team in its final game in the Aloha Bowl in Hawaii. On Christmas morning, Mason called athletics director Vince Dooley and said he would not be taking the Georgia job after all. Before the end of the day, Jim Donnan, the highly successful coach at Division I-AA Marshall, accepted the job of becoming Georgia's next head coach.

November 16, 1996
Mike Bobo throws a 30-yard touchdown pass to Corey Allen on the last play of regulation to tie the game at Auburn and send it into overtime. The first overtime game in SEC history went four extra periods, and Georgia won 56–49. It was the lone bright spot in Donnan's first season at Georgia, when the Bulldogs went 5–6.

November 1, 1997
After seven straight losses to Steve Spurrier and Florida, Georgia dominates the Gators to win 37–17 in Jacksonville.

November 29, 1997
Mike Bobo throws a touchdown pass to Corey Allen with eight seconds left as Georgia rallies to stun Georgia Tech 27–24 at Bobby Dodd Stadium.

November 25, 2000
Georgia loses its third straight game to Georgia Tech 27–15 in Athens. Despite winning 40 games and four bowl trips in five seasons, Donnan was fired as head coach.

December 26, 2000

Mark Richt, the offensive coordinator at Florida State, is named the new head coach at Georgia.

October 6, 2001

"Hobnail Boot." Trailing 24–20 with 44 seconds left, the Bulldogs put together one of their best last-minute drives ever behind redshirt freshman quarterback David Greene. Georgia reached the Tennessee 6-yard line, and Richt called P-44 Haynes, a pass to the fullback Richt had developed at Florida State. Verron Haynes was wide open for the touchdown with only six seconds left as the Bulldogs stunned Tennessee 26–24 in Knoxville. Larry Munson screamed, "We just stepped on their face with a hobnail boot and broke their nose!"

September 15, 2002

Georgia's David Pollack makes one of the signature defensive plays in school history during a 13–7 win at South Carolina in Columbia. South Carolina had the ball deep in its own territory. Quarterback Corey Jenkins dropped back to pass in his own end zone. Pollack stripped the ball into his arms and fell into the end zone for a Georgia touchdown.

October 5, 2002

Earlier in the week former Auburn coach and Georgia All-American Pat Dye wondered publicly if Georgia was "man enough" to go to Alabama and win against the Crimson Tide. As it turned out, Georgia was "man enough" to win the game. Trailing 25–24, Georgia drove the length of the field and Billy Bennett kicked a 32-yard field goal with 38 seconds left to give the Bulldogs a 27–25 victory.

November 16, 2002

"Touchdown! Oh, God, a Touchdown!" Georgia knew a win at Auburn would send the Bulldogs to the SEC championship game for the first time in history. Georgia trailed 21–17 with only 3:06 left. A 41-yard completion from David Greene to Fred Gibson put Georgia in position to score. Then Greene lofted a perfect 19-yard pass and Michael Johnson outjumped two Auburn defenders to make the touchdown catch and give Georgia a 24–21 win.

December 7, 2002

Georgia dominates Arkansas 30–7 at the Georgia Dome in Atlanta to win its first SEC championship in 20 years. Georgia went on to beat Florida State in the Sugar Bowl to finish 13–1. Georgia's only loss that season was to Florida in Jacksonville, 20–13.

December 6, 2003

Georgia reaches the SEC championship game for the second straight year, but the Bulldogs are no match for No. 3 LSU. The Tigers won 34–13 and then went on beat Oklahoma in the BCS national championship game at the Sugar Bowl in New Orleans.

October 30, 2004

Georgia defeats Florida 31–24 in Jacksonville for only its second win against the Gators since 1989. Earlier in the week Florida announced that coach Ron Zook would be stepping down after the season.

January 1, 2005

Quarterback David Greene leads Georgia to a 24–21 win over Wisconsin in the Outback Bowl. Greene ended his career with an NCAA record 42 wins as Georgia's starting quarterback.

December 2, 2005

Despite back-to-back losses to Florida (14–10) and Auburn (31–30), Georgia reaches the SEC championship game, where the Bulldogs upset LSU 34–14 to win their second SEC championship in four seasons. Senior quarterback D.J. Shockley, who had waited three years behind David Greene for his chance to play, was the MVP of the game.

November 11, 2006

With four losses in its past five games (including a 24–22 defeat against Vanderbilt), Georgia was given no shot on the road at No. 5 Auburn. But freshman quarterback Matthew Stafford led the Bulldogs to a dominating 37–15 win at Jordan-Hare Stadium. Georgia closed the season with three straight wins, including a 31–24 victory over Virginia Tech in the Chick-fil-A Bowl.

September 22, 2007

Stafford stuns Alabama with a 25-yard touchdown pass to Mikey Henderson in overtime to give the Bulldogs a 26–23 victory over the Crimson Tide at Bryant-Denny Stadium.

October 27, 2007

After Knowshon Moreno scores to give Georgia a 7–0 lead against Florida in Jacksonville, the entire Bulldog team leaves the bench and storms the end zone. Georgia was penalized for unsportsmanlike conduct, but the message had been sent. Georgia went on to dominate the game and win 42–30. Georgia had lost 15 of its last 17 games to the Gators previous to the win. The following Monday, Georgia coach Mark Richt apologized to SEC commissioner Mike Slive.

Georgia players storm the field following the first touchdown in the first quarter against Florida in Jacksonville. The Bulldogs won 42–30. *Photo courtesy of AP Images*

November 10, 2007

For the first time in school history Georgia takes the Sanford Stadium field wearing black jerseys. Georgia warmed up in its traditional red jerseys and then switched to black right before kickoff. With the Sanford Stadium crowd at a fever pitch, Georgia dominated Auburn 45–20.

January 1, 2008

Georgia finished the regular season tied with Tennessee in the SEC East but did not go to the SEC championship game because of a 35–14 loss at Knoxville earlier in the season. Georgia dominated undefeated Hawaii 41–10 in the Sugar Bowl, finished No. 2 in the final 2007 polls, and was a preseason No. 1 in 2008.

August 17, 2008

For the first time in school history, Georgia is No. 1 in the preseason Associated Press football poll.

September 27, 2008

Georgia was 4–0 and ranked No. 3 in the nation when No. 8 Alabama came to Sanford Stadium. As added motivation, Georgia started the game in the black jerseys that had been so successful the year before against Auburn. This time, it didn't work. Alabama scored on its first five possessions to take a 31–0 lead at halftime. Georgia finished the year at 10–3 and beat Michigan State in the Capital One Bowl on New Year's Day. But based on preseason expectations, it was a disappointing year that also included losses to Florida (49–10) and Georgia Tech (45–42).

September 8, 2010

A.J. Green, Georgia's star receiver, is suspended by the NCAA for four games for selling one of his old jerseys for $1,000.

October 2, 2010

Green finally returns to action and plays well, but it is not enough for the Bulldogs to win at Colorado. Georgia lost 29–27 to start the season at 1–4.

December 31, 2010

Central Florida defeats Georgia 10–6 in the Liberty Bowl, and the Bulldogs finish with their first losing record (6–7) since 1996. Mark Richt finished his 10th season at Georgia with a record of 96–34.

chapter 3
THE TRADITIONS *of* GEORGIA

WEBSTER'S DICTIONARY DEFINES TRADITION as "a set of customs transmitted from one generation to another." No university has a greater set of football traditions than the University of Georgia.

And what makes these traditions so special is that behind every one there is a personal story to be told. Here are just a few of those stories.

THE ARCH AND THE CHAPEL BELL

by Walter Corish

I arrived on campus in the fall of 1961, which was an interesting time to be at Georgia. Johnny Griffith had just taken over as head football coach from Wally Butts. And before I graduated in 1965 Coach [Vince] Dooley had come and started to turn things around. By the time I earned my master's degree in 1967, we had won an SEC championship. It was a special, special time to be on campus.

As a freshman, there were certain traditions that you absolutely had to observe. Freshmen had to wear "rat caps," and they were real caps, not like those beanies they wore at the North Avenue Trade School [Georgia Tech].

Another great tradition was the arch. It served as the gateway from North Campus to downtown, and we were told that we could not walk under the arch until we had graduated. Now nobody was there with a camera enforcing the rule, and I was tempted to walk under it a number of times. But I waited until I graduated before walking under it. That was a proud day.

Last season I took my grandchildren down there and explained the tradition to them. And no, they did not walk under the arch. But that is how a tradition gets passed down from one generation to another.

Back then the freshmen men lived in Reed Hall, and one of our responsibilities was to ring the chapel bell after a home win. The freshmen men's counselor instructed us on exactly how to do it. After a regular win, we would ring the bell until midnight. But if we beat Georgia Tech, we would ring it all night long. The problem was, in my first three years at Georgia (1961 to 1963), we only won 10 total games and never beat Tech. So there wasn't a whole lot of ringing going on. Fortunately, that changed when Coach Dooley came in 1964. [In 1964 Georgia won seven games and beat Georgia Tech 7–0.]

I do remember that when we went to Michigan and won in 1965, everybody decided to make an exception to the rule and ring the bell all night long.

Those are great memories of two great Georgia traditions. I was very lucky to be a part of both.

Walter Corish is an insurance executive who lives in Savannah.

Between the Hedges
by Vince Dooley

During my 41 years at Georgia as a head coach and athletics director, I had to make a lot of tough decisions. But the decision to remove our beloved hedges from Sanford Stadium was one of the toughest of all.

We knew early on that it had to happen. Once Atlanta had been awarded the 1996 Olympic Games and once the decision had been made to host the medal games for soccer in Sanford Stadium, we knew that the field configuration with the hedges would not be big enough.

Now the Georgia people love their hedges. They were in place when Sanford Stadium was dedicated in 1929. I believe it was the famed sportswriter Grantland Rice who first wrote that Georgia was going to play somebody "Between the Hedges," and since then everybody associated the hedges with our school. Those hedges are extremely important to our people.

I consulted a couple of our faculty representatives, Bill Powell and Gary Couvillon. Bill was actually a plant pathologist. They inspected the hedges and reported that the hedges actually had nematodes, which can spread disease throughout the hedges. So it became clear that we were going to have to deal with this problem down the road and this gave us a chance to address it at the proper time. We would remove the diseased hedges and replace them with new healthy hedges taken from the cuttings of the originals.

Because the hedges were sacred, it was very important to take the utmost care as we took cuttings from them. We decided to grow those cuttings at Tom Dudley's nursery in Thomson, Georgia. Tom is a Georgia grad and understood the magnitude of the task at hand.

University of Georgia fans collect pieces of the hedges that surround Sanford Stadium after the last game of the 1995 season. The hedges were replaced with cuttings from the originals the following summer. *Photo courtesy of Getty Images*

Then we took more healthy cuttings and grew them in an undisclosed location in Florida. We did that so that we would have a backup, just in case anything went wrong at our primary location in Thomson.

But everything went fine, and most of the Georgia people accepted what we did. The sons and daughters of the original hedges were nurtured and grew very fast. They were installed before the 1996 season as "Hedges II" and continue to thrive today.

There is no more beautiful setting in college football than a game at Georgia Between the Hedges.

Vince Dooley was Georgia's head coach from 1964 to 1988 and its athletics director from 1979 to 2004.

The Dawg Walk

by David Pollack

All players go through their ups and their downs. There are simply days when you don't feel 100 percent. But if you don't feel you are ready to play, you will be ready after you go through the Dawg Walk. That is the one opportunity that you have to be close to the Georgia people. And when you look them in the eye and you see how important being a Bulldog is to the people, if you don't feel some kind of responsibility, then you're crazy.

Some people wonder what the big deal is. We get off the team bus (on Lumpkin Street) and walk through a human corridor made by the fans and the Redcoat Band. But after you do it for the first time as a player, you realize that it is a very big deal.

You feel honored to walk through all those people, and you say to yourself, *Man, I can't let these folks down.* You already have a responsibility to your teammates and coaches. But these people have made a major investment to be at the game. And without them it is just practice.

When you're young, you don't quite get the full importance of the Dawg Walk. But when you get to Senior Day, it hits you how incredibly blessed you are to be a Georgia Bulldog. I still get chills thinking about it today.

David Pollack was a three-time All-American for Georgia from 2002 to 2004.

GLORY, GLORY TO OLD GEORGIA AND HUGH HODGSON

It is Georgia's best-known and much beloved fight song. It was sung in some form during the 1890s but was composed in its current form in 1915 by Hugh Hodgson, the well-known Georgia composer and legendary music educator.

Born in Athens in 1893, Hodgson was a musical prodigy on the piano by the age of four. By the age of 14 he was studying the piano in Europe, and by 22 he had played in Carnegie Hall in New York.

The university's school of music and its main performance hall (located on East campus) are named after Hodgson, who became a professor of music at Georgia in 1928. He later became head of the newly created department of music and remained in that position until he retired in 1960.

"Glory, Glory" is sung to the tune of "The Battle Hymn of The Republic":

"Glory, Glory to old Georgia...

"Glory, Glory to old Georgia...

"Glory, Glory to old Georgia...

"G-E-O-R-G-I-A..."

"I've been gone from Georgia for a long time, but when I hear that song, the chills still go up and down my spine," said Bill Krug, a Maryland native who played defensive back at Georgia from 1975 to 1977. "Running through the Redcoat Band while they play 'Glory, Glory.' Man, there is nothing better than that."

The Junkyard Dawgs, 1975

by Dicky Clark

We just weren't very good on defense in 1974. So before the 1975 season, Erk Russell, our defensive coordinator, said he was looking for a few good men to help him improve the defense. "We need some people to come up and help, and we think you can," Erk told me.

Now I was a backup quarterback to Matt Robinson and Ray Goff, and I didn't know if I was going to get back on the field.

You have to understand how the players felt about Erk Russell. He is the greatest motivator I have ever seen. And when Coach Russell asked you to do something, you really wanted to do it. If he had asked me to play nose guard, I would have given it a shot.

We had a little scrawny defense in 1975. I barely weighed 215 pounds, and I think the biggest guy we had was Ronnie Swoopes (who weighed 245). But we were tough and pretty quick.

So Coach Russell wanted to come up with a catchy name to describe this little defense that would get after you. So that summer he started calling us "the Junkyard Dawgs" after that old song [by Jim Croce] that included the line "meaner than a junkyard dog."

We got off to a pretty good start that year. We lost to Pittsburgh and Tony Dorsett in the opener [19–9] but settled in and started to play well.

After a few games, the Junkyard Dawg mania took off. Yeah, we gave up a lot of yardage that year, but we tended to tighten up when teams got near the goal. The perfect example of that was our game with Florida. They ran up and down the field on us with that great offense, but after an early score, we kept them out of the end zone for the rest of the game. The Junkyard Dawgs kept it close so that we could beat them with the famous Appleby-to-Washington play.

That team ended up winning nine games and going to the Cotton Bowl. And the tradition of the Junkyard Dawgs was born. I was proud to be a part of it.

Dicky Clark played at Georgia from 1974 to 1976 and later served as an assistant coach for the Bulldogs for 15 seasons.

Bulldogs in Their Own Words

RANDY JOHNSON

GUARD, 1973–1975

I am the classic example of how going to a place like Georgia can turn somebody's life around.

When I came to Georgia in 1971, I wasn't much of a student. I didn't know anything about hard work. I didn't know how to work out properly to become a better football player, and at one point I even quit the team.

When I left Georgia, I was an All-American, and I eventually got my degree and became a teacher. None of that would have been possible without the help of the people I met at Georgia. Sometimes when I look back, it's hard to believe that all those things really happened to me.

For a lot of reasons, I got off to a pretty rough start at Georgia. I didn't care a whole lot about school. I was married when I got there. I stayed in the dorm for two quarters before I brought my wife down. I just had a hard time getting adjusted to college life.

After my freshman season, in 1971, I came back for two-a-day practices in the summer of 1972. I went to the morning practice on the first day and decided I was going to quit before the afternoon practice. I had a good-paying summer job back in Lindale, so I was going to go home and do that.

As I was walking out the door to go home, I saw Coach [Vince] Dooley walking in. I told him what I was going to do, and he started talking to me about the opportunities I would be giving up if I left. He made some good points, but I was too stubborn and left anyway.

I lasted about six weeks, and then I went back to Athens to ask Coach Dooley for another chance. He told me that he'd give me another chance, but then he said, "Quite frankly, I don't think you're going to make it." We still get a good laugh about that today.

I came back during the 1972 season and practiced for two weeks on the scout team. Then I had an emergency appendectomy, which kept me out for the rest of the year. I took a redshirt so I would have three years of eligibility left.

Things finally began to start looking up for me in 1973. I was a second-string guard and still not in really good shape when we went up to Tennessee. That game really got my career started, I think. We won the game [35–31] when Andy Johnson picked up a loose ball and ran it in for a touchdown. The next day in the paper there was a picture of me and Chris Hammond blocking. I'm in the linebacker's chest, and his feet are about six inches off the ground, and our back is running right off of us. After that game I became a starter and stayed a starter for the rest of my career.

Randy Johnson quit college football for six weeks as a sophomore, but came back and left Georgia as an All-America guard.

The 1974 season was a nightmare year for us [6–6] that I hope everybody has forgotten by now.

In 1975 we came close to winning an SEC championship but slipped up. We lost our first game to Pittsburgh [19–9], which was a better team than most of us thought. We had to reevaluate a lot of things after that loss.

We lost at Ole Miss [28–13] in a game where everything that could go wrong did go wrong. Allan Leavitt hurt his leg, and I had to kick off. I had done it in high school and could usually get the ball to the 5-yard line. I was really excited when the game began, probably too excited. My first kickoff hit one of the up men for Ole Miss right in the chest. In fact, Butch Box almost recovered the ball for us. If Butch had recovered, I'm sure I would have been a hero. As it was, my place-kicking career was over at that point.

Nobody gave us a chance to beat Florida, but I went into that game thinking that there was no way that we were going to lose. That was just the way we felt about that game back then. Once Richard Appleby hit Gene Washington to give us the lead, the fun really began. I remember being on the field when we were running out the clock. We were smiling at each other in the huddle and reminding each other not to jump and create a penalty. What a great feeling!

Then in the Georgia Tech game, I finally got my chance to do what every lineman lives for—carry the football! Coach Bill Pace put in the "Randy Rooskie" play, where I would pull and pretend to run into Ray Goff, our quarterback. I would bend over like the wind had been knocked out of me, and Ray would give me the ball and keep running in the other direction. Then I would take off running.

The play worked except for one thing: Richard Appleby, our tight end, was supposed to run at the defensive back on that side and block his vision. Instead, Richard blocked on the outside, and the defensive back saw me. I only gained six yards. I always think how neat it would have been to score a touchdown on national TV!

I always tell people that I left Georgia in 1975 and finally graduated in 1984, and that was possible because of Coach Dooley. After playing pro football for a while, I thought the world owed me a living. I quickly found out how wrong I was about that. So I went back to school to get my degree, and Coach Dooley found a way to put me back on scholarship for a year. I don't know how he did it, and I never asked. All I know is that when I needed some help, he gave it to me.

Because of that I will love that man with all my heart for as long as I live; I owe him everything that I have. I got my degree and I have been a teacher for more than 20 years.

And the thing is, Coach Dooley never asked for anything in return. To me, that's what being a Bulldog is all about. When you're a Bulldog, you're part of a big family that looks out for each other when times get tough. Coach Dooley and Georgia gave me discipline at a time when I really needed it. I will always be grateful for that.

Randy Johnson was an All-America guard in 1975. He played for the Seattle Seahawks and the Tampa Bay Buccaneers. Today he is a teacher living in Lindale, Georgia.

THE GEORGIA REDCOAT BAND

It is halftime at Sanford Stadium, and at most college football venues it is good time to stretch, take a restroom break, and start getting ready for the second half. But before Georgia fans can move, they hear the clear voice of Tom Jackson:

"*Keep your seats everyone. The Redcoats are coming!*"

Georgia's Redcoat Band began in 1905 as 20 military cadets and today has more than 350 members who bring color and pageantry to the home games in Athens and a reliable show of support on the road for the Bulldogs.

The band has a long and colorful history, but here are just a few notable items from its website:

- Georgia's band was a fairly modest size until 1935. In that year LSU came to Athens for a game on November 16. Famed Louisiana Governor Huey Long was a big supporter of football at LSU and had declared long ago that the school's "Golden Band From Tigerland" would travel with the team. Georgia's alumni were not happy seeing their band dwarfed by the group from LSU and stepped up to help the Bulldogs band grow.
- There are a number of stories about how Georgia's band got its name, including one where a reporter from one of the Atlanta newspapers referred to Georgia as "the red coated band" because of their striking uniforms.
- Georgia's band was known as the "Dixie Redcoat Band" until 1971, when the word "Dixie" was removed from the title.
- The seminal moment in the band's history came in 1955 when Roger Dancz became director and his wife, Phyllis, took over as director of auxiliaries. He was in charge of the band. She formed the "Georgettes," who performed along with the band. Under the direction of the Danczes, the Redcoat Band became one of the very best in the country.

Dancz was the director of the Redcoat Band for 36 years and retired in 1991. He passed away in 1998.

"He started his first Redcoat Band rehearsal with 25 people, and I know a lot of band directors who would've found another job on that second day," said Dwight Satterwhite, who replaced Dancz as director. "But he had been hired to bring pizzazz and flash and style to the University of Georgia band program. I think he did."

- Game day is a busy one for band members. They form a human corridor for the "Dawg Walk" as players enter the stadium. They do their traditional pregame and halftime shows and play throughout the game.
- The Redcoat Band's most popular tradition is its postgame concert. While the fans head to their cars, Sanford Stadium is filled with such favorites as "Georgia On My Mind," and "Sweet Georgia Brown." The Redcoat Band brings game day in Athens to an end with its stirring rendition of "Tara's Theme" from *Gone with the Wind.*

"Sometimes when I would hear my players complain about practice in the summer I would point over to where the band was practicing," said former coach Vince Dooley. "I reminded the players that the band was out there before we got to practice, and they would be there long after we left. *Those* people knew how to work."

THE SHAVED HEADS OF 1976

by Matt Robinson

We kind of knew going in that 1976 had a chance to be a special year. Normally in a class of freshmen only about 10 or 12 make it all the way through, but if I'm not mistaken, about 22 guys in my freshmen class were still there in 1976, and about 17 or 18 of them were starters.

The team bonded at the beginning of training camp when Mike Wilson and Ken Helms shaved their heads. We saw them and laughed, and after about 15 minutes it was like a shark-feeding frenzy. They would take those electric clippers and run them down the middle of your head, so you couldn't change your mind. The next thing you know, they've done 28 guys.

Right after that, we went to practice and noticed that Coach [Erk] Russell was not there. Coach Russell was the original bald man, and we wanted him to see this. After a few minutes, through the gate came a figure wearing a full-blown shoulder length blond wig. It was Coach Russell. He told us that some of us had set bald heads back 20 years.

What was great was that every time we won a game, one of the coaches agreed to have his head shaved. They were really starting to get into it. Finally, Coach Dooley said that if we won the SEC championship, he would shave his head. None of us thought he would really do it.

We did win the championship, but honestly a lot of us forgot that Coach Dooley had said that. But when we had the team banquet that year out at Poss's, he showed up, and it was obvious he had a wig on. Coach Dooley got up and gave one of the most emotional speeches I have ever heard, and at the end he pulled the wig off to show his bald head. The room almost collapsed from people laughing and yelling so hard. It's an incredible memory.

Matt Robinson played quarterback at Georgia from 1974 to 1976. He played 10 seasons in the NFL and USFL. Today he lives in Jacksonville, Florida.

Bulldogs in Their Own Words

MIKE WILSON

TACKLE, 1974–1976

The amazing thing to me about my time at Georgia was that it almost never happened. When I got to Georgia in 1973, I hated football. By the time I left, I loved it again. That was one of the many things that Georgia gave me in my four years there.

I think Georgia found out about me by accident. Coach [Vince] Dooley and Coach Mike [Castronis] were up in the Gainesville area recruiting Tommy West [who would later go on to Tennessee]. I played at South Hall against Tommy's team at Gainesville. They must have spotted me, because I got a letter from them the following week.

When I was a senior at South Hall, we got a new head coach who was a Clemson man. So we made a road trip there, and he showed me everything. Clemson recruited me really, really hard.

But I knew Georgia was the place for me. It was only 45 minutes away, and so many of the people I knew were Georgia fans. I'll never forget the day I made my commitment to Georgia. Clemson immediately sent some coaches down to the school and tried to talk me out of it. I didn't budge despite their pressure. It was the smartest move I've ever made.

But it didn't start out that way. When I was a senior in high school, the coach made us practice three hours a day and just beat up on each other. Even on the day before a game we were hitting. It really took all the fun out of the game.

When I started playing freshman ball at Georgia, it was more of the same. It seemed like we went through two-a-days for a month. I was thinking, *Here is the same old crap again.* I just didn't like the game anymore. In fact, I quit five times in my first quarter. Every time I would quit and go home, Coach Mike would come get me.

Finally, after the last time I quit, Coach Dooley asked me to stay after practice so we could talk. We went over to the grandstand around the track, and we talked for about an hour or so. At that point I still didn't like football, and I was thinking about getting on with my life and being a carpenter or something.

Coach Dooley understood what I was going through. He told me to stick it out through this first quarter, because it would get better. He was right. I stayed, things got better, and everything turned out pretty well for me. So I owe a lot to Coach Dooley and his patience. I guess he saw something in me that I really didn't know about. He knew that I could play and contribute to the team.

When I was a sophomore, in 1974, I played mostly on defense. Coach [Erk] Russell asked me to help him out, and I was glad to do it. But our defense was pretty mangled up that year. We really didn't stop people the way a Georgia defense is supposed to.

The 1974 season was just miserable. We got the crap kicked out of us at the end of the year. It was the low point of my time at Georgia, and everybody knew that the following spring we had to get things turned around.

In the following spring they moved me back to offense. I didn't really like the move at the time, because as a player you like to have your name called out, but if you're a lineman, you really only get that on defense. It was disappointing until the day my dad came down to practice. There was a scout from the Houston Oilers hanging around that day, and he told my dad that my best chance of playing pro ball was on the offensive line. After practice, my dad and I went out to supper, and he told me what the scout had said. I didn't think about the defensive line after that.

We all agreed in the spring of 1975 that it was time to get to work. We were at Georgia to play ball and to get an education. We were doing a lousy job as football players. We had too many people looking at us to keep failing.

There have been some pretty good offensive lines at Georgia, but I will take the two I played on in 1975 and 1976 and stack them up with any others. In 1975 I played with guys like Randy Johnson, who was an All-American, and Steve Wilson, who played a bunch of years in the pros. In 1976 Cowboy [Joel Parrish] and I held down the left side, and George Collins was on the other. We had a lot of good linemen back then. Jimmy Vickers was our line coach, and if you would bust your butt for him, he would do whatever he could for you. He was a very good coach and a special man.

There are a lot of good memories from 1975. Everybody remembers the shoestring play that we ran at Vanderbilt. We all got a big kick out of it when they put the play in during the week, but a bunch of us thought we were going to look like fools if we actually tried it in the game. I was over there laughing, saying, "This ain't never gonna work." And darned if it didn't.

We beat Florida on the Appleby-to-Washington pass play that was set up and executed perfectly. Again, that was a little bit of a trick play, and we didn't know if it would work. But it did, and it was a great day to beat those guys because they were really good.

But we lost in the Cotton Bowl, which reminds me of my only regret at Georgia. I played three years and never won a bowl game.

We lost a lot of good football players after the 1975 season. Guys like Appleby, Glynn Harrison, Steve Wilson, and Randy Johnson. But early in spring practice it became obvious that we were going to reload with some very good football players. I think we all knew that we had a chance to have a special team in 1976.

Mike Wilson was so frustrated with football that he quit several times during his early days at Georgia. He came back and left Georgia as an All-America lineman in 1976.

People always ask me about the head-shaving episode in 1976, and there are a lot of stories about it. Here is exactly how it happened.

Ken Helms was a center for us, and one day he walked in as we were getting ready for practice. He had just gotten his hair styled and had gotten a brand new dryer to keep it styled. So I decided to give him a hard time about it. Well, one thing led to another, and he finally said, "Let's just shave our heads." It didn't bother me, so I said, "Hey, let's go."

We had a couple of sets of clippers and did each other's hair at the same time. The first thing we did was cut a gap right down the middle so there would be no backing out. Then all these guys started coming by and saying, "Do mine! Do mine!" Next thing you know, we've got 20-some guys with bald heads. I think that team bonded over that experience because we went on to be pretty good.

One of the highlights of my entire career at Georgia was when we beat Alabama in Athens in 1976. You have to understand that my dad is from Alabama—a little town near Birmingham, named Jasper. I've got a bunch of relatives over there, and they are all Alabama people. Back then Bear Bryant was the dominant coach in college football and Alabama was the dominant team, but we knew we were good enough to beat them.

I'll never forget the practice on Friday before the game. We were at the stadium, and there were already several hundred people on the railroad tracks. We all had chills just watching those people up there getting ready.

I don't think any of us slept that night. We could hear the noise outside as people were getting ready for the game. And when we took the bus to the stadium the next day, there were about 5,000 people on the tracks waiting for us. By the time we got off that bus and got through those people, Alabama never had a chance, and we won 21–0.

The party that night was the greatest one that Athens has ever seen. I know I'll never forget it as long as I live.

We went down to Jacksonville to play Florida, and at halftime we were behind 27–13. What I remember most is that nobody was yelling and nobody was nervous. We knew we were the better team, and we made up our minds at halftime that we were going to win. Once our offense got rolling, they were not going to stop us. We beat them [41–27], and then we went down to Auburn and clinched the SEC championship.

The best part of winning the SEC title was the team banquet. Coach Dooley had promised us that if we won the championship, he would shave his head. We really didn't think he would do it, but at the banquet he got up and gave a speech and pulled off his wig to show his bald head. The room went nuts. That's one of the things that is special about Coach Dooley: he is a man of his word. If he tells you he is going to do something, you can count on it.

I think we were ranked No. 4 when we played No. 1 Pittsburgh in the Sugar Bowl. I think *Sports Illustrated* told us they would definitely make us No. 1 if we won. We didn't compete very well, and they outcoached us and outplayed us. Basically, we got spanked.

Still, after a shaky start at Georgia when I wanted to quit, things turned out pretty well. I was lucky enough to play 12 seasons in the NFL, but I often tell people that it was nothing like the four years I spent in college. Your college years are the most impressionable ones of your life. The people you meet and the friendships you make will last for the rest of your life.

And when you play on a championship team, like we did in 1976, you really bond with that group of guys. They become your family forever.

What I will always remember and what I am most grateful for is that at Georgia I got my love for the game of football back. If it hadn't been for Coach Dooley and Coach Mike, there is no telling how my life would have turned out. How do you possibly repay something like that?

Mike Wilson was a two-time All-SEC tackle in 1975 and 1976. He was an All-American in 1976, after which he played 12 seasons in the NFL. He was inducted into the Georgia Sports Hall of Fame in 2001. Today Wilson lives in Gainesville, Florida, where he is in private business.

THE SHOESTRING PLAY, 1975
by Ray Goff

Everybody likes to talk about the shoestring play that we ran against Vanderbilt. We really have to give credit to Coach Jimmy Vickers for that play. He noticed on the film that on defense Vanderbilt would always huddle right next to the ball and hold hands. So he came up with this play and explained it to me.

He said: "The first thing you're going to do, Ray, is run a sweep outside the hash mark, and nobody is going to block for you."

I really didn't like that idea at all.

I was supposed to run outside the hash but not go out of bounds. The official would then put the ball on the hash mark, and that's where Vandy would huddle. I was supposed to then walk over to the ball and lean down like I was tying my shoe. While all this was going on, Gene Washington was across the field, lining up behind our offensive line. I was supposed to just lean down and shovel the ball to him, and he would have a convoy to the goal line.

It was early in the game, and we weren't playing all that well. We were up 7–3 when the shoestring play was called. I did my job and ran the sweep with no blocking and, of course, they killed me. The official put the ball down, and sure enough, Vanderbilt got in a huddle and held hands. When I knelt down next to the ball, one of the Vandy players asked me what I was doing.

I said, "Nothing," and shoveled the ball to Gene. He went into the end zone and nobody ever touched him.

We tried a variation of that play in the Cotton Bowl against Arkansas, but that time it didn't work. We were ahead 10–3, and Gene was supposed to take the ball from me and hand it on a reverse to Richard Appleby, our tight end. I was an eligible receiver, and he was supposed to throw it back to me. But the ball was fumbled, and Arkansas recovered. They knocked in a touchdown right before the half and tied the game 10–10. We lost the momentum and never got it back. They killed us 31–10.

It's funny how all these years later, people still remember the Shoestring that worked...and the one that didn't.

Ray Goff played quarterback for Georgia from 1974 to 1976. He was Georgia's head coach from 1989 to 1995.

The World's Largest Outdoor Cocktail Party

by Jeff Dantzler

About 10 or 12 years ago, we ran into some guys during our annual visit to Jacksonville for the Georgia-Florida game. For years these guys had picked one game away from home to visit. They had been to Michigan–Ohio State and several other great rivalries in college football, but this was their first Georgia-Florida game. They have been back every year since.

The Georgia-Florida game is really unlike anything else on the college football map. The tickets are divided evenly—40,000 for Georgia and 40,000 for Florida. I know Georgia people who leave for the game on Monday or Tuesday and fill up the hotels and condos on St. Simons, Jekyll Island, and Sea Island. For many of the Georgia people, it is a vacation that they always look forward to.

I can't speak for the Florida people and I wouldn't want to. But the Georgia people know how to have a good time. The game used to be called "The World's Largest Outdoor Cocktail Party" because that is exactly what it was. We're not supposed to call it that anymore. [After two alcohol-related deaths during game week in Jacksonville, officials at both schools asked that the media stop using the "Cocktail Party" reference when referring to the Georgia-Florida game.]

The game on the field is always intense, and for most of its history one side has dominated. We dominated the 1970s and '80s under Coach Dooley. I'll never forget during that stretch the Florida fans wanted to move the game out of Jacksonville. They said that we had a home-field advantage in a stadium that was about an hour from their campus in Gainesville.

Coach Dooley retired in 1988, and we hired Ray Goff. In 1990 Florida hired Steve Spurrier. Then the rivalry changed. Spurrier dominated us, like he did the rest of the SEC, and we fell behind. We are still trying to catch up. [Steve Spurrier went 11–1 against Georgia in his 12 years as Florida's coach. Florida is 18–3 in its last 21 games against the Bulldogs.]

We have had some tremendous wins in Jacksonville, none bigger than the famous 1980 game that gave us "Belue to Scott" and set us up to win the national championship. Sometimes I'm still nervous about watching the end of that game because I'm afraid Lindsay is going to drop the ball or something is going to go wrong.

But there is also the 1981 game [won by Georgia 26–21] when Herschel Walker carried the ball 47 times. In 1982 we won 44–0 when a lot of people thought we were going to lose.

But in this recent period, we have lost games that just defy description. We were so much better than Florida in 2002, and Steve Spurrier was gone. But we found a way to lose that game [20–13], and there is no doubt in my mind that it cost us a shot at the national championship.

We've had an entire generation of Georgia fans grow up not knowing how we used to dominate the Gators, but hope springs eternal. Urban Meyer is gone as Florida's head coach. He's been replaced by a Georgia boy, Will Muschamp, but he's never been a head coach before. We have a golden opportunity now to get back on the positive side of the World's Largest Outdoor Cocktail Party. I hope we take advantage of it. Going to Jacksonville for this game is always a lot of fun. But Georgia fans everywhere will tell you that it is a lot *more* fun when we win.

Jeff Dantzler, a noted historian on all things Georgia Bulldogs, is the sports editor of Bulldog Illustrated *magazine and hosts a daily radio show in Athens. He is also the voice of Georgia baseball and Georgia women's basketball.*

The Track People

by Larry Munson

One of the great things about Georgia is that there are so many traditions that are still going strong today. And after investing more than 40 years of my life in the place, tradition means something to me.

But you know the one I really miss? It's those crazy damned people who used to sit on the railroad tracks across the street [East Campus Drive] behind that end zone. I'm telling you, those people were what Georgia is all about.

I had heard all the stories from the former players and their experience with the track people. Remember that the players used to dress for the game over at the Coliseum and then get on a bus and come down to the stadium. They would park the bus on the street, and when the players got off, those damn people would go absolutely nuts! Now understand that most of those people had been out there on those tracks all night long and had been drinking for two days!

Mac McWhorter told me one time that if you weren't ready to play for Georgia after that, you probably were never going to be ready.

Joe Tereshinski, our old center, told me about the track people right before we played Alabama in that huge home game in 1976. The players went to the stadium on Friday to do their little walk around, and the track people were already there. They already had their damn game face on! Of course we killed Alabama [21–0] the next day. The track people had to get an assist on that one.

Then 1980 rolled around, and we decided to renovate and close off that end of the stadium. So the tradition of the track people was going to come to an end. We were undefeated and ranked No. 1 when we played Georgia Tech in the last game of the regular season—the last for the track people. I was staying at the Ramada Inn, and I told the folks I was going to drive down there and see the track people one last time. I didn't think anything of it, but the Georgia State Patrol guys wouldn't let me go alone. So they took me down there and kind of hung around to get me back.

Let me tell you, it was a wild damn scene. Some of those kids had been out there all night. I saw some guy lose his balance and just roll down the hill behind the tracks. I talked to a few of them and told them how we were going to miss the tradition.

Yeah, I know, progress. Nothing lasts forever because of progress. But the track people were something. They really were.

Larry Munson was Georgia's radio voice from 1966 to 2008.

UGA I–VIII: Damn Good Dogs

by Sonny Seiler

Since 1956 Georgia's official mascot has been a purebred white English Bulldog that goes by the name of UGA (pronounced "UH-gah). There have been a total of eight UGAs since 1956, all owned by Savannah attorney Sonny Seiler, his wife Cecelia, and the Seiler children—Swann, Charles, Sara, and Bess.

In the 56 years since he first started roaming the Georgia sidelines, UGA has become an international celebrity. On April 28, 1997, he appeared on the cover of Sports Illustrated *as the No. 1 mascot in all of college sports. UGA V appeared as himself in the Clint Eastwood–directed movie* Midnight in the Garden of Good and Evil.

As this book was going to press, the Seiler family was still mourning the sudden death of UGA VIII, who passed away on February 4, 2011, from lymphoma. The Seilers work with several breeders who are keeping the UGA lineage alive.

UGA V appeared on the cover of *Sports Illustrated* on April 28, 1997. The magazine proclaimed what the entire Bulldog Nation already knew: UGA is college football's greatest mascot.

It's really unfortunate that all of the UGAs can't speak for themselves because, I assure you, after all these years of taking UGA all over the country, they are very much like humans. When we lose a game, they can sense that their family is down, and they get down. And when we win and there is a lot excitement in the air, they get excited too and want to play.

Now throughout this discussion I will allude only to one dog because that is the way we see it. All of the UGAs are connected to form the spirit of one dog. That is the dog who represents the University of Georgia.

UGA has had so many great adventures. Over the years I think we've only missed a few regular season games. I remember that in 1958 we couldn't take him out to Texas when Fran Tarkenton made his debut. I've had to miss a game or two when I was in court, but somebody from my family will always take him. My son Charles has been helping me hold UGA down on the field since he was 15.

I think the only bowl he missed was our bowl out in Hawaii in 2000. I got a call saying that if we took him, he'd have to be quarantined for two weeks once he got out there. Well, we weren't going to do that, so we both missed out on a great trip.

In 1982 UGA went to New York to attend the Heisman Trophy winner when Herschel won the award. He had a great time. The dress was formal, so we had a white collar and a black tie made for him. And I'll never forget all the stares from those New Yorkers when I was walking him down to Central Park.

Another thing you need to know about UGA is that he loves a parade—especially when he is in it. He knows that a lot of people are paying attention to him.

UGA has had his moments on the silver screen. He pretty much played a starring role—at least I thought it was—in *Midnight in the Garden of Good and Evil*, which was shot in Savannah and directed by Clint Eastwood.

UGA and Clint Eastwood hit it right off. Clint came down to Savannah before shooting to check on a couple of things, and he asked if he could meet UGA and sort of size him up to make sure he would work in the movie.

Well, as soon as Clint saw UGA, he immediately dropped down to this knees and starting wrestling on the floor with him. UGA was loving it! Finally, Clint looked at UGA and said, "UGA, I'm going to make you a celebrity!"

That's when my wife, Cecelia, said, "Oh, Mr. Eastwood! UGA is already a celebrity!"

By the time Clint finished shooting down in Savannah, he found out that Cecelia was right.

I could go on and on, but what UGA would want you to know is this: he is proud to be a Bulldog. He is proud to be chosen to do what he does. And he does it with great dignity. Just watch sometime and you will see that he stands at attention for "The Star Spangled Banner" like everybody else.

Sonny Seiler teamed with Athens writer Kent Hannon to write Damn Good Dogs, *the story of UGA. There is also a DVD version of the story. Both can be purchased at the University of Georgia bookstore (www.uga.bkstr.com).*

THE "G" ON THE HELMET AND THE SILVER BRITCHES

by Vince Dooley

When we got to Georgia in [December] 1963, they had been struggling for several years. So a new head coach wants to change some things in an effort to bring some new enthusiasm and excitement to the program.

Georgia's football uniform had looked the same for a pretty long time under Coach [Wally] Butts with the silver helmets with the "block G" along with silver pants. I wanted something that was a little more modern and a little more exciting as we began to build our program.

I had seen the "G" on the helmet of the Green Bay Packers and liked the forward-looking design. I thought that general design would be something that might work for Georgia.

John Donaldson, a former Georgia player in the '40s, was on my first staff. And when I discussed the desire for a change of the helmet, he was very enthusiastic. His wife, Anne, had a degree in commercial art and volunteered to help us come up with a design.

I spoke to Anne and gave her some of the general parameters of what I was looking for. She came back with a very good design the first time out, and we went with it.

I should point out that while our new Georgia "G" has some significant differences than the one belonging to the Green Bay Packers, I asked our athletics director, Joel Evans, to contact the NFL to make sure they were comfortable with what we were going to do. The Packers gave their permission, and we opened the 1964 season with a red helmet with our "forward-looking G." I might also add that over the years the Packers have made changes in their design, so that the current version looks remarkably like ours.

One of the things we really liked about the new helmet was the black "G" against the white background on the red helmet. You could see it from just about anywhere in Sanford Stadium.

Another change we made on the uniform was to go with white pants. Georgia had been wearing the silver pants since Coach Butts came to Georgia in 1939. I thought the white pants looked good with the red jerseys and the red helmet when we were at home. We wore white pants and white jerseys on the road.

Now what a lot of people don't know is one of the reasons we went away from the silver britches in the first place. After I got to Georgia, I learned that one of the yells from the cheerleaders was "Go, You Silver Britches!"

Then I also learned that there was a variation of that yell that was not appropriate and wasn't what we were all about. [The variation of the yell was "Go, you Sons of ——, a word that rhymes with "britches."] So we got away from the silver britches, and they didn't have that yell any more.

In 1980 we decided that 17 years was long enough. Prior to the start of the season, we went back to the sliver britches that Georgia had worn for so long. Of course, that team went 12–0 and won the national championship, so we kept the pants. I still think we have the best-looking uniform in college football.

THE SEAGRAVES PARTY, 1980

by Hugh Nall

Our 1980 national championship team was special in a lot of ways. I have to say that is the closest group of guys in my time at Georgia. And one of the things that bonded that team in 1980 was something that we always called "the Seagraves Party."

It was a tradition on the Georgia football team to blow off some steam at the end of spring practice with a party at one of the local farms. No, we didn't tell the coaches about it, and yes, there were usually some adult beverages involved. Basically, the rising seniors were in charge of it, and we had a pretty good class coming up.

It used to be that the party included beverages only. But that year some of us thought the party needed some food. That's where the hog came in.

Five of us were involved: Scott Woerner, Chris Welton, Frank Ros, Nat Hudson, and me. Woerner was the big hunter and knew that we could go to this pig farm about three miles out of town near the botanical gardens. We had a great plan. I was going to handle the bow and arrow, all of us would get the pig out to Poss's place, and Nat Hudson was going to be the cook. Nat showed up in his cook's uniform, and, man, that was a sight.

To make a long story short, we went out to the farm, got the pig, and cooked it. But eventually we got caught because some of the freshmen—John Lastinger was in that bunch—took the hog head on campus and went to Brumby Hall to scare the girls. Campus police already knew that a hog was missing, so it didn't take long for them to put two and two together.

Coach Dooley was livid. He threatened to kick us off the team. Instead, he made us move out of our apartments and into the dorm. I remember Coach Russell addressing the five of us and then looking at Chris Welton and saying, "Chris, I understand that we killed a pig." That was Coach Russell's way of telling us that we were all in this thing together.

We had to paint the wall around the practice field. Coach Dooley would come by in his big car and tell us that we didn't do it good enough and make us do it again. We had to paint the bleachers at the baseball stadium. It was the hottest summer I can ever remember.

It was no fun going through it at the time, but "the Seagraves Party" of 1980 bonded that team in a way that is hard to describe. And you know the rest of the story. We went on to go undefeated and win the national championship.

Today those guys remain my closest friends. I talk to Welton and Woerner almost daily. And here is what's funny. It's been 31 years, and people still come up to me and say, "Killed any hogs lately?" They remember the Seagraves Party. I would much rather be remembered as the center on the 1980 national championship team, but I know that party bonded us in a way that made it possible to win that championship. So I will take that.

By the way, I still have that bow. I wonder what I could get for it on eBay.

Hugh Nall was the center on Georgia's 1980 national championship team. He went on to become an offensive line coach at Ole Miss and Auburn.

chapter 4

THE PEOPLE *of* GEORGIA

THEY WEREN'T PLAYERS. They weren't head coaches. But they are people you should get to know if you want to understand the complete history of football at the University of Georgia. Each has made a special contribution in his or her own way.

The stories of these special Georgia people are told by the ones who knew them best.

BARBARA DOOLEY

by Derek Dooley

Where in the world do you possibly start when the subject is my mother?

Everything you really need to know about my mother is contained in one story: the year was 1979, and I was 11 years old. We were sitting in the stands at a home football game at Georgia. Well, the game was not going well, and you know how fans are. They started saying negative things about the head coach, who happened to be my father [Vince Dooley].

Well, if there is one thing you don't do in front of my mother, it is to be openly critical of my dad. She just won't stay silent. She immediately stopped watching the game and went on a full verbal assault of those people. She was not going to put up with that.

Barbara Dooley is the wife of Vince Dooley, Georgia's Hall of Fame coach (1964–1988) and the mother of Derek Dooley, the current head coach at Tennessee.

I went to my daddy and begged him not to make me sit in the stands with my mother again. So he let me stay down on the sideline with him during the game, and eventually he had to put her in a private box with the rest of the family. It was the best thing for everyone involved, especially those folks in the stands.

But here is what you need to know about my mother and why she fought so hard to protect my father. She knew how hard he worked and how much family life he gave up to be a head coach at a place like Georgia. My father was incredibly invested in doing the best job he could, and my mother sacrificed having him home because that was what he needed to be the best that he could be. She understood that and was willing to make the sacrifice. I believe that was an incredible gift to the university, because unless you've lived that life, you have no idea how hard it can be.

My mother is comfortable in her own skin and has always had her own personality and way of doing things. My father never really got upset when she did things that may have embarrassed him because he wanted my mother to be her own person. He knew that everybody understood, "That's Barbara."

She is an extraordinary woman and, now that I'm a head coach, trust me when I tell you that nothing's changed. She is going to speak her mind.

Derek Dooley, who is now 43, is the head football coach at the University of Tennessee. Barbara and Vince Dooley attend most of Tennessee's home games, where they sit in a private box. Derek Dooley is the youngest of Vince and Barbara's four children. His mother still calls him "Precious."

Barbara and Vince Dooley recently celebrated their 50th wedding anniversary. A former candidate for the U.S. House of Representatives, she is the author of Put Me In, Coach, *a book about her life as a coach's wife. She has four children and 10 grandchildren. She remains one of the most popular after-dinner speakers in the South. For more information on Barbara Dooley, go to www.barbaraandvincedooley.com.*

Joel Eaves, Athletics Director, 1963–1979
by Vince Dooley

Before Joel Eaves became my boss as the athletics director at Georgia, he was my basketball coach at Auburn. I had signed to play football at Auburn, but Coach Eaves had seen me play in the state tournament and so he sent me a note asking me to consider also coming out for the basketball team. I really loved basketball.

Joel Eaves (left) was hired as Georgia's athletics director in November of 1963. He immediately hired Vince Dooley (right) as the Bulldogs' head football coach. The two had worked together at Auburn. Eaves remained as Georgia's AD until 1979, when he was succeeded by Dooley.

I played basketball for Coach Eaves as a freshman at Auburn and then became a starter as a sophomore. But my basketball career was cut short by a knee injury. I had hurt the knee before and thought it was completely healed. But one day I was going in for a layup and came down wrong and just tore the knee to pieces. They would have to operate. I was able to recover well enough to keep playing football, but my basketball career was done.

After my playing days at Auburn, I went off to the military and then came back to Auburn as an assistant football coach. Coach Eaves and I became the head scouts for the team.

We both held that job for five years, which meant that every Friday during the season we would travel somewhere to scout a future opponent. We would carry an old 16-millimeter Kodak projector and all of the game films we could get of that team. We would watch the film on Friday night, go to the game on Saturday, and return to Auburn and present the scouting report on the opponent.

It was great for me because I had a chance to study a lot of football with someone who was a great analyst and a true perfectionist. He was extremely well organized. I can remember being on a plane, and as soon as we landed he pulled a schedule for the entire weekend out of his pocket. He had every minute of that weekend planned. He once asked me on a Friday: "Do you think we should get a wakeup call for 6:18 Sunday morning?" Of course, I said yes because he had already thought all of this through.

He finally got out of coaching, and in 1963 Georgia hired coach Eaves as the athletics director. Georgia had fallen on some hard times financially and needed someone who was highly organized and a real straight shooter to run their department. Coach Eaves was perfect for that job.

He needed to hire a head football coach at Georgia because Johnny Griffith had been let go. He called and told me that he wanted to recommend me for head coach at Georgia but wasn't sure his athletic board would agree. I was only 31 years old at the time and was the coach of the freshman team at Auburn. Having worked with me all those years, he knew what was beneath the surface. But he just wasn't sure if he was willing to stick his neck out for someone so young.

What changed his mind was a phone call from Frank Broyles, the head coach at Arkansas. Frank was looking for an assistant coach to replace Doug Dickey, who had left his staff to become the head coach at Tennessee. Frank called Coach Eaves looking for me. I think that put Coach Eaves over the edge. He called me and offered me the head coaching job at Georgia. Then he said, "Oh, by the way. Frank Broyles called. Do you want to be an assistant coach at Arkansas or a head coach at Georgia?" Needless to say, after I took five minutes to talk to Barbara, I accepted the head coaching job at Georgia.

I told Coach Eaves, "If you're dumb enough to stick your neck out for me, I guess I'm dumb enough to take the job."

The only thing we haggled about was the length of the contract. He wanted to give me three years, and I wanted four. He gave me the four years with a starting salary of $12,500 per year. I still have the contract in a frame hanging in my office.

To understand the history of athletics at the University of Georgia, you have to appreciate the importance of Joel Eaves. He brought stability and fiscal discipline at a time when we really needed it. Coach Eaves was known to be very frugal, but that was what was required at the time. He was the right man at the right time in our history. He was a straight shooter and a man of unquestioned integrity. I was proud to call him my friend, and I was honored to replace him as athletics director when he retired in 1979.

Joel Eaves served as Georgia's athletics director from 1963 to 1979. He passed away on July 18, 1991.

Vince Dooley, who was Georgia's head football coach from 1964 to 1988, took over as athletics director in 1979 and remained in the position until he retired in 2004.

Claude Felton
by Mark Schlabach

In every institution there are unsung heroes. These are people who do extraordinary work every single day and quietly make the institution what it is.

At the University of Georgia, one of those people is Claude Felton, their longtime sports information director.

I met Claude when I was a 19-year-old student at Georgia working for the *Red & Black*. I thought I might want to get into sportswriting. I didn't know anything.

But Claude helped me, just as he helped a lot of young reporters who came before me and who have come to Georgia since I left. And he did it in a quiet and understated manner that sometimes makes people unaware of how effective he is and how good he is at his job.

When I was a young reporter, Claude's door was always open and it still is. He always answered his phone and he still does. If he doesn't know the answer to your question, he will find a way to get you the information. And if, as a reporter, you screwed up—and I certainly screwed up—he wouldn't pick up the phone and scream at you. He would calmly explain how you had gotten it wrong and he would never, ever hold a grudge.

The only thing about working with Claude as a student is that when you get into the real world as a reporter, you think every sports information director will be like Claude. You quickly find out that it's not true. If it were, our jobs as reporters would be a lot easier.

I have so many good memories with Claude. I used to spend a lot of time in his office, putting golf balls and waiting for practice to start. Most guys would run you out of the building.

Claude Felton (right), Georgia's Hall of Fame sports information director, with Herschel Walker in 2005.

If you had a problem with a coach or a player, Claude knew how to walk that fine line and to serve as a buffer between the two. He worked for the university but was also there to *help* the media. Some guys simply can't do both.

I still remember him driving that old blue Maverick all over campus. I thought I wanted to be a sports information director, but when I saw what Claude was driving, I decided to go in another direction. And when Claude finally broke down and bought himself another car, he made his son drive the Maverick. Priceless.

I don't think people truly understand how valuable an employee Claude Felton has been to the athletic department at the University of Georgia. He is a big part of the success Georgia has enjoyed in athletics. And I don't know of anybody who loves Georgia more than Claude.

I have said it many times: Claude Felton is the best sports information director in the country, period. All of us who have worked with him so long are just very lucky that he happens to work for the University of Georgia.

Mark Schlabach, a 1996 Georgia graduate, is the national college football writer for ESPN.com and a former writer with the Washington Post *and the* Atlanta Journal-Constitution. *He lives in Madison, Georgia, with wife, Heather, and their three children.*

Claude Felton, who holds two degrees from Georgia, came back to his alma mater in 1979 as sports information director and today is the associate athletics director of sports communication. He has received every major honor in his profession, including induction into the College Sports Information Directors Association (CoSIDA) Hall of Fame. Claude and his wife, Cathy, have three children.

LEWIS GRIZZARD, 1946–1994

by Loran Smith

Lewis Grizzard was a remarkable talent. I've never read anybody who could weave humor into a story as well as Lewis. But in addition to his unique personality, Lewis also benefitted from some really good timing.

When Lewis came back to Georgia (after working in Chicago), he began writing about what he loved. He loved country music, he loved beer, and he loved barbecue—which most of us love. At that time, though, those kinds of things just weren't being written about in the major newspapers such as the *Atlanta Journal* and the *Atlanta Constitution.*

Lewis wrote about the things that made him unique. He had a troubled early life. His parents were divorced. He was very close to his mama. He was constantly in search of his father, who must

THE QUINTESSENTIAL BULLDOG

Lewis Grizzard was born in Moreland, Georgia, and from very humble beginnings became one of the most successful writers of his generation. He became the executive sports editor of the *Atlanta Journal* at the age of 23. He then became the executive sports editor of the *Chicago Sun-Times* but decided that living in the North during college football season was not meant for him. That's when he wrote the book *If I Ever Get Back to Georgia I'm Going to Nail My Feet to the Ground.*

Lewis did come back to Georgia in 1977 as a sports columnist at the *Atlanta Constitution*. Several months later, at the prodding of executive editor Jim Minter, an old sportswriter, Grizzard became a general columnist of the first order.

And that's when Lewis became a star, publishing 25 books and becoming one of the most in-demand speakers of his era. One of those books was *Glory, Glory*, which he coauthored with Loran Smith after Georgia's 1980 national championship season.

He made a guest appearance on the television show *Designing Women* and also had an appearance on *The Tonight Show with Johnny Carson*.

But more than anything, Lewis was, by any definition, the quintessential Bulldog. He made no pretense of objectivity when Georgia was playing a football game. Besides, it was always more than a football game. It was, as Lewis said in a famous column: "Our way of life against theirs."

have been a rambling man. He had a couple of marriages that failed, and he wrote about that. In many ways, Lewis was like a country-western performer. Lewis liked the sad songs and liked to sing the sad songs. When Lewis wrote about his past, he made himself vulnerable, and people immediately identified with him.

But there was another side to Lewis that those of us who knew him were able to see. He also loved to sing the happy songs. He

The late, great Lewis Grizzard was passionate about the University of Georgia and Bulldogs football.

had a great desire to identify with the lighter side of life. He loved a good laugh and a good story.

Lewis enjoyed being the center of attention at parties. He was a great raconteur. He enjoyed his friends and he didn't want to be confined in his life. He wanted to be free to spend time with his friends. It was probably the reason one or two of his marriages broke up. The daily routine of marriage wasn't meant for him.

The one misconception I think people had of Lewis was that he was this hard-drinking, hard-living kind of guy, and that's why he died so early [at the age of 47]. The truth is that he had had a defective heart valve since birth, and once it was replaced, any infection would give him trouble. He had bad wisdom teeth, and I still believe if he had had them pulled he might be with us today. I just don't think this representation of him living a hard life is accurate.

He was just an exceptional talent, and we all miss him.

Loran Smith was the longtime executive director of the Georgia Bulldog Club. He cowrote Glory! Glory! *with Grizzard in 1981.*

DANIEL HAMILTON MAGILL JR.: THE GREATEST BULLDOG OF THEM ALL

by Greg McGarity

There is one thing that all of us who love Georgia can agree upon: Coach Dan Magill is the greatest Georgia Bulldog who has ever lived.

He is the most unique personality I have ever met. And it's not even close. He is one of those rare, selfless people who don't care about making money or getting credit for what he has done. All he cares about is making other people the best they can be and then doing what is best for Georgia.

I began working for Coach Magill at the tennis courts when I was only 10 years old. He would let a bunch of us pick up tennis balls and pick up bottles and trash and other stuff around the courts. In exchange for that, he would give us a dozen old tennis

In addition to being the greatest of college historians, Dan Magill is the most successful coach in the history of men's college tennis.

balls that we could use to practice our serves. Then he would sit up in the stands and give us lessons. There is no telling how much money he could have made by charging our parents for those lessons. But Coach Magill didn't think like that. He wanted to develop tennis in the city of Athens and maybe someday some of those young people would be able to help Georgia. That was always the way his mind worked.

Just think of everything Coach Magill has done to help Georgia. He started the Georgia Bulldog Clubs in every county in the state—all 159 of them. He was our sports information director. He became the most successful men's tennis coach in history. By the sheer force of his will, he got the Collegiate Tennis Hall of Fame built on our campus. And very rarely does his name get in the headlines. He is always the worker bee who is trying to help others.

I am so pleased that there were two events this year to honor Coach Magill because too many times we don't take the time to tell people how much we appreciate them while they are still around. His 90th birthday celebration in February [2011] was something really special. Then later in the month he was honored by both houses of the Georgia General Assembly. A lot of people had the opportunity to tell Coach Magill how much we love him, and that was good to see.

Think about this: he's 90 years old and he still goes to his office at the Hall of Fame almost every day. And while he is there, Coach Magill is trying to think of new ways to help Georgia. There has never been—and there will never be—another one like him.

Greg McGarity, a letterman on Georgia's 1973 tennis team, is the director of athletics at the University of Georgia.

ERK RUSSELL, DEFENSIVE COORDINATOR, 1964–1980

by Bill Krug

If you are lucky, you will meet a handful of people who are unforgettable and have a direct and positive impact on your life. I was one of the really lucky ones because I got to play for Coach Erk Russell at Georgia.

I didn't grow up in Georgia. I was a guy from Maryland who fell in love with Georgia. I didn't know about the legend of Erk Russell when I signed to play for the Bulldogs.

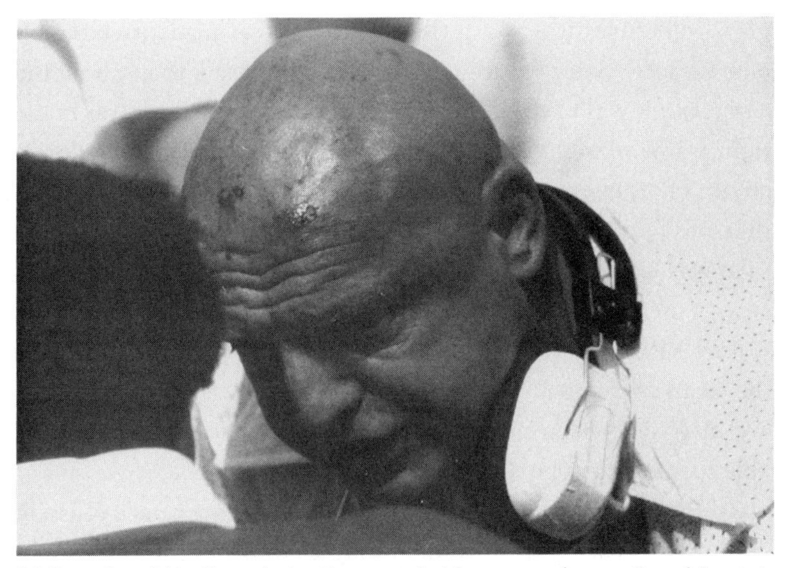

Erk Russell could be fierce during the game, but for 17 years he was Georgia's most beloved assistant coach.

In fact, I really didn't have a whole lot of contact with Coach Russell as a freshman because I didn't make the varsity that year [1974]. But I did hear the older players talk about him. They loved him and were in awe of him.

Coach Russell was simply the greatest motivator of people that I have ever met. He exuded confidence in way that I have never seen from another coach. Yeah, he was intense, but at the same time he was playful. He was tough, but at the same time you knew he had a tender heart for his players. He knew when to kick his players in the butt and then exactly when to put his arm around them and reassure them. I've never been around anyone quite like him.

Coach Russell was incredibly funny. He always came up with something right before the game to relax us and get us ready to play. Sometimes it was a little risqué, but that made it even funnier. Coach Dooley was usually the last one to talk to us about the game, but it was Coach Russell who made sure the team was in the right frame of mind to play. I have to give Coach Dooley a lot of credit. He was secure enough to let Coach Russell be himself, and that was good for Georgia.

It was Coach Russell who came to us about being the Junkyard Dawgs in 1975, my sophomore year. He had heard the term from Jimmy Matthews, one of our big boosters. A Junkyard Dawg is the meanest, scrawniest dog of all, and that described our defense. We may have given up a bunch of yards that year, but we were able to keep the score close for our offense.

It's hard to put into words how we felt about Coach Russell. He loved to kid around, and as long as you gave him the right kind of effort in practice, he let you have fun. But if you started slacking off, he would turn really serious and say, "All right, men. Now we're going full speed." You didn't want to hear Coach Russell say that.

It's been more than 30 years since I played my last game for Georgia, and Coach Russell is one of those people who just stick with you the rest of your life. Like I said: I was one of the lucky ones. It's hard to believe he's gone.

Bill Krug was an All-SEC defensive back for Georgia from 1975 to 1977.

Erk Russell was Georgia's defensive coordinator from 1964 through the national championship team of 1980. In 1981 he left to build a program at Georgia Southern, where he won three Division I-AA national championships. Russell retired after the 1989 season and passed away in 2006 at the age of 80.

Mr. Bulldog: Herschel Scott

by Tony Barnhart

Back in the '90s I was serving as the college sports editor of the *Atlanta Journal-Constitution*. In our preseason special section we wanted to honor the "Super Fans" of college football. Those are the fans for whom the sport—and the loyalty to their team—borders on the obsessive.

When I started looking for that kind of fan to represent the University of Georgia, I kept getting the same name from my friends: Herschel Scott.

The University of Georgia has been playing college football since 1892, and in that time there have been hundreds of thousands of loyal fans who would go to the ends of the earth to support their beloved Bulldogs. But there has never been another fan quite like Mr. Scott, who passed away on November 7, 2003, at the age of 82. It was my privilege to sit down with him for an interview several years before his death.

Mr. Scott had business cards printed up that declared him to be "Mr. Bulldog." When we met for the first time, he promptly handed me one. He lived in Monroe, Georgia, and his listing in the local phone directory was simply "Mr. Bulldog." I know. I looked it up.

At the time of his death, Mr. Scott had attended 471 consecutive Georgia football games both home and away, a streak that started in 1962. His last game was at Tennessee on October 11, 2003. He missed the following week's game at Vanderbilt to have surgery. Three weeks later he was gone.

"We've lost one of the greatest of all Bulldogs," athletics director Vince Dooley told me at the time. "It just won't seem right not seeing Mr. Bulldog around anymore."

At the time of his death in November 2003, Herschel Scott, also known as "Mr. Bulldog," had attended 471 consecutive Georgia football games. *Photo courtesy of the* Atlanta Journal-Constitution/*W.A. Bridges*

Mr. Scott made sure that his love for Georgia would continue after he was gone. Several years before his death, he had a red-and -black marble gravestone created. It reads: "A Bulldog Born, Bulldog Bred. Here I Lie, a Bulldog Dead. How 'Bout Them Dawgs!"

That says it all.

Frank W. "Sonny" Seiler

by Swann Seiler

For all of his great accomplishments as an attorney, I suppose my father is best known as the owner of UGA, the University of Georgia mascot. Owning all the UGAs and taking care of them has been a labor of love for my dad, my mother Cecelia, and the entire Seiler family. And we want to do it as long as the university wants us to do it. It has become a very important part of our lives.

But I want to tell you some things about my father that you probably don't know. We are an extremely close family. I know all families think they are close, but we really are. I have a brother, Charles, and two sisters, Sara and Bess, and Daddy checks in with all of us almost every day. And we all check in on our mother just about every day. We are that close.

My father has a very strong faith. We are all Lutheran, and Daddy is very much a disciplinarian. They expected us to behave, and nothing had to be said. We just did it because it was expected of us. He expected us to be involved in community activities. We were not allowed to just sit around the house. When we came home from school, we did our homework and then were outside doing *something*.

Daddy lettered in swimming at Georgia and taught us all how to swim. We were lifeguards and summer camp counselors. We were encouraged to make the most of the free time that we had.

While Daddy gets a lot of the attention, I want to use this opportunity to point out that my mother is truly the unsung hero when it comes to UGA. She made the shirts for the dog until real jerseys started being made for him. She was in charge of the feeding, and she treated UGA just like one of her children. She was the one who could look at a litter of puppies and pick out the next UGA. It was just instinctive on her part. The dogs were very loyal to her. She is a very genteel lady, a gourmet cook, and a meticulous housekeeper. When we were growing up, she expected a lot of us, and we are much better off for it.

Taking care of UGA has really become a year-round job for the Seiler family, but, as I said, it remains a labor of love. My brother, Charles, should get a lot of credit because he takes UGA to all of the away games. You'll remember that Charles was (kind of) holding UGA when he went after the Auburn player [Robert Baker] in 1996. That moment, and when he appeared on the cover of *Sports Illustrated* [April 28, 1997] really launched UGA's popularity. I talk to Charles every day, and he and Daddy and all of us work hard not to overexpose the dog. But we want him to be there when Georgia needs him.

I often get asked what it is like to be Sonny Seiler's daughter. I tell the people that it is an honor but it does put pressure on you. I work very hard to meet his expectations. But he and my mother have given me and my brother and sisters much more than we could ever give back to them.

Swann Seiler is a community relations manager for the Georgia Power Company and a former president of the University of Georgia Alumni Association. In 2011 she received the Dean's Medal for Communications Leadership from Grady College, the School of Journalism and Communications at the University of Georgia. She lives in Savannah.

Swann Seiler, former president of Georgia's Alumni Association, poses with her father, Sonny, who has owned UGA, the Georgia mascot, since 1956.

Frank W. "Sonny" Seiler is a graduate of the University of Georgia School of Law and a former president of the University of Georgia Alumni Association. He and his wife, Cecelia, have owned every UGA since UGA I made his debut in 1956.

LORAN SMITH

by Neil "Hondo" Williamson

This book contains the knowledge you must have to call yourself a Georgia Bulldog. Well, I would say that you can't be a true Georgia Bulldog unless, at some point in your life, you have done an impersonation of Loran Smith.

They don't do impersonations of people who aren't unique. And Loran is a special and unique guy. He is the most understated of great Bulldogs in the pantheon of great Bulldogs.

Every time that I introduce him in public, I tell people that I have never known anybody who loves the University of Georgia more than Loran. He has done so many things for our beloved university that nobody knows about.

One of my bosses once said that people think that change comes in great leaps and bounds. But the reality is that the people who bring about change and help move an organization forward are the ones who do a thousand little things to make it better. That's Loran because every day he wakes up looking for another way to make Georgia better.

He helps Georgia in so many ways. He is really the glue that has held the lettermen together. He was the one who stayed in touch with everybody and has chronicled everything.

And when the team from 25 or 30 years ago comes into town, he is every bit as comfortable with the backup tackle as he is with the stars. He will treat a swimmer from the '50s with the same

Loran Smith came to Georgia as a track star in the 1950s. He went on to become the executive secretary of the Georgia Bulldog Club and the sideline reporter for UGA's radio broadcasts.

dignity as he would No. 34 [Herschel Walker]. That's because every one of those guys contributed something to making Georgia better.

One of my favorite stories about Loran happened early in my involvement with the tailgate show. He was interviewing a guy who had played in the early '60s under Johnny Griffith. The guy was hard of hearing, and Loran was at his sickest [Loran Smith is a cancer survivor and founded the Loran Smith Center for Cancer Support at Athens Regional Medical Center], so his voice wasn't strong. Both men were struggling to hear and understand each other, and finally Loran reminded the player of a big block he had made in a game a long time ago. The player said, "Loran, I didn't remember that until you called me on Thursday."

That's the point. Loran remembers an important moment in Georgia history better than the guy who did it.

Loran also gets guests for us that other people can't get. When the Braves were having their great run, we could get [manager] Bobby Cox on the morning of a game. In our pregame show before the 2003 Sugar Bowl, we had [Miami coach] Larry Coker, who was playing for the national championship, Darrell Royal, Vince Dooley, and Bobby Bowden. We have that kind of star power on our show because Loran knows everybody, and everybody likes Loran.

I remember one time Loran was interviewing one of our players, Charles Johnson of Hawkinsville, Georgia. Loran said to Charles, "You must be the most famous person to come out of Hawkinsville."

Charles said, "No, that would be [rapper] Young Jeezy."

Loran never missed a beat and said, "Yes, Young Jeezy."

Loran had no idea who Young Jeezy was, but he was going to go with the flow.

A friend of mine who works with me went to Auburn. He told me all of us really didn't get how wonderful it is to have someone like Loran involved in our broadcast. He brings a unique flavor that other schools simply do not have. My friend said the Bulldog Nation is going to mourn the days when he's not in the broadcast and look back in fondness.

The biggest compliment I can give Loran is this: during his 43 years as Georgia's radio voice, the great Larry Munson had a number of people who were his color men and sideline reporters. But when people impersonate Munson, it is always, "Whaddaya got, Loran?"

Not, "Whaddaya got, Neil?" or "Whaddaya got, Joe?" It has always been, and will always be, "Whaddaya got, Loran?"

Neil Williamson, a Georgia graduate, is a veteran of more than 25 years in sports broadcasting in Georgia. He is the director of sports marketing at WSB Radio and cohosts Georgia's popular Tailgate Show *with Loran Smith.*

Loran Smith, a former captain of the track team at Georgia, has dedicated his professional life to the university. Among his many titles at Georgia have been assistant sports information director, business manager of athletics, and executive director of the Georgia Bulldog Clubs. He was the sideline reporter for Georgia's radio broadcasts for 36 years. He remains the cohost of Georgia's Tailgate Show.

Dean William Tate

by Charlayne Hunter-Gault

On January 9, 1961, Charlayne Hunter and Hamilton Holmes became the first African American students to enroll at the

Dean William Tate, Georgia's beloved dean of students, with the school's Homecoming Queen in 1974.

University of Georgia. In those difficult early days of desegregation, one of the people who stepped up to face the protestors and made Hunter and Holmes feel safe on campus was William Tate, Georgia's beloved dean of students. On the 50th anniversary of this historic event, Charlayne Hunter-Gault shares her memories of a Georgia icon, Dean William Tate.

It's too bad that Hamp [Hamilton Holmes, who died in 1995] is not here, because the two of them were so much alike. Hamp and Dean Tate were purists. Hamp was a purist in terms of academics and how he carried himself. He was serious about who he was and wouldn't tolerate people who would not acknowledge him for who he was.

Dean Tate believed in the law. It may not have been his personal view before the law was made, but once the decision came down, he was going to live by the law.

The memories I have from those first tumultuous days include Dean Tate being willing to put his body between us and the mob. Now there were people there who were just curious, but there were also people there who were mean and vicious. There is a picture somewhere of me and Hamp sitting in a car. And there is Dean Tate standing there with his body—and he had a peculiarly shaped body—in front of the car, pushing those students away.

People have asked me many times if I was afraid during that time. I tell them I really wasn't. I'm sure part of it had to do with the fact that I was young and the feeling of invincibility that comes with youth. But a lot of it had to do with my confidence in this big, white barrel of a man whose job it was to take care of Georgia's students—all the students. He was protecting me, and I had enough confidence in his amazing, giant presence to think that it was going to be all right.

I don't know what kind of price, if any, Dean Tate paid for that kind of support. But you have to wonder if taking that kind of stand hurt him with any of his peers. I never asked him about it. Dean Tate, like Hamp, was a man's man. He didn't have a whole lot to say about those kinds of things, and I didn't expect him to. I'm sure there were students at Georgia at the time who didn't appreciate the way he handled it. But I know I did.

It is hard to believe that it has been 50 years since that incredible time. But there are so many things to remind me of how important it was for me and Georgia. Not long ago I met a young black woman who graduated from law school at Georgia. I was at the airport in Atlanta when a young black man walked up to me and said, "I'm a heart surgeon because of you."

Other Memories of Dean Tate

"I remember that Dean Tate told me about being in Athens at the end of that game [Georgia winning at Michigan 15–7 in 1965]. He told me that as Ed Thilenius counted down the final seconds on the radio, he stepped outside and could hear the game all over town. Nobody was on the street. When the game was over, campus security kept calling him because guys were riding up and down the street with kegs of beer in their trucks. Dean Tate just told the police to leave them alone and make sure they didn't hurt anybody." —Preston Ridlehuber, quarterback, 1963–1965

"Dean Tate was a greater miler and two miler at Georgia and was a hero to the high school runners in the state. One of them, Bob Young, wrote him asking for advice on how to run the mile, and Dean Tate started corresponding with him and giving him tips. Later on Young showed up at the mile race at the Southern AAU meet in Birmingham. Young put on a burst of speed at the end and beat Tate in the mile. This did not make Tate's track coach at Georgia, Herman Stegeman, very happy. He asked, 'How could you lose to that high school boy?'

Tate said, 'I guess he just had a smarter coach than I did.'"—Dan Magill

Just the other day I was going through security at the airport in Johannesburg [Hunter-Gault now lives in South Africa]. I looked over at the line next to me and saw a young black couple. She was wearing a T-shirt that said "Georgia Dawgs!"

I yelled, "Go, Dawgs!!"

Fifty years ago none of that would have been possible, and today it is. What happened at Georgia happened because of a whole lot of people. Dean Tate deserves his place in that history.

Dean William Tate retired from the University of Georgia in 1971 as one of the most beloved figures in school history. He could be gruff, and his dorm raids (looking for illegal alcohol use and improper fraternization with the opposite sex) made more than one UGA male curse his name. But when a student was truly in need, they had no bigger advocate than Dean William Tate. The Tate Student Center at the University of Georgia is named for him. Each academic year, 12 freshman men and women are inducted into the Dean William Tate Honor Society. It is the highest honor a freshman can receive at Georgia. Tate died on September 21, 1980.

Charlayne Hunter-Gault graduated from Georgia in 1963 with a degree in journalism. She worked for the New York Times *before joining the* MacNeil/Lehrer Report *on PBS as a national correspondent. In 1997 she moved to South Africa with her husband, banker Ronald Gault. In 2001 the academic building where she registered for classes was renamed the Holmes-Hunter Academic Building. Her 1992 book* In My Place *tells the story of her childhood and her time at Georgia. Hunter-Gault and Holmes established an academic scholarship for African American students at Georgia.*

Georgia's Voices

Eight different men have served as the radio voice of the Georgia football team. Each of them has bonded with the Georgia people in his own special way. Here are the stories of three of these men.

Larry Munson (1966–2008)

by Scott Howard

Like a lot of kids who grew up in the state of Georgia, I spent a lot of time listening to Larry call Bulldogs games on the radio. One of the staples of my routine on game day was to make sure I took my

Larry Munson was the voice of the Georgia Bulldogs from 1966 to 2008.

transistor radio with me to the stadium. And like everyone else, I listened to Larry make the call while I watched the action on the field.

When I started working in Athens in 1989, Larry would come in to my station about once a week. He was working for WSB radio in Atlanta but had a weekly cable TV show in Athens. So on those days, he did his WSB radio show from our station and sort of hung out for about three or four hours. That is really when I got to know Larry. It was a great thrill to sit in the news room while he told his stories.

By the time I was given the opportunity to work with him on the [Georgia] network broadcasts [in 1994], I felt like I knew him well. At first it was a little intimidating, and basically what I did [as his color man] was try hard not to step on his toes. When you work with Larry, it is not a traditional broadcast where one guy did the play-by-play and the other guy did the color and analysis. Larry was so good that he could do both. My role was to stay out of his way and provide statistical information that he did not have. But Larry was very easy to work with.

Larry was effective as a broadcaster because he showed so much emotion when calling a game. He was pulling for Georgia and there was no doubt about that. Some guys use it as a point of pride that they are not a homer. But, quite frankly, if you don't want to be a homer, you probably shouldn't be in college broadcasting. Larry believed his role was to be cheering for the Bulldogs and to give our listeners the Georgia point of view. And nobody did it better than Larry. He was so descriptive and was such a great storyteller. He could put you right on the edge of your seat. I always looked forward to having a close game because I knew we would get vintage Munson.

The bond Larry had with the Georgia people was something very, very special. When you think of Georgia icons, you always think of UGA, Coach Dooley, Herschel Walker, and Larry Munson—not necessarily in that order.

When the time came [in 2008] and I got the opportunity to sit in Larry's chair, I knew I could not be him. I could not replace

Larry, and I certainly couldn't fill his shoes (his feet were a lot bigger than mine.) I'm not there to give people their Munson fix, so I never tried to do that.

I have always believed that it is just a cool thing that I got this opportunity to follow such a legendary voice. All I can do is take what he taught me and use it to be the best that I can be because, after all, there is only one Larry Munson.

Larry Munson was the radio voice of the Georgia Bulldogs from 1966 through the first two games of the 2008 season. He is a member of the National Sportscasters and Sportswriters Hall of Fame.

Scott Howard is a 1984 graduate of Georgia who joined the broadcasts of Bulldogs football as a color analyst in 1994. Howard did the play-by-play for Georgia road games in 2007, and when Munson stepped down in 2008, Howard took over play-by-play duties.

Ed Thilenius

by Loran Smith

Larry Munson is the man most people remember when they think of Georgia's radio voice, but I knew Ed Thilenius, and he has a special place in Georgia history.

Ed was just terrific. He had the most wonderful baritone voice. If he had grown up in Pittsburgh or Chicago, that great voice would have given him the recognition he never got while announcing some poor University of Georgia teams.

In the time Ed was calling the games for Georgia [1955 through 1965], we had a couple of decent teams, but not many. He got to call the 1959 SEC championship season and was in place for the first two years under Vince Dooley [1964 and 1965], when we came back to prominence.

From 1957 to 1964 Bill Munday (left) did the color on Georgia broadcasts with Ed Thilenius (right). Thilenius left Georgia in 1966 to work for the Atlanta Falcons and was replaced by Larry Munson.

But he was also a victim of some bad luck. He left Georgia to work for the Atlanta Falcons and their NFL broadcasts when the Falcons began their franchise [in 1966]. New NFL franchises don't do well, and so Ed had to call some really bad football. Then not long after he started, the NFL did away with regional broadcasting crews, and he didn't make the cut.

He really wanted his old job back, not to unseat Larry [Munson], but he just wanted to be a part of the broadcasts again. He called me and asked if anything could be done, and eventually he and Larry talked about him coming back and doing the color. That didn't work out.

But the thing about Ed was that he was always so prepared. Dan Magill once said that Ed was so authoritative that even if he was wrong, you would believe that he was right. I just loved his voice. I have never heard one better.

Ed Thilenius was the Georgia radio voice from 1955 though 1965.

BILL MUNDAY

by Furman Bisher

The thing you need to know about Bill Munday is that in the late 1920s he was considered to be as good as any broadcaster in America. He was a pioneer in his field and right up there with legends like Graham McNamee. He was the first sports director at NBC and started working the Rose Bowl for NBC in 1929. I remember listening to his call of that Rose Bowl when the California player [Roy Riegels] ran the wrong way against Georgia Tech.

Now, Bill had a different style. He grew up in Cedartown, Georgia, and never lost his southern drawl. He would talk about a team "going to the promised land" when they were getting close to scoring.

But eventually alcoholism—the sauce—did him in. I didn't meet Bill until I got to Atlanta in 1950, and by then he had pretty much hit rock bottom. Some of the local politicians got him a job running the elevator at city hall. When he would go to lunch, he would drop by the office and talk. I asked him to do some writing for us because I thought with his experience Bill would have something interesting to say. So he wrote one piece a week for us with his byline on it. It got him started back, and eventually the Georgia people got him back on the air.

I do have one regret about my relationship with Bill Munday. I remember one day I was hurrying to get to the office and I saw him

Bill Munday, shown here during the late 1920s, called the 1929 Rose Bowl for NBC. He was a native of Cedartown, Georgia.

across the street. I didn't take the time to stop and say hello and I just kept going. About a week later he fell dead of a heart attack.

Bill Munday was a very talented man, and you have to give him a lot of credit. He got about as far down as you could get and made a great comeback.

Furman Bisher, one of the greatest sports columnists of all time, worked for the Atlanta Journal *and the* Atlanta Constitution *from 1950 until his retirement in 2008. He lives in Fayetteville, Georgia, with his wife, Linda.*

After winning his battle with alcoholism, Bill Munday returned to the booth to work with Ed Thilenius as a color man for Georgia football. He worked the Georgia-Florida game in 1964 and died suddenly in February 1965.

OTHER GEORGIA PLAY-BY-PLAY BROADCASTERS: Jim Wood, George Therenger, Stan Raymond, Marcus Bartlett.

COLOR ANNOUNCERS: Eric Zeier (current), Scott Howard, Neil Williamson, Dave O'Brien, Phil Schaefer, Loran Smith, Howard Williamson, Bob Yongue, Jim Koger, Bill Simpson, Marcus Bartlett.

chapter 5
BULLDOGS *in the* COLLEGE FOOTBALL HALL *of* FAME

THE UNIVERSITY OF GEORGIA has been playing football since 1892, and in that time 16 former players and coaches have distinguished themselves by being named to the College Football Hall of Fame.

The College Football Hall of Fame is currently located in South Bend, Indiana, but in March 2013 will relocate to a new facility in Atlanta. It is only fitting that these great Bulldogs will soon be honored so close to home.

FRANK SINKWICH, RUNNING BACK, 1940–1942
1942 Heisman Trophy Winner

Sinkwich, who grew up in McKees Rocks, Pennsylvania, was part of a huge wave of Pennsylvania players recruited to Georgia by Coach Wally Butts. Sinkwich, in fact, was part of Butts' first recruiting class at Georgia in 1939.

After a sophomore season (1940) that saw him gain 373 yards on 63 carries, Sinkwich exploded in 1941 to become one of college football's very best players. In 1941 Sinkwich set an SEC rushing record with 1,103 yards. Georgia finished the regular season at 8–1–1 and then went on to the Orange Bowl, where Sinkwich put on a show for the ages. He completed 9 of 13 passes for 243 yards and three touchdowns. He also ran for 139 yards as Georgia beat TCU 40–26. Sinkwich's 382 yards of total offense is an Orange Bowl record that still stands 60 years later. It is also worth noting that Sinkwich suffered a broken jaw in the third week of the 1941 season and played the final eight games with a protective mask.

In 1942 Sinkwich teamed with sophomore Charley Trippi to lead the Bulldogs to an 11–1 season, Georgia's first-ever SEC championship, and a national championship according to some recognized news services. Sinkwich ran for 795 yards and passed for 1,392 yards (an SEC record at the time). Sinkwich went on to become the first player in Georgia history to win the Heisman Trophy.

Despite playing with two sprained ankles, Sinkwich scored a touchdown in his final college football game, a 9–0 win over UCLA in the Rose Bowl. He was inducted into the College Football Hall of Fame in 1954. His No. 21 jersey is one of only four that have been retired at the University of Georgia. He died on October 22, 1990, at the age of 70.

Charley Trippi, Running Back, 1942, 1945–1946

1946 Maxwell Award Winner

Georgia went back to Pennsylvania (Pittston) to find the man considered by many as the greatest player in Bulldogs history. Trippi was only 160 pounds as a high school senior, and so Notre Dame, among others, took a pass on him.

Despite Trippi's slight build, Coach Wally Butts and his staff saw something they liked in Trippi. Trippi agreed to sign with Georgia after spending a year at LaSalle prep in New York.

Trippi was a sophomore on Georgia's 1942 SEC championship team. Despite sharing the backfield with Frank Sinkwich, who

Charley Trippi is in both the College Football and Pro Football Halls of Fame.

won the Heisman Trophy that season, Trippi rushed for 672 yards and averaged 6.9 yards per carry.

Trippi would have been one of college football's superstars in 1943 but left Georgia to begin his military service. He returned to school for the final seven games of the 1945 season. In 1946 Trippi rushed for 744 yards and led Georgia to an 11–0 season and another SEC championship. He finished second in the Heisman Trophy voting to Army's Glenn Davis. He won the Maxwell Award, which goes to the nation's best college football player. He went on to play nine seasons with the Chicago Cardinals of the NFL.

Trippi, who still lives in Athens, is a member of the College Football Hall of Fame, the Pro Football Hall of Fame, the Rose Bowl Hall of Fame, and the Georgia Sports Hall of Fame. He was inducted into the College Football Hall of Fame in 1959.

Bulldogs in Their Own Words

CHARLEY TRIPPI

Growing up in Pennsylvania, I basically had two choices in life. I could find a way to go to college or I could work in the coal mines like my dad.

I saw what the coal mines did to my dad as he tried to support five children. Some days when he got home, he would have to lay on the couch for an hour before he could eat dinner. I decided that was never going to happen to me.

The University of Georgia gave me the opportunity to play football and get an education, and it completely changed my life.

As a senior in high school, I wasn't recruited all that much. I only weighed 160 pounds. I went to Georgia on a recruiting visit in 1940, but coach Wally Butts had just taken over, and I was a little apprehensive about where the program was going.

But when I got back home, I got an invitation and a scholarship to attend LaSalle Military Academy near Long Island, New York.

Everything would be paid for, and I would get a chance to develop more as a football player. I told the Georgia coaches that my plan was to go to prep school and then I would enroll at Georgia. It was the smartest thing I ever did.

I went to LaSalle and got heavier and stronger. I also played on a really good team and was named to the All-Metropolitan team in New York. Then the other schools really started paying attention to me.

But I had given my word to the Georgia coaches. Also, when I was being recruited, a big Georgia alumnus who worked for Coca-Cola promised me that if I went to Georgia I would always have a job in the summer. I remember graduating from high school on a Friday, and the next Monday morning I was driving a Coca-Cola truck. I was making more money than my dad, who was earning about $90 a month from the WPA. I was making about $25 to $30 a week.

I remember telling my dad about the football scholarship to go to Georgia. He said, "You mean they are going to pay all of your expenses to knock you down?" Of course he was elated because not many people in my area could afford to go to college.

But I also told him that once I got down there I was not coming back. I had to ride 800 miles on a bus to get to Athens. It took two days, but I thought it was the chance of a lifetime.

When I got to Georgia, I really didn't know Coach Butts. I had not met him during my recruiting trip, but I certainly knew his reputation. I knew a guy who had tried to play at Georgia and had left. He said, "Buddy, when you go down there, it will be like a slaughterhouse." I figured that if they were making the linemen work that hard, I had a chance to be a pretty good back.

I will never forget my freshman year, in 1941. We started out with 65 freshmen, but we ended the year with only 18 scholarship

They Said It

"Bobby Dodd, Georgia Tech's legendary coach, said that Charley Trippi was the greatest football player he ever saw. Trippi could do it all. He had incredible speed and could get up to full speed in just a few steps. I have a great deal of respect for Herschel Walker, but a lot of people believe that Charley Trippi is best player that Georgia has ever had."
—Dan Magill

guys and two walk-ons to play the freshman game with Georgia Tech. But I will say this—the guys who were left, you could go to war with. We made a tremendous sacrifice to stay there, and we took some awful beatings.

The 1942 season was a great one for us. I started out playing the same position [tailback] as Frank Sinkwich. He was a great inside runner, but I was a little bit faster on the outside. After making a few token appearances in the first few games, I stayed at tailback, and Frankie was moved to fullback, where he went on to win the Heisman Trophy.

The only game we lost all season was to Auburn, when we were ranked No. 1. Auburn was a T formation team, one of the few around, and we didn't know how to stop it. They beat us fair and square, but we still got an invitation to play UCLA in the Rose Bowl.

I was fortunate enough to play in a lot of special games. I played in three bowl games, four college all-star games, and a pair of NFL championship games. But nothing has ever compared to playing in the Rose Bowl.

It's just a special event, and anybody who plays college football has always wanted to play in that game. I can't describe the feeling of stepping on that field for the first time, other than the adrenaline started flowing and I really wanted to play. I remember playing 58 minutes in that game, and we beat UCLA 9–0.

In 1943, like a lot of guys, I went into the service, but I was one of the lucky ones. I got into a good program where I was able to play baseball and football during the war. The services were really competing for talent, and they would move you all over the place. I was finally based in Tampa, at the headquarters, and it was all football. I lived in Clearwater Beach with my family. We would commute in the morning, have practice, have lunch, and go home. That was my job.

I came back to Georgia in the middle of the 1945 season, right before we were going to play LSU in Athens. Coach Butts had gone to the T formation that season, and I didn't know anything about it. I only practiced two days before we had to play LSU. I almost got killed, and we lost 32–0. But believe me, after that I learned what to do in a hurry. Once I got the hang of the offense, I kind of liked it.

Going into the 1946 season, we knew we had a chance to have a pretty good team. And once we started winning and got the momentum going, we were hard to stop. I remember beating Alabama and Harry Gilmer in Athens 14–0. Gilmer was a great quarterback, but I don't think we allowed him to complete a pass that day.

I will always remember the Sugar Bowl, which was my last game for Georgia. We were playing North Carolina and their great running back, Charlie Justice. "Choo Choo" could go the distance any time he touched the ball. He was good enough to beat you by himself.

At halftime we were behind 10–0, and I was really mad. I could see an undefeated season slipping away. I was the captain of the team, so I chased the coaches out of the locker room. I told the players, "If we don't win this ballgame, we're going to be characterized as just another football team, even though we won 10 games. What we've done up to this point won't mean a damned thing. Anybody who doesn't think we're going to win then just take your damned uniform off and sit on the bench."

We went back out there and won 20–10 to finish 11–0. It was a great way to go out.

So many people influenced me at Georgia, but I have to start with Coach Butts. I learned how to play football when I came to Georgia, and from him I learned the level of commitment you had to give to the game in order to be really successful.

Coach Butts hammered that into me day after day. He would say things like, "Trippi, you're starting to believe everything they write about you." He would never let me get complacent.

I didn't really get to know Coach Butts until I left college and came back to coach for him. He was awful on the football field because he wanted to win so badly, but he had a big heart. If anybody was in need, he came to the rescue. He never let anybody down.

They call us "Wally's Boys," and every year before G-Day [spring game] we try to have a reunion and swap stories. I look forward to that gathering every year.

What does it mean to be a Bulldog? Well, I came to Georgia a poor boy. My first year in Athens I wore Coca-Cola work pants and a T-shirt all the time. That's all I had. But Georgia completely turned my life around. It gave me a chance to excel in football, and I was able to turn that into a very successful career in professional football.

And when my playing days were over, I came back to Athens, where I had always had a home, and I was able to enjoy some success in real estate.

It's simple, really. My time at Georgia was the best thing that ever happened to me. That's why I'm still here.

Bob McWhorter, Halfback, 1910–1913

Georgia's First All-America Player

In 1913 Bob McWhorter became Georgia's first All-America player. And, along with Frank Sinkwich, he was the first Bulldog player to be inducted into the College Football Hall of Fame in 1954.

The first of eight members of the McWhorter family to play football at Georgia, Bob McWhorter played under Coach W.A. Cunningham and led the Bulldogs to their first sustained success in football. He scored 61 touchdowns in four seasons as his teams went a combined 25–6–3.

Born in Athens, McWhorter was the first athlete in school history to be the captain of both the football and baseball teams, which he did as a senior. He graduated Phi Beta Kappa and was offered a contract to play professional baseball. Instead, he attended law school at the University of Virginia. He returned to Athens to practice law and was elected to four terms as the city's mayor. He died on June 29, 1960, at the age of 69.

McWhorter was inducted into the Georgia Sports Hall of Fame in 1964.

Glenn "Pop" Warner, Coach, 1895–1896

Led Georgia to First Undefeated Season

Glenn Scobey "Pop" Warner played his college football at Cornell, where he was called "Pop" because he was older than most of his teammates. Georgia hired Warner right out of college for

$34 per week. A little-known fact about Warner is that while he was coaching Georgia, he was also helping to coach the team at Iowa State.

Warner's first Georgia team went 3–4, but in the second season Georgia was 4–0.

Warner returned to Cornell in 1897 and eventually coached at eight different schools, where he won 319 games. Among those schools was the Carlisle Indian Industrial School in Pennsylvania (1899–1903), where he coached the great Jim Thorpe.

Warner, who was inducted into the College Football Hall of Fame in 1951, founded the Pop Warner Youth Football League, the largest in the country.

He died on September 7, 1954.

VERNON "CATFISH" SMITH, END, 1929–1931

Scored All of Georgia's Points in a Historic Win over Yale

According to Mark Schlabach's book *Georgia Football Today and Yesterday*, there are two stories explaining how Vernon Smith got his nickname:

One version claimed that a classmate at Macon's Lanier High bet Smith that he could not eat an entire raw catfish. The other story was that Smith just bit the head off a catfish on a dare. Regardless of which story is true, the name stuck with Smith for the rest of his life.

Smith was All–Southern Conference for all three of his varsity seasons at Georgia, but will always be remembered for his performance against Yale in the dedication game for Sanford Stadium on October 12, 1929.

Smith scored all of Georgia's points in a 15–0 win: he caught a touchdown pass, recovered a blocked punt in the end zone for a touchdown, kicked an extra point, and tackled Yale star Albie Booth in the end zone for a safety.

After college, Smith went into coaching for 10 seasons.

He was inducted into the Georgia Sports Hall of Fame in 1966 and the College Football Hall of Fame in 1979. He died on September 28, 1988, at the age of 80.

Bill Hartman, Fullback, 1935–1937

Enrolled in Graduate School at Age 77
So That He Could Still Serve Georgia

Few athletes had a lifelong association with the University of Georgia like Bill Hartman. A star in the early 1930s at Madison (Georgia) High School, Hartman was one of the most highly recruited players in the South. He chose Georgia, and right up until the time of his death in 2006, one day away from turning 91, Hartman was still serving the university.

He was an All-American in 1937 and played briefly for the Washington Redskins before coming back to Georgia as an assistant coach under Wally Butts.

Hartman coached part-time until 1956 and then became very successful in the insurance business.

In 1970 Coach Vince Dooley asked Hartman to work with Georgia's kickers as a volunteer. He coached a number of All-America kickers, including Kevin Butler, the only place-kicker in the College Football Hall of Fame. In 1992, when the NCAA banned volunteer coaches, Hartman enrolled in graduate school so that he could continue to work for Georgia as a graduate assistant.

Bill Hartman was buried at the Oconee Hill Cemetery, just across the street from the east end of Sanford Stadium. During the graveside ceremony, the public address system at the stadium broadcast some of Hartman's best plays at Georgia, reenacted by Larry Munson, Georgia's legendary radio voice.

The spirit of Bill Hartman continues on today. The Georgia Student Educational Foundation, which Hartman took over in 1960, has been named for him. The Bill Hartman Award is given to former student-athletes at Georgia who have distinguished themselves professionally. Among the recipients of the Hartman Award are Fran Tarkenton and Billy Payne.

Bulldogs in Their Own Words

BILL HARTMAN

FULLBACK, 1935–1937

In many ways it always seemed like I was destined to go to Georgia.

When I was growing up, we lived in Columbus, Georgia, for a while, and back then Georgia was playing Auburn in Columbus every year. My father took me to see my first Georgia game against Auburn in 1925. I had never seen anything quite like it.

I was still very young, but I remember Georgia going to play Yale in New Haven, Connecticut, in 1927, and Georgia won the game 14–10. Yale was a power back then, so it was a tremendous accomplishment for Georgia to go up there and beat them. But that was also the same year that we lost to Georgia Tech 12–0, and it cost us a trip to the Rose Bowl and the national championship.

There are not many of us still around, but I was in Athens on that day in 1929 when Sanford Stadium was dedicated. Yale came down to help Georgia dedicate the stadium, and we beat them 15–0. That was such a glorious day.

They Said It

"My father loved the University of Georgia so much that at age 24, after an impressive rookie season with the Washington Redskins, he chose to return to the university as an assistant coach to Wally Butts over a bright career in the NFL. He loved living in Athens. He loved Georgia and gave it his all until the day he died in 2006. He loved my mother more, but UGA came in a close second." —Bill Hartman Jr.

I was a lucky fellow growing up. I was the captain of the 1931 team at Madison [Georgia] High School, and then I went on to Georgia Military College [GMC] for prep school. I spent a couple of years there and was the captain of the 1933 team. Wallace Butts, who would become the head coach at Georgia in 1939, was my coach at GMC.

When it came time to pick a college, I had a lot of options. Little did I know that when I picked Georgia, it would start an association that would last a lifetime.

I began to be heavily recruited in my first year at GMC in 1932. Ralph "Shug" Jordan was the freshman coach at Auburn, and he would referee some of our games. I remember during one of those games I got knocked down, and he ran over to pick me up because he wanted to recruit me for Auburn.

I was only 17 years old, so Coach Butts talked me into coming back to GMC for another season in 1933. That was the year that Bobby Dodd left Tennessee and went to Georgia Tech as an assistant—and he started recruiting me, too.

I thought seriously about going to Tech. They were going to get me a job in the off-season, and the idea of working in Atlanta appealed to me.

General Robert Neyland, the legendary coach at Tennessee, offered me a job with the Tennessee Valley Authority in the summers that would pay $50 a week. That was really good money for a boy who used to work for a dollar a day at the grocery store. Neyland also said he would put me up in the Andrew Johnson Hotel in Knoxville so I wouldn't have to live in the dorm. All that kind of stuff was legitimate back then.

Then I met Mr. Harold Hirsch Jr., an executive with Coca-Cola and a big Georgia supporter, who offered me and three of my GMC teammates summer jobs with his company. We would make $75 a week, plus expenses, traveling as investigators for Coca-Cola. I liked Mr. Hirsch and I liked Georgia, so I decided to become a Bulldog. It was the best decision I ever made in my life.

The campus at Georgia was so different then. There were only 3,000 students—1,500 girls and 1,500 boys—and it seemed like everybody knew everybody else. Football players were not isolated as they are now but were part of the social scene. We all belonged to the various fraternities and honor societies that were so much a part of campus life. It is the most enjoyable time that I can remember.

On the field there were a lot of memories, too. I remember that in 1934 we lost the freshman game to Georgia Tech before 40,000 people. The score was 20–14, and we lost the game on a mistaken decision by the referee.

In 1935, when I was a sophomore, I played in most of the games. I clearly remember one game against Alabama. Paul "Bear" Bryant was a senior on that Alabama team and was supposedly playing on a broken leg. We ran the ball up and down the field, but they beat us 17–7.

In 1936 we went up to New York and played a Fordham team that was supposed to be heading to the Rose Bowl. They called

Bill Hartman has been associated with the University of Georgia since he enrolled as a freshman in 1934.

their offensive line "the Seven Blocks of Granite," and one of those blocks was Vince Lombardi. Their offensive line coach was Frank Leahy, who would go on to be the head coach at Notre Dame.

We were just a bunch of little Georgia boys, and they had a marching band with about 100 people in it. I remember they kept playing the song "California, Here We Come" because the Rose Bowl was supposed to invite them after the game.

We led 7–0 for most of the game, but they came back and tied us 7–7. We knocked them out of the Rose Bowl, though. We took the train back to Athens and got there about 5:30 Monday morning. There were more than 10,000 people there to meet us.

One of my favorite memories of 1937, my senior year, was when we played Holy Cross at Fenway Park in Boston. Holy Cross had a great All-America fullback named Bill Osmanski, who played the same position as I did. The Boston papers were calling the game "Wild Bill H. versus Wild Bill O." I played about 58 minutes in that game, but they beat us 7–6.

I will always remember my last game in Athens. Tulane was a power and about a three-touchdown favorite over us. They ran up and down the field on us, but we beat them 7–6.

In my last game against Georgia Tech, I remember that the score was tied 0–0 at the half. Coach Harry Mehre was late getting out of the locker room and was still in the end zone when Tech kicked off to us to start the second half. While Coach Mehre was arguing with one of the stadium guards, I ran the kickoff back 93 yards for a touchdown. But Tech scored a touchdown in the fourth quarter to tie the game 6–6.

I went on to play some pro football with the Redskins [in 1938], but Georgia was never far away for me. Back then guys in the NFL couldn't also coach in the SEC, but Georgia Tech coach Bill Alexander asked the league to waive that rule, so I got to help Coach Butts when he took over in 1939.

I really enjoyed coaching. Probably the most important thing I did as a coach was to talk Frank Sinkwich out of quitting. One day he didn't show up at practice, and Coach Butts sent me to the dorm to get him. Frank said he didn't think he had the ability to play in the Southeastern Conference, but he came back, started to work a little harder, and became Georgia's first Heisman Trophy winner in 1942.

I went into the service in 1942, and all during the war I thought about coaching at Georgia. When I came back in 1946, I coached part-time and started selling insurance. By 1956, I decided to go full-time in the insurance business in order to make some money for my family.

But I was lucky. Later in life I got the chance to be the volunteer kicking coach under Coach Vince Dooley, and I got to work with some great players. I was also given the honor of being the chairman of the Georgia Student Educational Fund.

All of those things kept me close to Georgia for my entire life, and for that I will always be grateful.

Fran Tarkenton, Quarterback, 1958–1960

Drew Up a Play in the Dirt to Beat Auburn in 1959

Francis Tarkenton was an Athens native, the son of a minister, and admired what Wally Butts was doing in the passing game at Georgia, the hometown team. But when the time came to make a decision on college, Tarkenton said that he seriously considered going to Georgia Tech.

"You have to understand that it was the Bobby Dodd era. Tech was the hot school and the team that everybody wanted to play for," Tarkenton said. "I think my second choice was Auburn."

But Tarkenton and his family were close to Mae Whatley, the wife of Georgia assistant "Big" Jim Whatley, who convinced Tarkenton that he needed to stay at home and play for the Bulldogs.

"Deep down I knew I wanted to go to Georgia, but I guess I was fighting it," Tarkenton said. "But Coach Whatley came over

They Said It

"On fourth down, Francis stepped into the huddle and said, 'All right, we're going to win the football game.' That's exactly what we did. Francis drew up a play in the huddle to go to Bill Herron and then hit him for the touchdown. We had quite a celebration that night."—All-America guard Pat Dye on Fran Tarkenton's winning touchdown pass against Auburn in 1959

to my house one night and basically flipped the switch. He made me uncover my feelings that I really wanted to go to Georgia. I still thank God that he did."

Tarkenton was a two-time All-SEC quarterback for Georgia and led the Bulldogs to the 1959 SEC championship and a spot in the Orange Bowl. He is best remembered at Georgia for a 13-yard touchdown pass to Bill Herron, a play that he literally drew up in the dirt, to beat Auburn 14–13 and clinch the 1959 SEC championship.

Tarkenton went on to an 18-year career in the NFL, where he played in three Super Bowls. He retired from pro football with 47,003 yards passing and 342 touchdowns. Then he had an ultra-successful third act of his life in business. He is a member of the College Football Hall of Fame and the Pro Football Hall of Fame. In 1998 he was inducted into Georgia's Circle of Honor. In 1986 he became Georgia's first recipient of the prestigious Silver Anniversary Award from the NCAA. It goes to a distinguished former student-athlete on the 25th anniversary of their senior year.

Vince Dooley, Coach, 1964–1988

Georgia's All-Time Winner

It was December of 1963 and, after four straight losing seasons, there was a lot of negative energy around the football program at Georgia.

First, Georgia officials replaced athletics director Wally Butts, who coached Georgia from 1939 to 1960, with Joel Eaves from Auburn. Coach Johnny Griffith was let go, and Eaves hired an unknown Auburn assistant coach named Vince Dooley. Dooley was only 31 years old.

Twenty-five years later, Dooley would retire with 201 victories, six SEC championships (1966, 1968, 1976, 1980, 1981, 1982), and one national championship (1980).

After retiring as head coach at the age of 57, Dooley would remain as Georgia's athletics director until 2004 and would build the Bulldogs' total program into one of the best in the nation.

Dooley was inducted into the Georgia Sports Hall of Fame in 1978 and the College Football Hall of Fame in 1994. He has won just about every major award that is given to a college athletics administrator, including the John L. Toner Award.

Dooley has written more than a half-dozen books on football and gardening, which is his favorite hobby. He earned his master's in history at Auburn and is a student of Civil War history. He remains active in athletics today as a consultant to Kennesaw State University's new football program, which will begin play in 2014.

Wallace Butts, Coach, 1939–1960

"The Little Round Man"

Of all the men who have served as Georgia's head football coach, James Wallace "Wally" Butts is the greatest enigma.

"The Little Round Man" was short in stature but powerful in personality. His practices could be brutally tough. Some players thought Butts was too tough and that Georgia sometimes left its best games out on the practice field.

"Some guys didn't like the fact that Coach Butts was so tough on them," said Art DeCarlo, who was an All-SEC safety at Georgia in 1952. "I didn't. I understood where he was coming from. He knew that whatever we chose to do in life we would have to be willing to work hard at it. So when I got to pro ball, I was able to handle everything that they threw at me. I had already been through the toughest part of my career at Georgia."

But as tough as Butts could be, the vast majority of the men who played for Butts remain fiercely loyal to him. Every year "Wally's Boys" have a reunion in Athens.

"They say Coach Butts was a complex man, but he was only complex if you didn't know him," said Jimmy Vickers, an end at Georgia from 1957 to 1959. "There was no mystery about Wally Butts. If you laid it on the line for him, he would lay it on the line for you. And to me, that's what it really means to be a Bulldog."

In the eight seasons from 1941 to 1948, Georgia was as good as any team in the country, winning 69 games and three SEC championships.

After winning his fourth and final SEC championship in 1959, Butts was forced to retire after the 1960 season with 140 career victories, still second only to Vince Dooley. He remained as Georgia's athletics director until 1963 and then launched a successful insurance business.

Butts was inducted into the Georgia Sports Hall of Fame in 1966 and the College Football Hall of Fame in 1997. He died of a heart attack on December 17, 1973.

HERSCHEL WALKER, RUNNING BACK, 1980–1982

1982 Heisman Trophy Winner

It has been almost 30 years since Herschel Walker played his last game for Georgia, but even today his numbers are staggering:

- 1,891: still the SEC record for most rushing yards in a season (1981)
- 5,259: still the SEC record for most rushing yards in a career (and he did it in only three seasons)
- 385: still the SEC record for most carries in a season (1981)
- 994: still the SEC record for most carries in a career

There are a lot more numbers, but you get the picture. When Walker's career ended at Georgia, he held 41 University of Georgia records, 16 SEC records, and 11 NCAA records.

But here is Herschel Walker's most impressive number of all: in the three seasons he played for the University of Georgia, the Bulldogs were 33–3 with three SEC championships and one national championship.

"Herschel Walker is the best player in the history of college football," said teammate Frank Ros, the captain of the 1980 national championship team. "I just don't think there is any doubt about that."

Georgia's fans can recite Walker's career highlight reel from memory. But he will always be remembered most for his performance in the January 1, 1981, Sugar Bowl, when the Bulldogs played Notre Dame for the national championship. Walker dislocated his shoulder on a hit early in the game. Trainer Warren Morris told head coach Vince Dooley that Walker was done for the day. But on the sideline, Walker told the trainers to pop the

THEY SAID IT

"I have always believed that talented people can be overachievers too—those are your superstars—and there is no better example than Herschel Walker. For all of his great gifts, and he was an immense talent, nobody worked harder and nobody was mentally tougher or had more self-discipline than Herschel. I just called him 'Old Man River' because he just kept on rolling along. The tougher the game, the more he liked it. As a coach, you hope to have one player in a lifetime like Herschel."
—Vince Dooley

shoulder back in place and returned to the game. Walker ran for 150 yards against a Notre Dame defense that had not given up a 100 yards against a *team* all season. Georgia won the game 17–10 and the national championship.

He won the Heisman Trophy in 1982 when Georgia went undefeated during the regular season and played Penn State (and lost) in the Sugar Bowl for the national championship.

Walker did not play his senior season at Georgia in 1983 because he signed a professional contract with the New Jersey Generals of the fledgling USFL.

He was inducted into the College Football Hall of Fame in 1999. Today Walker lives in Dallas, Texas, where he is involved with several charitable causes.

Bulldogs in Their Own Words

HERSCHEL WALKER

I remember when the call came, telling me that I had just been named to the College Football Hall of Fame. My first reaction was that I thought they were kidding. I really didn't think I had done anything yet because I still felt so young. That's because I felt that my freshman year at Georgia wasn't really all that long ago. I laughed when I got the news because I thought that you were supposed to be old to get those kinds of honors.

I'm so humbled by all the things that have come my way in life because I feel I still have so much to learn. Time goes by so fast. You just have to remember to stop and count your blessings along the way, and God has really given me more than my fair share.

When it comes to the memories, it's hard to know where to start. There are so many wonderful football memories because we were able to have some success while I was at Georgia. But what sticks with me today, and what I am most grateful for in my life, are the people I met at Georgia and how good they were—and still are—to me. Georgia was the best place in the world for me because I always knew that the people there cared about me as a person first. I never had any doubt about that.

The list of people is too long, but I always have to give thanks to Coach Dooley and Coach Mike Cavan, and teammates like Frank Ros, who have remained close to me. Ros is like a brother to me, and he has always been there for support.

People ask me all the time, if I were 18 years old, would I want to go back to Georgia and do it all over again? I don't think we're meant to live our lives over. One shot is all we get, and we have to make the most of it. If I did go back, though, I wouldn't want to change a thing.

I really, really enjoyed my time at Georgia. As everybody knows, I wasn't sure if I was going to go to Georgia. But once I got there, I knew that Georgia was the only place for me. It was an experience that will always be with me, and I will always be grateful for it.

I look at Georgia as a huge family. My sister was there. I met my wife, Cindy, there. And once you are part of the Georgia family, you remain in that family for the rest of your life. No matter what happens, they will always be with you.

And it was at Georgia where I learned to grow up and be a man. We had some good times at Georgia, but we also had some trials and tribulations. Those made me a much better person and built me into the kind of man I am today.

People ask me if I miss football and if it was hard to give up playing. It really wasn't. I don't miss the game, but I really miss being with the guys in the locker room. I miss seeing their faces after we have won a big game. I miss the crazy stories they would tell. I miss being with a group of guys that has a common goal. When talented people work together and care about each other, it's amazing what they can accomplish. That is what I miss.

And that is exactly what happened at Georgia in 1980, my freshman year. Georgia had had a tough season the year before [6–5], so nobody thought our team could be special in 1980. But that group of guys was really close. We stayed together as a team. No matter how tough things got, we always believed that if we just kept playing as hard as we could, we would find a way to win. That's what we did for every single game that year. That is why my freshman year at Georgia is still my No. 1 moment in sports.

Because I went to Georgia and because I played for Coach Dooley, I received some opportunities in life that other young people don't get. So I guess that's why I have always felt it was up to me to make a difference in this world. There are so many young people out there who need support—who just need a chance like the chance I got at Georgia.

Herschel Walker led Georgia to the national championship in 1980 and became the Bulldogs' second Heisman Trophy winner in 1982.

After all, when I get to heaven, God is not going to ask me how many Heisman Trophies I won or how many yards I gained. He's going to ask me what I did for my fellow man. I would like to have a good answer for Him.

Bill Stanfill, Defensive Tackle, 1966–1968

1968 Outland Trophy Winner

Stanfill came to Georgia in 1965 as a member of one of the school's most talented freshman classes ever. He left in 1968 with two SEC championships, an Outland Trophy, and the foundation that allowed him to play on two Super Bowl champions for the Miami Dolphins during an eight-year NFL career.

As a sophomore in 1966, Stanfill teamed with All-American George Patton to give Georgia one of the best defensive tackle combinations in all of college football. That was confirmed later that season when the two combined to make life miserable for Florida quarterback Steve Spurrier, who would later win the Heisman Trophy. Georgia beat Florida 27–10 on the way to winning the SEC championship. Stanfill still calls it the most important memory of his college career.

"I remember Bill Yeoman, the former Houston coach, telling me that Bill Stanfill was the only player he had ever seen who could take away all three options in the triple option. He was that good," said Dooley. "Bill was one of the greatest athletes we ever recruited to Georgia."

After his playing days, Stanfill retired to Leesburg, Georgia, where he became a real estate broker. He was inducted into the College Football Hall of Fame in 1998.

Bulldogs in Their Own Words

BILL STANFILL

I'll never forget the day I signed my scholarship to go to Georgia. I was recruited by a bunch of schools, but pretty quickly I narrowed it down to three: Auburn, Georgia, and Florida State.

Yeah, Coach [Ray] Graves at Florida did call. But I told him in no uncertain terms that I had no interest in becoming a Gator. Never did care much for the Gators, but I'll talk more about that later.

When it came down to signing time in December, I decided on Georgia. I liked the Auburn coaches, and Florida State had some good offers on the table. But I was a Georgia boy, and that's where I figured I should go to school.

I called Coach Sterling Dupree and Coach Dooley, and they came to my house. I signed my scholarship on Coach Dooley's back while Hal Herring, the Auburn defensive coordinator who was recruiting me, sat in the living room and watched. He told me he wanted to see it with his own eyes, and then he left.

Georgia has had a bunch of good recruiting classes, but the group of guys I came in with in 1965 had to be one of the best. Not only did we have a lot of great football players, but we had some quality people who went on to become doctors and lawyers and successful politicians. And before we were done, we also won a couple of SEC championships.

I was a freshman in 1965 and couldn't play on the varsity. I just remember that Jake Scott was my roommate. Now, that was an experience. Jake may have been the single greatest athlete to ever play at Georgia. He could do everything on a football field. He was very intelligent, but he didn't like school. As a result, he

Bill Stanfill won the Outland Trophy at Georgia in 1968 and went on to a great career with the Miami Dolphins.

wasn't eligible in 1966 when the rest of us finally got a chance to play. They had to redshirt him.

A lot of great things happened in 1966, my sophomore year, but my fondest memory of that year—and probably my whole college career—was when we went to Jacksonville to play Florida. I was hurt, and I wasn't really supposed to play. It was the night before the game, and I was rooming with George Patton. There was a knock on the door; it was Coach Dooley and the team doctor. I was thinking, *Uh-oh, what's going on here?*

Well, I always said that Coach Dooley was a miracle worker when it came to injuries. The next day, I was in the game playing Florida, and the Super Gator—that's what we called Steve Spurrier—was their quarterback.

They led us 10–3 at halftime, and all they had to do was beat us to win the SEC championship. But in the second half we took that boy to the woodshed and won [27–10]. That was a great day.

Next we went on down to Auburn, where we clinched Coach Dooley's first SEC championship. Then we got to play Georgia Tech when they were undefeated in Coach Bobby Dodd's last year. Tech had already accepted a bid to play Florida in the Orange Bowl. And we beat both of them.

I'm proud to say that in my three years we never lost to Tech and we never lost to Auburn. We beat Florida twice.

In 1967 I thought we had a pretty good team, but we lost some close games. We lost to Houston by a point and to the Gators by a point. What I most remember about that Florida game was their All-America tailback, Larry Smith. During the game, I hit him with a flipper and knocked him out. The Florida media called it a cheap shot and were raising all kinds of noise.

The next week Coach Dooley brought me into his office. He said, "Bill, it was not a cheap shot, but let's try to quiet this media down somewhat. I want you to write Larry Smith and apologize to him."

I thought he was kidding. I told Coach Dooley that was the way he taught us to play the game—tough and physical. Finally he said that he would write the letter, but he wanted me to sign it.

And I did. I didn't understand it at the time, but as I got older I appreciated what Coach Dooley was trying to do.

In 1968 we had a helluva team. We started out the season with a tie against Tennessee on that damned rug in Knoxville. Man, I hated that AstroTurf; it was like playing on a pool table. I got a strawberry on my leg that turned into a staph infection. I had boils up and down my leg and had to go to the hospital several times to get IVs. That's how bad it was.

We had a couple of ties, but we won the rest of them. We beat Florida again. We beat Auburn again and clinched another championship. And we beat Tech again.

The only downer was the bowl game. Some of the guys were let down because they thought we were going to the Orange Bowl. Instead we went to the Sugar Bowl and played Arkansas. I heard all the stories about guys being on Bourbon Street the night before the game, but I don't think it's true. I was married and in my hotel room with my wife. Arkansas just beat us [16–2].

For the record, I don't like New Orleans. I lost a Super Bowl there, too. [Miami lost to Dallas 24–3 in Super Bowl VI on January 16, 1972.]

There were so many funny things that happened off the field when the game was over. I guess it's safe to talk about them now—at least the statute of limitations has passed.

At the end of the Georgia-Florida game in 1966, people went pretty crazy. I hit old Spurrier so many times that people kept coming up to me wanting to show their gratitude. By the time I got to the locker room, I looked down and my helmet was full of money. One guy actually tried to buy my helmet from me, but I figured I'd better not do that.

In 1968 we were down in Jacksonville playing Florida in a monsoon. We got up something like 35–0 at halftime. After the first possession of the second half, the coaches told the first-team defense that we were through for the day. So a bunch of us got our Gatorade cups and stood by the fence while the Georgia fans filled them up with liquor. Then we would stand on top of the bench so nobody could look down into the cups while we enjoyed ourselves.

I had a great experience at Georgia. It prepared me for the NFL and for life after the NFL.

Quite frankly, when I first got there, I thought Coach Dooley was out of his mind. But as I got a little older, I realized where he was coming from and what he was trying to get us to do. He was trying to shape us, not only as football players but as men. When you're young, you just don't understand or appreciate that.

I was lucky. In my career I got to play for three great coaches: Vince Dooley, Erk Russell, and Don Shula. It doesn't get any better than that.

It's funny. I had to give up a lot to play football. I played four years at Georgia and eight years in the NFL. I have four discs fused in my neck. I have one bad disc in my lower back. In January of 2001 I had my left hip replaced. In November of that same year I had my right hip replaced. In 2003, for the first time in a long time, I was finally pain-free.

And you know what? If I were 18 years old right now, I would be glad to do it all over again. That's how much I loved going to Georgia.

Terry Hoage, Defensive Back, 1980–1983

From Playmaker to Winemaker

Terry Hoage's road to the College Football Hall of Fame, where he was inducted in 2000, has to be the most unusual in Georgia football history.

Terry Hoage, the last player to sign a scholarship at Georgia in 1980, was called "the greatest defensive player I have ever seen" by Coach Dooley.

It was the spring of 1980, and Georgia still had a couple of scholarships left over after putting together what would be a highly rated signing class. One of those scholarships was reserved for Herschel Walker, who would eventually sign on Easter Sunday.

Coach Vince Dooley told his coaches to go back over their recruiting lists and find somebody who could play but was also a strong student. They found Hoage.

When he graduated from high school, Hoage, a native of Huntsville, Texas, had decided to enroll at the University of Texas and give up football. His plan was to go to medical school. His father was a biology professor, and to Hoage football was merely a fun diversion from a rigorous academic schedule.

By the time he left Georgia, Hoage was a two-time football All-American and a two-time academic All-American. He led the nation in interceptions with 12 in 1982. In 1983 he finished fifth in the Heisman Trophy voting.

Hoage was a third-round draft choice of the New Orleans Saints in 1984 and played in the NFL for 13 seasons.

"I've said this many times and I still believe it," said Dooley. "Terry Hoage is the best defensive player I have ever coached and possibly the best I have ever seen. That year [1980] we signed the most highly recruited player in the country [Herschel Walker]. Terry was one of the least recruited players because we were the only Division I school to offer him a scholarship. Now they are both in the College Football Hall of Fame."

Today Terry Hoage and his wife, Jennifer, own a vineyard in Paso Robles, California (www.terryhoagevineyards.com).

Bulldogs in Their Own Words

TERRY HOAGE

Not too long ago I asked Coach Dooley why he gave me a scholarship. Georgia didn't sign me in 1980 until well after the signing period was over. He said that they wanted somebody who was going to go to class and make good grades. I appreciated that answer because, in retrospect, I'm glad that Coach Dooley understood me enough to allow me to enjoy life on campus outside of football.

Still, I had no idea that the journey that I started at Georgia in 1980 would someday take me to the [College Football] Hall of Fame.

I looked at football a little differently than guys I played with in high school. It was something that was fun to play because I really loved competing in just about anything. But football was not something I was going to chase after in my life.

I didn't know anything about Georgia when they came to my hometown [Huntsville, Texas] and started recruiting me. My plan was to enroll at the University of Texas and probably go on to medical school. I would not have walked on as a football player at Texas. I didn't have the desire to play football so badly that I was going to go out of my way.

Steve Greer and Mike Cavan recruited me early, and then they went away, and I didn't hear from Georgia for a while. Then Georgia offered me a scholarship, so it was an easy decision. Bill Lewis came out and signed me, and before too long I packed up my pickup truck and started driving to Athens.

My role in 1980 was to basically be a live tackling dummy. I was on the scout team, and it was our job to give the varsity the best possible look at what the opponent for that week was going to do. I was really too stupid to know what was going on. Coaches would just show us a picture of what we were supposed to do, and I went out there and did it.

I vividly remember one day playing linebacker on a goal-line defense. I got the crap knocked out of me and was lying flat on my back in the end zone. Cavan came over and stood over me and said, "Welcome to the SEC."

The truth is, I was enjoying myself, because I was winning just as many battles as I lost against the varsity. There were no expectations of me, so I was free to take chances on the football field and have fun. If I messed up, I knew I wouldn't get yelled at because I wasn't supposed to be doing anything. That freedom to take chances is what eventually led to my blocking kicks in practice.

One day, an entire practice for the Sugar Bowl game against Notre Dame was dedicated to special teams. It was a live scrimmage against the place-kicking team, and I was told to sort of stand in the back of the defense and not do anything. This went on for a while, and then I started thinking to myself, *Why am I just standing here when I could run and jump over the line and block the kick?*

So I didn't tell anybody, I just did it. And I blocked the kick. A little bit later I blocked another one. I figured I had nothing to lose. What were they going to say? Don't do that anymore?

Finally, Coach Dooley came up to me and said, "Can you do that again?" I said, "Well, I've already done it twice." And that's how my whole kick-blocking thing was born.

Now coaches, you know, can really screw up a good thing. After I blocked a couple of kicks in practice, they started tinkering with ways to make it better. They got Frank Ros going down on his hands and knees, and they told me to step on his back and jump. All I did was kick him in the butt three or four times and really bruise his hamstrings.

Of course I was cocky and told them I didn't need a platform. All I needed the line to do was to take out the knees of the offensive line and lower the wall a little bit. They finally conceded that it was probably not a great idea to keep kicking Frank in the butt.

So I went on the Sugar Bowl trip, and that was my job. I didn't get the first kick, but the next time it worked, and we blocked it. But to tell the truth, I expected it to work. I didn't see any reason why it wouldn't work. I think I was able to block four or five kicks in my career.

In 1981 I was a sophomore and moved into the rover position, which really suited my talents. I was able to grow into the position. I felt comfortable doing the things they asked me to do because it was all within my physical capabilities. I didn't have to stretch myself. The defense was such that it put me into a position to be around the ball and make plays. That season was a lot of fun.

But the following spring [of 1982] I actually went to Coach Lewis during practice and had a conversation with him about not playing anymore. When I signed up to play football, I thought it would be confined to the fall. I had no idea that it lasted 365 days a year—right after football was off-season training. Then there was spring ball. That year, about halfway through spring practice, I was sick and tired of playing football and thinking football and everything in my life being about football. It was too much.

I basically tried to quit, but Coach Lewis wouldn't let me. He did take it easy on me. He didn't ask a whole lot of me for the rest of spring practice. He told me to just relax and not worry about things.

Still, after spring practice, I told him that I had no intention of coming back in the fall. I didn't have the desire to keep doing it at that level and at that pace. He was very nice and told me to think about it and to give him a call at the end of the summer. So I went to Colorado and basically backpacked all summer. I didn't think about football or anything. I didn't train, but I did carry a 60-pound backpack at a high altitude all summer.

August rolled around, and I was back in Texas seeing my folks. Now I had to make a decision. I really hadn't made any alternative plans if I decided not to go back to Georgia. So I just went back and looked up Coach Lewis. I asked him if I could come back and hang out with the football team. I wouldn't be first team anymore, but that was fine.

In many ways it was like being a freshman again. Because I wasn't a starter, I could just go out and play for the joy of playing. Consequently, I took a lot of risks and reaped a lot of rewards. [In 1982 Hoage led the nation in interceptions with 12 in 10 games.]

It was probably the best year I ever had playing football because I was able to let go of all the superfluous stuff that people attach to competitive football at the highest level. I was just able to play like a little kid and not worry because I didn't fill the "C" gap. I just had fun.

Because I had so much fun in 1982, I was in a much better frame of mind to come back in 1983. It was not as hard to go through the off-season weight training and, as it turned out, the upper-level genetics classes I was taking had labs only in the afternoon, which conflicted with spring practice. I think that saved my sanity. I was able to come back refreshed.

At the time a lot of noise was made about the fact that Herschel Walker left school early to turn pro. But we had a lot of other good football players on that team. So when Herschel was gone, I think a lot of us felt we could make up the difference. Not that I didn't miss him in our backfield, because he was a great player. But it was our team, and we were happy with it.

My favorite memory of the 1983 season was being so happy for John Lastinger in the Cotton Bowl. He had taken so much criticism throughout his career. I'm sure that Georgia has a special place in his heart, because he rode such an emotional roller coaster while there. It was really nice to see him go out that way. [Lastinger scored a touchdown on a 17-yard run late in the game as Georgia beat No. 2 Texas 10–9 in the Cotton Bowl.]

It was never my ambition to play professional football. When I showed up in the NFL, I don't think I even knew how teams made the playoffs. I just thought I would play a couple of years, bank a little money, and then go to medical school. I was as surprised as anybody when it turned into a 13-year career.

I have to be honest that when the call came about the Hall of Fame, I didn't know anything about it. I didn't understand how big a deal it really is. It is an unbelievably huge honor, and now that I understand it, I am really humbled by it. I'm still not sure I necessarily belong there.

I just remember my family being at the dinner in New York, and there I was standing next to all of these other football players who had accomplished so much more than I had. When I think about how many people play collegiate football and how few get this honor, it is still amazing to me.

Like I said before, the thing that I am most grateful for with regard to my time at Georgia is that Coach Dooley didn't handcuff me and keep me under his watchful eye every second. He allowed me to grow up and become responsible for myself. I know a lot of guys don't have that experience.

At Georgia I was able to have the best of both worlds. I was able to live in the world of football and reap those benefits, but I also lived as a college student in the academic setting, which is just as important to me. That was what I needed and wanted. I don't think I would have survived if it had been any different.

I remember missing curfew one night because I was across campus watching a play and it had gotten out late. I was hurrying back to McWhorter Hall and walked right into Coach Dooley. I thought I was in big trouble.

He asked me where I had been, and I told him I had been to see *A Midsummer Night's Dream.*

He said, "Okay, just get on to bed."

That was nice. Coach Dooley got it. He understood. I have always appreciated that.

Kevin Butler, Place-kicker, 1981–1984

First Place-kicker Chosen to the College Football Hall of Fame

The College Football Hall of Fame was founded in 1951 and for the first 50 years of its existence honored players at every position except one—kicker.

Place-kickers and punters have always been an important part of football. They can win games—and lose them—quicker than just about any other player. But for five decades there was a resistance to putting them into the Hall of Fame with all of the other great position players in the history of the game.

That changed in 2001 when the Hall of Fame Honors Court decided the time had come to enshrine a place-kicker. The kicker they chose was Kevin Butler from the University of Georgia.

It only made sense. Butler was a two-time All-American in 1983 and 1984. He was considered to be one of the best clutch kickers of all time: he made a 60-yard field goal with only 11 seconds left to beat Clemson in 1984. His last kick as a college player came in the 1984 Citrus Bowl, when he attempted a 72-yard field goal that would have beaten Florida State. The kick was right down the

THEY SAID IT

"He possessed an incredible confidence. Every time we would cross the 50-yard line he would start walking in front of me, just to remind me that he was available. A time or two I had to push him out of the way so I could focus on trying to score the touchdown." —Vince Dooley

middle and was only a couple of yards short. He made a field goal in the rain in the final seconds to beat BYU 17–14 in 1982.

As a rookie in the NFL, Butler was the kicker on a Chicago Bears team that won the Super Bowl in 1986.

Today Butler lives in Atlanta, where he is in private business. His son, Drew, is an All-America punter for the Bulldogs who will enter his senior season in 2011.

Bulldogs in Their Own Words

KEVIN BUTLER

I've always been one of those people who believe things happen for a reason, even if we don't understand it at the time. And looking back at it now, it seems like I was destined to go to Georgia.

As I started my senior year [1980], Georgia and Auburn were right there hand in hand. Then, on the last play of the first game of my senior year, I hurt my knee. I was playing quarterback [for Redan High School in Stone Mountain], and Harris Barton of Dunwoody [who would go on to play for the San Francisco 49ers] landed on my knee and screwed up my kicking leg.

I was in a hip cast for about six weeks, and let me tell you, that was depressing. Here I had worked all these years to put myself into a position to get a college scholarship, and now this. It was a tough situation to deal with, to be honest.

Georgia and Auburn both stuck with me and made it clear that the scholarships were still on the table, no matter what. Duke came in and made an offer that would allow me to keep playing soccer, which was something I loved. But, needless to say, their football was light-years behind the other two.

I was always leaning toward Georgia for a couple of reasons. One, Rex Robinson was finishing up and was the latest in a string of four-year kickers at Georgia. I could see myself taking over that job and holding it for the next four years. The other thing was the way Coach Dooley used his kickers. He had made Rex a big part of that national championship run. He believed in playing great defense and making his kickers an important part of the game plan.

So that's why I signed at Georgia. Ironically, getting hurt helped me in a way. Because I couldn't play the rest of the year as a senior at Redan, I doubled up on my work and was able to graduate early. So I enrolled at Georgia and was there for spring practice in 1981. It really gave me a leg up on the competition, because there were already five or six kickers there. We competed every day, but I was able to win the job.

My first big memories came early in the 1982 season. In the opener against Clemson I got a chance to kick a couple of field goals, and we won 13–7. Later on I heard that Strom Thurmond, the senator from South Carolina, had written a letter calling me "the most dangerous Butler since Rhett."

That game was on a Monday night, and we had to turn right around and play BYU on Saturday. Steve Young was their quarterback, and they moved the ball up and down the field, but our defense kept making big plays to stop them. It was a misty day, and I remember turning to Herschel Walker and saying, "It's going

Kevin Butler, who beat Clemson with a 60-yard field goal in 1984, became the first place-kicker ever to be inducted into the College Football Hall of Fame.

to come down to one of us." I told Herschel that if he would just get me in position, I'd kick a field goal and win this thing.

And that's what happened. [Butler kicked a 44-yard field goal with 1:11 left in the game to give Georgia a 17–14 victory over

BYU.] It was the first time I had ever kicked a field goal to win a game.

I didn't make a lot of big kicks in 1983, but every field goal mattered because of the way that team had to play. We had lost Herschel, so it came down to defense, field position, and kicking. We turned every game into a chess match and waited for the other team to make a mistake. Then we would pounce on it. That was never more true than when we beat Texas [10–9] in the Cotton Bowl. I was very proud to be a part of that team.

People like to talk about the field goal to beat Clemson [26–23] in 1984, but what they don't remember is what led up to that. Clemson was ranked No. 2 or something like that, and nobody expected us to win. And at halftime we were getting beat pretty badly [20–6].

I have never seen Coach Dooley as crazy or as emotional as he was in that locker room. He really jumped on us because we were playing so lethargically. He wasn't mad because we were losing. He was mad because we weren't conducting ourselves the way a Georgia team should in a big game.

Well, in the second half we took it to them and tied the game. We got the ball back late, put on a little drive, and got it to around midfield. It was fourth down. I remember being right next to Vince. He just looked at me and said, "Field goal."

It was going to be a little more than 60 yards.

At that point there wasn't a whole lot to say. Coach Dooley had confidence in me, and I had confidence in myself. Coach [Bill] Hartman, my kicking coach, knew I had the leg. So did my teammates. But it freaked out the people in the stands that we were trying it.

Jimmy Harrell was the holder, so I never worried about that. When it left my foot, I knew I had hit it solid. I watched it for about a second to make sure that it was going to keep its course. Then I raced down toward the student section and dropped to my knees. I knew it was going to be good and that we were going to win. You never forget kicks like that.

The disappointing thing was the way that season ended. We went down to Jacksonville and got exposed [27–0] by Florida. I had never been on a team that had been beaten that badly. Then we just sort of fell apart, losing to Auburn [21–12] and Georgia Tech [35–18]. At Georgia, those are the three games that define your season. We dropped the ball and laid a big egg, and that still doesn't sit well with me because I was a senior on that team.

We went down to the Citrus Bowl and played Florida State. All week the coaches had been telling us about their ability to block kicks, and darned if we didn't let it happen—they tied us up late [17–17].

It came down to the last play of the game, and we had the ball. I don't know exactly where it was. I just knew that we were looking at a 72-yard field goal!

I remember going out there and hearing the Florida State players chuckle over in their huddle. They were making comments about our mothers and how ridiculous the kick was going to be.

We got to the spot, and Jimmy Harrell looked at one goal post and then the other.

"Shoot, we can make this one left-footed," he said.

I said, "Yeah, but we've got to kick it that way," and pointed to the goal that seemed like a mile away.

Jimmy said that when he put the ball down, he was going to lean it back a little bit, to give it a little better trajectory. I told him that was a pretty good idea.

I went out fully expecting to make it, but it came up a yard short. I was mad because I thought I should have made it. My last kick at Georgia was a miss, but it could have been one of my most famous kicks.

I've often said that I'm one of the luckiest guys in the world. I got to play for a college coach who appreciated how to use a kicker, and I benefited greatly from that. I got to play on a Super Bowl champion team as a rookie. I'll never forget that Cathy and I were supposed to get married on January 25, the day before the Super Bowl. After I went to my first team meeting in Chicago, I called home and told her that we had to change the date. I knew that team was going to the Super Bowl.

And then, after all the great things that had happened to me, one day Coach Dooley called and said that I had been selected as the first kicker to be inducted into the College Football Hall of Fame. That was a very emotional day for me.

But it all started at Georgia. That's where I really learned how to play and to be an important part of the team, even though I was the kicker. I gained a lot of pride in what I did at Georgia, and those lessons carried me through the rest of my career.

Like I said in the beginning, I think I was destined to go to Georgia. Now I'm really glad I did.

John Rauch, Quarterback, 1945–1948

Started 45 Consecutive Games at Quarterback

Rauch had a remarkable career at the University of Georgia. A native of Yeaden, Pennsylvania, Rauch started every game in four seasons for Wally Butts. He led the Bulldogs to an 11–0 season and an SEC championship in 1946, and as a senior led the Bulldogs to a 9–2 season and another SEC championship in 1948. When Rauch left Georgia, his 4,044 career passing yards was an NCAA record.

He started 45 games for Georgia, and in those games he was 36–8–1. He was the SEC Player of the Year in 1948.

He went on become the head coach of the Oakland Raiders and took them to the Super Bowl in 1968. He also was the head coach of the Buffalo Bills.

Ironically, Rauch's football career almost ended at age 14 when doctors detected a heart murmur. But in the 11th grade another doctor cleared Rauch, and he was able to continue playing football.

Rauch had done it all in football. But he was more than overwhelmed in 2003 when the call came that he was going to be inducted into the College Football Hall of Fame as a Georgia Bulldog.

"I was really overcome. I couldn't believe it," Rauch said in an interview in New York just prior to his induction. "I thought about Coach Butts and all my teammates at Georgia and what all those people had done for me. Nobody gets to the Hall of Fame alone, and I'm living proof of that. Everything that I ever became in football I owe to Georgia and to Coach Butts.

"I never thought I could make it to the Hall of Fame, but I did, and it was because of the Georgia family."

Rauch died on June 10, 2008, at his home in Oldsmar, Florida.

Bulldogs in Their Own Words

JOHN RAUCH

My entire football career almost never got started. I grew up in Yeaden, Pennsylvania, a suburb of Philadelphia, and back then the first time you ever got a chance to play organized ball was in high school. I had played a bunch in the sandlots and around town and knew I had a chance to make the varsity early.

But when I was 14, a couple of days before the first practice, a doctor gave me an exam and said I couldn't play because I had a heart murmur. My dreams were dashed.

I was in the 11th grade when the football coach at Yeaden decided that he would get a second opinion on my condition. My parents agreed, and that doctor cleared me to play. So I got to play my junior and senior years in high school.

My parents didn't have the money to send me to college, but my coaches were determined to find a place for me to go to school and play ball. I visited Tennessee, but they really didn't seem all that interested.

My life changed when my high school basketball coach, John Naegli, met a Georgia alumnus during a wedding up in Pennsylvania. Harold Hirsch Jr. was a Coca-Cola bottler, and his father was a big Georgia booster. In that one meeting, my high school coach convinced Harold Hirsch Jr. that I could be a college football player.

The next thing I knew, Coach Naegli received a train ticket in the mail with a note. The ticket was to Athens, Georgia, and the note said for him to send me down there so that Coach Wallace Butts could take a look at me.

Part of me didn't want to go because I didn't know what I was getting into. But I got on that train anyway. It was pretty late when I got to Athens. I got off the train and had no idea where I was or where I was going. I woke up a taxi driver near the station and told him I was here to try out for the Georgia football team.

He knew exactly where to take me. We woke somebody up at the dorm where the football players were living. They gave us some sheets and showed us a room where I could stay. The taxi driver even helped me make up the bed. I tried to pay him but he said, "If you're going to be a Georgia football player, the ride is on me."

John Rauch started every single game during his four-year career at Georgia.

For the next three days I just sort of hung out with the guys. I ate at the dorm and even went to a few classes. In the afternoon we would play touch football, and I would be the guy drawing up plays. I had not seen a coach yet.

Finally, on the third day, we were out throwing the ball around, and a car drove up. Three men got out of the car, and one of the guys said, "The short one is Coach Butts."

We played for a while longer, and finally Coach Butts walked up and asked me who I was. Then I told him the story of how I got the train ticket and how I got to Athens.

That's when he told me that he planned to go to the T formation that fall, and he wanted to show it to me. So he showed me how to take the snap directly from center and some other things. Then we ran some plays while he watched. Finally, Coach Butts took me off to the side and asked me about my plans. I told him that my immediate plan was to get back home because I had to graduate from high school in two weeks.

That's when Coach Butts told me that if I came to Georgia, I would have a chance to be the starting quarterback that fall. All of his other quarterbacks were going into the service because of the war.

Then he called over J.B. Whitworth, the line coach.

"You go home with Johnny and stay with him until he graduates," Coach Butts said. "Then you bring him back."

And that's what he did. We flew back to Philadelphia, and Coach Whitworth stayed around until I graduated. Then we went back to Athens. The next thing I knew, it was a week before the first game, and I was the starting quarterback. I started the first game against Murray State in 1945 and then started every game for the rest of my career at Georgia.

That was an interesting year to be at Georgia. A lot of guys were coming back from the war. We got Charley Trippi back midway through the season, and it took us a while to teach him the new T formation. Coach Butts took some of the best plays from the T formation and some of the best plays that Trippi ran from the old single-wing and developed quite an offense.

But the 1945 season [9–2] just set the stage for 1946 [11–0] when we went undefeated and beat North Carolina in the Sugar Bowl. Most of the guys on that 1946 team were two or three years older than everybody else. There was a lot of talent on that team—Trippi at left half, John Donaldson at right half, Dick McPhee at fullback, Joe Tereshinski...the list could go on and on. There is nothing like ending the season as an undefeated and untied team. That will always be my fondest memory.

In 1947 we still had John Donaldson, and Billy Henderson was coming along, but we just lost too many big-play guys. We ended up losing four games, and that was certainly a letdown from where we had been the year before.

The 1948 team didn't have a lot of stars, but we knew how to play together. We went 9–1 and then got to play Texas in the Orange Bowl. We lost that game, but I couldn't complain. When I left Georgia, I was the only player who had ever started every college game, including four straight bowl games. I felt really lucky.

I tried coaching for a while, and I never forgot the lessons I learned from Coach Butts. He was way ahead of his time in the passing game. He also believed that you never achieved anything great without paying a price. That philosophy served me well, even if some of my players didn't agree.

I was an assistant at Tulane when Al Davis contacted me at the coaches' convention. He was about to get the Oakland Raiders job and wanted me to come on as an assistant. I didn't know if I wanted the job, but Al turned out to be the most persistent man I've ever met. He could sell refrigerators to Eskimos.

I had been in Oakland three years when I became head coach and had a chance to take the Raiders to the Super Bowl. It also helped that I had a couple of bright young assistants named Bill Walsh and John Madden.

Everything that I ever became in football I owe to Georgia and to Coach Butts. Yes, he was a man of many characters and could change very fast, but I always thought that he was pushing me to be better. Some guys just resented that.

He could be as tough as a football coach could be, but each one of us knew that if we were ever in trouble we could go to Coach Butts. He did so many good things that nobody ever knew about. There is only one man I respected more, and that was my father.

I've lived in a lot of great places in my life, and even though I was born in Pennsylvania, Athens and the University of Georgia will always feel like home. I never thought I could make it to the Hall of Fame, but I did, and it was because of the Georgia family. It was a team effort, and for that I will always be grateful.

Jake Scott, Safety, 1967–1968

Still Holds Georgia Record for Interceptions

Coach Vince Dooley called him "the best athlete I ever coached." Scott was a consensus All-American in 1968 and led the SEC in interceptions in 1967 and 1968. He also led the SEC in punt return yardage in 1968. After a great junior season in 1968 Scott, who was known as the freest of free spirits, defied conventional wisdom and signed with the British Columbia Lions of the Canadian Football League. After a year in the CFL, Scott signed with the Miami Dolphins. In six years with the Dolphins Scott played in three Super Bowls and was the MVP of Super Bowl VII in 1972. He played his final three NFL seasons with the Washington Redskins. He was inducted into the State of Georgia Sports Hall of Fame in 1986. On May 17, 2011, the National Football Foundation announced that Jake Scott had been voted as the 12th player from Georgia to be inducted the College Football Hall of Fame.

JIM DONNAN, COACH, 1996–2000

Won 1992 Division I-AA National Championship at Marshall

Jim Donnan played his college football at North Carolina State, beating Georgia in the 1967 Liberty Bowl. He was 40–19 in five seasons as Georgia's coach but earned entry into the Hall of Fame because of his work at Marshall (1990–1995), where he posted five straight seasons of 11 wins or more and the 1992 Division I-AA national championship. He was inducted into the Hall of Fame in 2009.

PAT DYE, GUARD, 1958–1960

Won Four SEC Championships as Coach at Auburn

Pat Dye, from Blythe, Georgia, was an All-America guard in 1959 and 1960 for the Bulldogs. Dye, one of three bothers to play at Georgia, was named to the College Football Hall of Fame as a coach in 2005. Dye coached at East Carolina, Wyoming, and Auburn (1981–1992) for a total of 19 seasons. He won 153 games overall and four SEC championships in 12 seasons as the head coach at Auburn.

chapter 6

PLAYERS WHO MADE a DIFFERENCE

WHILE THERE ARE 12 FORMER PLAYERS in the College Football Hall of Fame, there are literally hundreds who have had a profound impact on the history of the sport at Georgia.

This list just scratches the surface, but if you're going to call yourself a Georgia Bulldog, these are players that you need to know.

BREAKING THE COLOR BARRIER

by Horace King

In 1971 Georgia signed its first recruiting class that included African American athletes. Horace King, a star at Clarke Central High School in Athens, was the first African American to sign, followed by his teammates, tight end Richard Appleby and linebacker Clarence Pope. Georgia also signed defensive back Larry West of Albany and defensive lineman Chuck Kinnebrew of Rome. King, who went on to play for the Detroit Lions, recalls that historic time.

I remember not too long after we got to Georgia, Loran Smith wrote a story and called us "pioneers." I remember swelling up with pride because then I understood what we were doing.

For a while, though, I didn't know if I was going to Georgia. It was coming down to the last days of the signing period [in 1971], and I was getting ready to go visit Michigan State.

Coach Mike Castronis was recruiting me for Georgia, and it was decided that we would all have a meeting. Appleby was there. Our assistant principal, Walter Allen, was there. We all sat down and decided to put everything on the table.

My main issue was that I didn't want to be a token person on campus or be considered unique or special when it came to being a football player. I wanted to be a member of a team. That's all. Then my mom reminded me that if I went off someplace far away, she would never get to see me play.

Finally, I looked at Richard and said, "I'll go if you go." It was just like that.

It turned out to be one of the greatest decisions I have ever made. Even though I went there with some concerns and doubts about how real my opportunity would be at Georgia, things just fell into place.

Now I'm not trying to say that everything was perfect. Getting comfortable and getting adjusted at Georgia was a long process. Still, I can't imagine having gone to school anywhere but Georgia. Georgia prepared me for pro football, and I was able to live out a dream. It rounded out my life as a young man and prepared me to move into adulthood.

Horace King was an All-SEC running back in 1974. He went on to play eight seasons for the Detroit Lions of the NFL.

FATHERS AND SONS

When current punter Drew Butler arrived on campus in 2008, he became the latest son to play football at this father's alma mater.

Georgia Football: It's All in the Family

Georgia has had 20 players who followed their fathers' footsteps and became football lettermen at Georgia. In fact, there have been several fathers who have had sons and then grandsons play for Georgia:

- Morton Hodgson Sr. (1906), son Hutch (1933), and grandson Pat (1963–1965, All-SEC tight end in 1965).
- Joe Tereshinski Sr. (1942, 1945–1946), sons Joe Jr. (1974–1976) and Wally (1976–1977), and grandson Joe Tereshinski III (2004–2006).
- Forrest "Spec" Towns (1936–1937), son Bobby (1957–1959), and grandson Kirby (2000–2003).

Like his father, Kevin, who was Georgia's place-kicker from 1981 to 1984, Drew Butler was an All-American by his junior year.

Here are some of the other father-son combinations who have played for Georgia. The years they lettered are in parentheses.

Marion Campbell (1949–1951) and Scott Campbell (1983). Marion Campbell was known as the "Swamp Fox," and after a career as an NFL head coach returned to Georgia as defensive coordinator in 1994.

James Cavan Jr. (1936–1937) and Mike Cavan (1968–1970). Mike Cavan led Georgia to the SEC championship as a sophomore quarterback in 1968. He was a longtime assistant under Vince Dooley and later the head coach at Valadosta State, East Tennessee State, and SMU.

Knox Culpepper Sr. (1954–1956) and Knox Culpepper Jr. (1981–1984). The senior Culpepper was the captain of Georgia's

1956 team. The junior Culpepper was the captain of Georgia's 1984 team.

GLENN CREECH (1964–1965) and GLENN CREECH JR. (1986).

LEROY DUKES (1962–1964) and DAVID DUKES (1984–1987). Leroy Dukes played on Vince Dooley's first Georgia team in 1964 and remained one of Georgia's biggest supporters as the owner/manager of the Ramada Inn in Athens. David Dukes was a star quarterback at Clarke Central High School in Athens and played quarterback for the Bulldogs.

STEVE GREER (1967–1969) and MICHAEL GREER (1997–1999). Steve Greer was an All-America nose guard for the Bulldogs in 1969 and was later a longtime assistant coach for Vince Dooley. Michael was an outstanding receiver.

BILLY HENDERSON (1946–1949) and JOHNNY HENDERSON (1976–1977). The elder Henderson played on two SEC championship teams at Georgia (1946, 1948) and went on to become one of the most successful high school coaches in the history of the state. Johnny Henderson was a starter at defensive back on Georgia's 1976 SEC championship team.

OLIVER HUNNICUTT SR. (1937–1939) and PAT HUNNICUTT (1962–1964). Oliver Hunnicutt was a three-year letterman at Georgia who went on to a very successful career (187 wins, two state championships) as a high school coach at Gainesville and LaGrange. He is a member of the Georgia Sports Hall of Fame. His son, Pat, was a defensive back and an All-SEC Academic selection in 1964. He went on to become a dentist in LaGrange.

John Kasay Sr. (1965–1966) and John David Kasay (1987–1990): John Kasay Sr. was a starting guard on Georgia's 1966 SEC championship team. He came to Georgia from Johnstown, Pennsylvania, and never left. Today he works with the school's strength and conditioning program. John David Kasay was an All-SEC place-kicker at Georgia in 1990 and went on to success in the NFL. He is still with the Carolina Panthers.

Cliff Kimsey (1939–1941) and Bucky Kimsey (1969). Cliff Kimsey was an All-SEC quarterback (third-team) in the same backfield with Frank Sinkwich.

Don Leebern Sr. (1936) and Don Leebern Jr. (1957–1959): The junior Leebern was a tackle on Georgia's 1959 SEC championship team. As the president of the Georgia Crown Distributing Company, Don Leebern became one of Georgia's biggest benefactors. He later became chairman of the University of Georgia Board of Regents.

Tom Nash Sr. (1925–1927) and Tom Nash Jr. (1969–1971). Tom Nash Sr. was an All-America end on Georgia's 1927 "Dream and Wonder" Team. Tom Nash Jr. was a three-year starter and a two-time All-SEC tackle (1970–1971). The junior Nash is an attorney living in Savannah.

Porter Payne (1946–1949) and Billy Payne (1966–1968). Both were All-SEC players in their senior seasons. Billy Payne went on to law school at Georgia and eventually became the chairman of the 1996 Olympic Games in Atlanta. He currently is the chairman of the Augusta National Golf Club.

"BIG BOB" POSS (1942) and "LITTLE BOBBY" POSS (1969–1971). "Big Bob" Poss was one of the most beloved personalities to play at Georgia and established a famous barbecue business with his son in Athens. Big Bob played on Georgia's 1942 team that won the SEC and the national championship. His most famous quote about that team, which included Frank Sinkwich and Charley Trippi: "I was third-team and I was good."

RAY RISSMILLER (1962–1964) and SCOTT RISSMILLER (1990–1992): Ray Rissmiller, a native of Easton, Pennsylvania, was an All-America tackle in 1964, Vince Dooley's first season at Georgia. Scott Rissmiller played tackle during the Ray Goff era at Georgia.

LANGDALE WILLIAMS (1959–1961) and TODD WILLIAMS (1982–1984, 1986): Both father and son were quarterbacks for the Bulldogs. Todd Williams was the starter on Georgia's 1984 team.

THE MCWHORTER FAMILY

It is the First Family of Georgia football, as a total of eight McWhorters have lettered at the University of Georgia. J. Vason McWhorter was the first to earn a letter in 1903. Bob (1910–1913) was Georgia's first-ever All-American. Mac (1971–1973) was the last McWhorter to receive a letter and was an All-SEC guard in 1973. He became a longtime assistant football coach before retiring at the end of the 2010 season.

McWhorter Hall, which was built in 1967 to house athletes at the University of Georgia, was named after Bob McWhorter.

Bulldogs in Their Own Words

MAC MCWHORTER

GUARD, 1971–1973

When your name is McWhorter, people say you have no choice—you're going to play for Georgia.

There have been eight McWhorters to play for Georgia, and I was the last. My great-uncle, Bob McWhorter, was the first football All-American in the history of Georgia. The athletic dorm at Georgia is named after him. My dad signed a football scholarship to play at Georgia, but was drafted by the Milwaukee Braves and decided to play baseball.

So I guess you'd have to say that when it came time for me to go to college, my path was pretty certain. Oh, I thought about Georgia Tech, but that thought was very fleeting, I can assure you. I chose to be a Bulldog, and I have never regretted it.

There were so many people who helped me at Georgia that I can hardly count them all. I came there as a linebacker. I played freshman ball in 1969 and got redshirted in 1970, and the next thing I knew, they were moving me to offensive guard.

I'll never forget that when I made the move, John Kasay, our strength and conditioning coach, came up to me and said, "If you ever think you're going to play in the SEC at guard, then you better live with me."

So I did, and he worked me to death. I cussed that man every day, but he bulked me up to around 230 pounds, and in 1973 I made All-SEC. I would have never played as well as I did or accomplished as much as I did without John Kasay. That's why I named my oldest daughter, Kasay, after him. I think there are about six players who have named children after him.

Coach Erk Russell was really special to all of us. I was an offensive player, and he coached the defense; still, he really touched me. My parents still have a handwritten letter he wrote them when I graduated. They had it laminated, and it still hangs on a wall in their home. He coached guys hard, and he was very demanding, but he had this way about him that let you know that he really cared.

There are so many memories I hardly know where to start. I was a backup guard in 1971, but in the Auburn game in November, Royce Smith hurt his knee. Now, Royce was an All-American and a great, great player, but I had to take his place for the rest of that game with Auburn and then start on Thanksgiving night against Georgia Tech.

Everybody remembers that game because Jimmy Poulos went over the top to score with just a few seconds left. What they don't know is that, with the game on the line and time running out, the coaches called "44 lead," which was an isolation play right over me, the sophomore guard. To this day I'm convinced they thought Royce was still in there instead of me. Thank God Jimmy got into the end zone and we won the game.

Later on that year we played in the Gator Bowl, which matched Coach Dooley against his brother, Bill, who was the head coach at North Carolina. We were 10–1 and had a pretty good football team. What I remember is that Coach Dooley really wanted to win that game. He stuck us in a Hilton way out of town and didn't let us have cars or anything.

Well, one night a bunch of us decided to have a party in our own room. So we got a huge suitcase and took a cab down to the package store. We proceeded to fill that suitcase up with the beverage of our choice. Then we decided, what the heck...we'll just ice down the beer in the suitcase so it will be cold when we get back to the hotel.

Mac McWhorter, an All-SEC guard in 1973, is one of eight McWhorters to play football at Georgia.

So we snuck back into the hotel and got to the elevator. We almost made it, but when the elevator door opened, who do you suppose was inside? It was Coach Dooley and Barbara, Erk and Jean, and Pat Hodgson and his wife, Nancy.

It was one of those huge elevators, so they insisted that we get on board. Nobody was saying anything about the suitcase. I got as far into the corner as I could, and I noticed that Erk was standing next to me. I looked down, and water was starting to drip from the corner of the suitcase!

Still, nobody said a word. The coaches' floor came first, so Erk held the door and let everybody off while the players and the suitcase stayed on. As he walked out the door, Erk said, "You boys have fun."

The elevator door was almost shut when suddenly in popped a hand with a cigar in it. It was Erk's, and he said, "One more thing, Mac. Next time you go wash your clothes, make sure to dry them before putting them back into the suitcase!" He smiled again and let the door shut.

That was his way of letting us know that we hadn't gotten away with anything.

I remember that at the beginning of every season Coach Dooley would lay down the law. He would list a bunch of "establishments" in Athens where players could not go because previous players had had trouble there. Then he would leave, and Erk would come and tell us to add Cooper's to that list of off-limits places. Cooper's, you see, was his place, and he didn't want us in there.

Then there was the annual party after spring practice, where freshmen would get initiated. Well, I guess the statute of limitations has run out on this one. Back then the juniors were in charge of getting the "product" for the party. So we would go around to all the different establishments in Athens, and we would tell them what it was for. They were more than happy to make a donation.

I still have a picture at home from that spring. I was living over in married housing, and we had cases of beer stacked up to the ceiling! I was on top of the stack. It was just unbelievable the fun we had!

We struggled in my last two years—1972 and 1973. I remember in 1973 we were playing at Vanderbilt and not doing very well. We couldn't run the ball because they had the line of scrimmage stacked. I looked up on one play, and there was a linebacker in front of me and the safety was right behind him. At halftime Coach Dooley was really upset.

"We're not running the ball the way Georgia is supposed to run it, and we're not going to throw until we do," he said.

That same year we beat Tennessee up there, after we got a lucky break. They faked a punt, and we got possession deep in their territory. The ball was on about the 10-yard line, and Andy Johnson was supposed to run a down-the-line option. When you're on the offensive line, you don't see a whole lot, and the next thing I knew, Andy was in the end zone, and we'd won the game [35–31]. We looked at film the next day and saw that Andy had actually fumbled the ball, and that it bounced right back up into his arms. We couldn't believe it.

I'm a Georgia boy, but Bill Curry at Georgia Tech gave me my first job in college coaching. I remember my first game with Georgia as a Tech assistant. It was in 1980. Georgia was really good, and we were really bad, but I was all excited about going back to my alma mater and being back in Sanford Stadium.

Well, it never occurred to me that some of the Georgia people might not be happy to see me come back. When we got off the bus at the railroad track end of the stadium, all hell broke loose. These people were throwing things and calling me everything, including a traitor. All of the players scurried down the hill, and we finally got into the locker room. Then they looked at me.

All I could say was, "Hey, guys. I'm on your side now."

I'm lucky in that I eventually got to go back to Georgia as an assistant coach. Part of me thought I would just retire there and coach the offensive line. At least that was my hope, because I do love Athens. But it didn't work out that way. That's just the nature of our business.

I am so grateful for the years I did have at Georgia. If I hadn't spent those five years at the University of Georgia, I certainly wouldn't have done the things I've done since then. Everything that I have accomplished, professionally and socially, I can credit to the time I spent at Georgia.

I tell my players today that their college experience is just a blur—it goes by so fast. Still, it will be the foundation of your life.

And, like we used to say, there is nothing like being a Bulldog on Saturday night. That is one thing that will never change.

Mac McWhorter was an All-SEC guard in 1973 and the offensive captain of Georgia's 1973 team. McWhorter came back to Georgia as an assistant coach for five seasons (1991–1995). He retired from coaching in 2010.

THE BAILEY BROTHERS

In eight seasons between 1995 and 2002 at least one of the three Bailey brothers from Folkston, Georgia, was in the starting lineup for Georgia:

Ronald Bailey was a starting cornerback for the Bulldogs in 1995–1997.

Roland "Champ" Bailey was an All-America cornerback for Georgia in 1997–1998 and one of the most versatile players in school history. In 1998 he participated in more than 1,000 plays as a cornerback, wide receiver, and special teams player.

Rodney "Boss" Bailey was an All-America linebacker and captain of Georgia's 2002 SEC championship team.

Bulldogs in Their Own Words

CHAMP BAILEY

DEFENSIVE BACK, 1996–1998

When I look back on it, I guess there were all kinds of reasons for me to go somewhere other than Georgia.

Coach Ray Goff started recruiting me early, but during my senior year, he was let go. Coach Glen Mason came in for a week and recruited me, but then on Christmas Day of 1995 he decided he was going to stay at Kansas. I really didn't know what to think.

But Coach [Jim] Donnan came and really made me feel like he wanted me at Georgia. I know some coaches will tell you anything to get you to come to their school, but that wasn't Coach Donnan. He stood by his word. I was really blessed to have him as a coach because he pretty much let me do what I wanted to do on the football field.

That first season [1996] was pretty tough. [Georgia was 5–6 in the 1996 season.] We really had some growing pains as everybody got adjusted to the new staff. But it helped me to have my older brother, Ronald, already there. He was a starter and just kind of showed me what to do. I just followed in his footsteps and tried to get a feel for things.

We had some good wins when I was a freshman, like the game at Auburn where we beat them [56–49] in four overtimes. Nobody expected us to do that. But I think after that game we knew that if we did what Coach Donnan and the staff asked us to do, we'd eventually be a good football team.

I will always remember my sophomore season in 1997. By then I felt I had pretty much mastered what they wanted me to do at cornerback. That's when Coach Donnan started to use me some on offense and special teams. I really loved it.

In high school I had played a lot of offense, and once Coach Donnan gave me a taste of it, I didn't want to go back. I really liked making plays and getting the ball in the open field.

The two greatest memories of that year were the Florida game and the Georgia Tech game. I know a lot of people didn't expect us to beat Florida because we hadn't been able to win against the Gators for a long, long time. But, growing up in south Georgia, you pretty much learn to hate Florida, and I was really looking forward to that game.

We knew we were good enough to beat Florida. We had a lot of guys on that team—guys like Robert Edwards, Matt Stinchcomb, Hines Ward, Chris Terry, and myself—who went on to do well in the NFL. When we got up on them 14–3 at halftime, we knew we had a great chance to beat them, and we did [37–17].

After that game there was such a great celebration. Out in the parking lot of the stadium in Jacksonville, people just stayed around and had another great party. Most of the players on my team were going back to Athens, but I got in my dad's car and rode home with him. I remember walking out to the car and the people were just so happy. I had never seen anything like it.

If you're a Bulldog, beating Georgia Tech is always great. But it's even better when you win the way we won down there in 1997. Tech thought they had us beat when they scored late to take the lead. [On November 29, 1997, Georgia Tech's Charles Wiley scored a touchdown with 48 seconds left to give Georgia Tech a

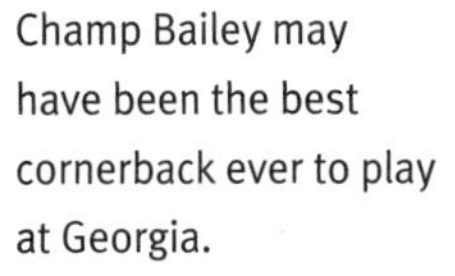

Champ Bailey may have been the best cornerback ever to play at Georgia.

24–21 lead at Bobby Dodd Stadium in Atlanta.] But we got the ball back in good field position when their guy kicked the kickoff out of bounds.

Coach Donnan put me into the game, and we ran what we called a "tunnel screen." I lined up at receiver on the right side and just came across the middle of the field and caught a pass from Mike Bobo. Now you never know what kind of opening you're going to get on that tunnel screen, but I was lucky to get a big one. I just wanted to get as many yards as I could so that we could at least get a field goal to tie the game. [Bailey took that pass 28 yards to give Georgia a first down at the Georgia Tech 37-yard line. Bailey then caught another pass from Bobo for seven yards, and Georgia was at the Georgia Tech 30-yard line with 29 seconds left.]

After I caught those two passes, it was pretty clear to me that we weren't going for the tie. We were going for the win! And that's what we did. We got it down there close after Tech was called for pass interference, and then Bobo hit Corey Allen for the winning score. The Tech people couldn't believe we had snatched that thing away from them. That was a sweet, sweet win.

We were so close to being a great football team in 1997, so a lot of us thought that 1998 would be our year. And when we started 4–0 and beat LSU [28–27] down in Baton Rouge, we were convinced that we were going to win the SEC. But Tennessee came to our place the next week and just beat us [22–3]. At the time we didn't know how good Tennessee really was, but they went undefeated and won the national championship.

We had a bad game against Florida [a 38–7 loss]. But the game that will always hurt was the loss to Georgia Tech [21–19]. We were so much better than they were. It didn't make sense for us to lose to them. I just couldn't believe we lost that one.

I knew pretty much at the end of my junior year that turning pro was going to be the right thing to do. There were reasons to stay. Boss, my little brother, was a freshman, and I wanted to sort of look after him. But it was the right thing to do. Coach Donnan was with me every step of the way and really helped me. I will always be grateful to him for that.

I've been lucky in my life. I come from a great family that has always been there to support me. And my brothers and I were lucky that we all played at Georgia. I'm still taking some classes at

Georgia, and the people there still treat me and all the members of my family well. When you come to Georgia, it is like being a part of a family, and that family is always with you.

I love Georgia. I grew up a Bulldogs fan, and I always knew I wanted to be a Bulldog. But the experience was everything I hoped it would be. Georgia was the perfect fit for me, and I felt like I had a great career there. I wouldn't change it for anything in the world.

Champ Bailey was perhaps the most versatile player at Georgia since the inception of two-platoon football. Bailey participated in more than 1,000 plays in 1998 as a cornerback, wide receiver, and special teams player. He was a first-round draft choice of the Washington Redskins in 1999 and was traded to the Denver Broncos in 2004. His brothers, Ronald and Boss, also played for Georgia.

Bulldogs in Their Own Words

BOSS BAILEY

Linebacker, 1998–2002

Because I had older brothers who played for Georgia, people have always asked me if I had a choice to go anywhere else. Sure, I had a choice, but the honest answer is that after Ronald and Champ played at Georgia, it just seemed like a second home to me.

Ronald and Champ never put any pressure on me. In fact, Champ wanted me to go to these other places and have some fun. But when I hurt my knee in high school, I decided to go ahead and tell the Georgia coaches I was coming.

I really enjoyed my freshman season, in 1998. Champ was still on the team, and it was nice having my brother around. I was basically a special teams player and a backup linebacker to Dustin Luckie. I got on the field a pretty good bit, and it was great to put on the uniform and be a football player at Georgia.

About the only real memory I have of 1998 is when we went down to LSU and beat them [28–27]. That put us at 4–0, and we came home to play a big game with Tennessee. That was an incredible day. ESPN brought *College Gameday* to Georgia, and people were really fired up.

Tennessee was undefeated, too, and we really didn't know how good they were until we got on the field. Our defense was concerned with stopping Tee Martin and Peerless Price, but Tennessee lined up and ran the ball against us with Travis Henry and Travis Stephens. They beat us pretty good [22–3]. Tennessee went on to go undefeated and win the national championship, so we can't feel too bad about that loss.

In 1999 I got my first chance to start, and I was really excited about that. That was the year, though, that Coach [Kevin] Ramsey came in as the new defensive coordinator. He brought in a brand-new system, and at first it was tough for us to learn. It took longer to adjust to what Coach Ramsey was doing than we thought it would. That's why our defense struggled. We had a lot of problems defensively, but I still think I had a chance to show the coaches what I could do.

After a so-so season in 1999 [8–4], I think we were all excited about what could happen in 2000. We knew that a little heat was on Coach [Jim] Donnan, but we really thought we were going to have a big year and that everything would be fine.

Unfortunately, my season ended during the first game, with Georgia Southern. That year Coach Donnan decided that some of the starters needed to play on special teams. I was on the kickoff team. On the opening kickoff I was running down the field and planted my foot to avoid the blocker. I felt my knee give way. Nobody ever even touched me.

As soon as it happened, I knew the knee was gone because I had hurt the other knee like that in high school. I knew that I was done for the season.

At first I was down about it, but it turned out to be a blessing in disguise. My young son was about to have heart surgery, and this gave me more time to spend with him. As soon as I got home after the game and saw him, I was through feeling sorry for myself. [Bailey's son, Kahlil, was born with a heart defect and underwent four hours of surgery in 2000 to correct the problem. Today, Kahlil is fine.]

It really surprised me when they fired Coach Donnan after the 2000 season. We didn't have a great season, but we were 8–4. That's not awful, either. We did have talent, and I guess they thought we should be winning more than that with the players we had.

I remember meeting Coach [Mark] Richt for the first time. I had heard a lot of things about him when he was at Florida State. We knew he was coming from a great winning tradition. I went up to his office and chatted with him. I was immediately impressed with how calm he was about life and how he went about his job. I knew there was something special about him.

Another reason I liked Coach Richt was that he never sugarcoated anything. He made it clear that he believed in hard work. The first thing he talked about was winning the SEC championship. He said we couldn't think about the national championship until we were good enough to win the SEC. I really respected that about Coach Richt.

The worst day of my college career was not when I hurt my knee. It was the day that I was introduced to mat drills in the

Boss Bailey, Champ's brother, overcame a serious knee injury to lead Georgia to the 2002 SEC championship.

off-season. [Mat drills are a series of strenuous exercises that are run on a conditioning mat. They are designed to push the player past the point of exhaustion and to test his ability to push through fatigue. Like basic training in the armed services, it also serves as a bonding experience for the players.] It was funny: they showed us videotape of the guys at Florida State running them, and I remember looking at Peter Warrick—he seemed to be enjoying it. So we were thinking, *Hey, this is going to be a lot of fun. This is something we can do together to get in shape.*

Well, I think they just showed us the good parts of the tape, because when we started running them ourselves it was no fun at all. I was wondering what kind of mess we had gotten ourselves into. Some of the guys were thinking, *Man, we should have played harder for Coach Donnan, and we wouldn't be doing this right now.*

I thought that day was never going to end, but it did and we survived. And the mat drills, as bad as they were, brought us together as a team. And that's where our motto was born: "Finish the Drill." It means that no matter how tired you are, you have to find the energy to finish the drill. Those mat drills made us mentally tough.

I think that toughness really paid off for the first time when we won at Tennessee that fall [of 2001]. Tennessee thought they had us beat when they scored late. Another team would have been tired and would have given up, but we had something left and found a way to win that game [26–24].

That game was the turning point for this team and this program. After that, everybody had the greatest confidence in the world in each other and in Coach Richt and the staff.

We didn't talk a lot about it publicly, but I really believed we had a chance to be pretty good in 2002. We had some great leaders on that team, guys like Tony Gilbert and Jon Stinchcomb and myself. And we had some younger guys who wanted to be good and would follow.

I think the turning point in our season was when we went to Alabama. I think that may have been the toughest place I've ever played. That was SEC football at its finest. We fell behind late, and Alabama was sure they were going to win. Then our offense really got rolling and just marched the ball down the field. Billy [Bennett] kicked the field goal, and we won [27–25]. It's hard to explain, but we really knew we were going to win that game.

That win was especially sweet because before the game Coach Pat Dye, who used to be the coach at Auburn, said that we weren't "man enough" to beat Alabama.

I had the exact same feeling when we played Auburn. We played a lousy first half, and late in the game we were still behind. But I just knew that somebody was going to step up and make a play. Then David Greene and Michael Johnson made the play [a 19-yard touchdown pass with 1:25 left] to give us the win and put us in the SEC championship game.

The night of the SEC championship game at the Georgia Dome was really, really special. I remember seeing the look on the face of Jon Stinchcomb. His brother [Matt] had played at Georgia with Champ, but they had never won an SEC championship. I remember looking at Jon, and we both thought, *This is for all those guys.* [On December 7, 2002, Georgia beat Arkansas 30–3 in the SEC championship game in Atlanta. It was Georgia's first SEC championship since 1982.]

I remember talking to my brothers after the game, and I think they were more excited than I was. It had been so long for Georgia, and to be a part of the team that finally brought the championship back to Athens was really special. I still have a picture of me, Stinchcomb, Tony Gilbert, and Burt Jones. We were the captains of that team and the captains for that game. That is something that I will always have with me.

I began to visit the University of Georgia when my brother, Ronald, went there in 1993. Ronald had his time. Champ had his time. And now I've had my time.

I just know that my brothers and I wouldn't trade anything for our time at Georgia.

I guess you could say that Georgia has been pretty good to the Bailey family. I hope that we have been good for Georgia, too.

Boss Bailey was an All-America linebacker in 2002 and the captain of Georgia's SEC championship team. Bailey was drafted in the second round by the Detroit Lions and played there until 2008. He then went to the Denver Broncos, where his brother, Champ, also played, and was released in 2009.

The Stinchcomb Brothers

When it comes to high achievers both on and off the football field, it would be tough to match the Stinchcomb brothers, Matt and Jon.

Matt Stinchcomb (1995–1998) was an All-America offensive tackle in 1997 and 1998. He was a two-time academic All-American who graduated with a 3.96 grade-point average. In 1998 he was the winner of the Draddy Award (now the William V. Campbell Award), which is given by the National Football Foundation to the top scholar in college football. In 1999 Stinchcomb was a first-round draft choice of the Oakland Raiders. He signed with the Tampa Bay Bucs in 2004 and retired after the

2006 season. Today he is a college football analyst for ESPN and lives in Atlanta, where he owns an insurance brokerage firm with former Georgia quarterback David Greene.

JON STINCHCOMB (1999–2002) was an All-America tackle in 2002 and a two-time academic All-American. He graduated with a 3.75 grade-point average in microbiology. At the time of his graduation Stinchcomb planned to attend medical school but put that on hold to play for the New Orleans Saints. He was a starting tackle on the Saints' 2009 Super Bowl championship team.

Bulldogs in Their Own Words

MATT STINCHCOMB

OFFENSIVE TACKLE, 1995–1998

I guess you could say that I went through one of the strangest times in the history of Georgia football. When I was a freshman in 1995, we ended up having three different head football coaches in about three weeks.

I was recruited by Mac McWhorter and head coach Ray Goff to come to Georgia. The truth is, they really didn't have to work that hard.

I started going over to Athens for games with my coaches pretty early in my high school career. I didn't have a family connection with Georgia, but for some reason I always felt comfortable when I was there. By the time I got to be a senior, it was pretty much a foregone conclusion for me: I was going to be a Bulldog. Nobody ever noticed, but when I would take my unofficial visits to other schools, I would always do it on the Saturday they were playing Georgia.

As a freshman in 1995, I was a backup to Paul Taylor at the tight-side guard. I don't know if Paul was a first-team All-SEC player that year, but he should have been. He was a great player.

That was really a tough year, and things really worked against our team. We started out great when Robert Edwards scored five touchdowns against South Carolina. And the next week against Tennessee we were running up and down the field when Robert got hurt. Then things just began to fall apart because of injuries. Before the season was over, we had Hines Ward, a wide receiver, at quarterback.

We finished the season 6–5 [6–6 after losing the Peach Bowl] and things began to get very strange and very surreal. In December Glen Mason was named the head coach. A week later, on Christmas Day, we heard that he was going to stay at Kansas.

I can say this now: I really and truly think that situation worked out for the better. The players liked and respected Coach Goff, and a lot of them told me that they weren't sure that Coach Mason would have been a good fit. We only had a very short time with Coach Mason, I know, but it just didn't seem like it was going to work.

A lot of stuff changed when Coach [Jim] Donnan came in. First of all, no one was retained from the previous staff, and that is always difficult. It would have been different if there had been a lack of respect for the previous staff, but this was a wholesale change. It was a tough transition, particularly for the older guys.

The first season was tough because we went 5–6, but we did have a couple glimmers of hope, as I recall.

We lost our first two games to Southern Miss and South Carolina and were behind at home late in the game to Texas Tech 12–7. We were looking right at 0–3, but Mike Bobo drove us 97 yards in the last two minutes, and we beat them 15–12. From an internal standpoint that was huge. We really needed that win—it gave the players a little confidence in the new coaching staff.

Then came the game at Auburn where we were behind 28–7 and just getting killed. Everybody thought we would probably fold up, because the week before we had been destroyed by Florida [47–7].

Mike Bobo didn't start the game, but he came on and somehow threw a touchdown pass on the last play of regulation to tie the game and send it into overtime. That ended up being the first four-overtime game in SEC history, and we won [56–49]. If I had to pick a game that was the most important one of my time at Georgia, it would probably be that one. At that point we were a beleaguered football team that really needed something good to happen. The win was a glimmer of hope that one day we were going to be good.

In 1997 good things finally started to happen. The biggest moment was when we went to Jacksonville and beat Florida for the first time in a really long time. I'm sure a lot of people didn't see it coming. I was rooming with Steve Herndon at the time. We were sitting in the hotel room the night before the game, and we just kind of looked at each other. I think I said, "Does it kind of feel different this time?" He agreed. It's hard to explain because you always feel you have a chance to win, but for some reason my gut felt really different.

Beating Florida [37–17] was a very pleasant surprise. It had been so long, and the Georgia people wanted it so badly.

After that game against Florida, we thought we might be in a position to do something pretty big, but the next week we lost to Auburn [45–34], and that kept us out of a big bowl.

When I was a senior in 1998, we thought we really had it going after we won at LSU [28–27] to go 4–0. We went home to play

Matt Stinchcomb, an All-America tackle in 1997 and 1998, also won the Draddy Award, which goes to college football's top scholar.

Tennessee, and everybody was really excited. *College Gameday* was in Athens. But then we went out and didn't play very well at all and got beat [22–3]. It was a huge letdown for everybody.

What we have to remember is that Tennessee had a great team that year. They went on to win the national championship. In fact, Tennessee was the biggest hurdle we faced during my entire career at Georgia. They had some very good teams, and you have to give them credit.

Of course, we went back to our old ways and lost to Florida again [38–7]. For some reason the guys wanted to wear black pants, as we had done in the Outback Bowl against Wisconsin. I wasn't for it. Maybe if we had worn the silver britches we would have won. I'm sure those black pants made a 31-point difference.

What I remember about that game is that Bill Goldberg came in and gave us his best pump-them-up speech. To his credit he stayed the whole game, because it was a bloodbath. They just jumped all over us.

I really don't want to talk about the Georgia Tech game in my senior year [a 21–19 loss]. Our senior class had made it a big deal that we weren't going to be the class that finally lost to those guys. I know this will come off as bitter, but there were a lot of strange things that happened in that game—and they all went against us. You can't go back and argue about it now, but that game and the loss the year before to Auburn were the two toughest losses I had at Georgia.

Still, I wouldn't trade anything for my four years at Georgia because it sort of set the stage for the rest of my life. I knew that I ultimately wanted to live in Georgia and that I would make a group of friends and contacts there that I would always have. Today my closest friends are the guys I played with.

Georgia is a great institution with great traditions, and I feel I was lucky to be a part of it and remain a part of it. Playing at Georgia really has become the centerpiece to everything else I've done in my life.

Bulldogs in Their Own Words

JON STINCHCOMB

Tackle, 1999–2002

My brother Matt and I have lived very similar lives, and to a lot of people it was a foregone conclusion that I would follow in his footsteps to Georgia. But the fact is, we are different people, and I wanted to look around a little bit more to make sure that I was going to get the right fit for me.

So I looked around to make sure a place like Auburn or Clemson wouldn't be better for me. But I just kept comparing every place I went to Georgia and what Georgia had to offer. I realized that no matter where I looked, there wasn't going to be a better place for me than Georgia.

Matt was really hands-off during the process. He and the rest of my immediate family were comfortable with letting me make the decision. Others were a little more pushy, especially living where we live with all those Bulldogs. Let's just say there were a lot of happy people when I made my decision.

I graduated from high school early so that I could come to Georgia in the spring of 1998. I did that for a couple of reasons. I needed to rehab a torn anterior cruciate ligament, but the main reason was so that I could spend more time with Matt. He was going to be a senior and the coming year would be the last chance to spend any significant time together.

I get asked a lot what having an All-America brother at Georgia meant to me when I got there. It meant a lot. To have a role model who is also someone you love is very special. Watching the way he worked and prepared was obviously a learning experience for me. I watched Matt and Chris Terry, Georgia's other tackle, and learned from them. There is no doubt in my mind that being around them created a work ethic in me and gave me the good habits that put me on the path to success.

I redshirted my first year in 1998, and today I'm thankful that I did. At the time I was a little bitter. I'm sure ego always comes into play, because when you're young you want to prove yourself. I took that year to get stronger and to get better. If I had played right away, I'm sure the comparisons to Matt would have started way too early, and that's not fair to an incoming freshman.

In 1999 I was the backup right tackle to Kelvin Williams, but then he got hurt. Suddenly I was in the starting lineup as we went to Tennessee. I remember that game because Shaun Ellis was the big dog of their defense that year, and it was going to be my job to block him most of the time. I'll never forget that on the trip Miles Luckie called me up to sit with him.

Miles said that at some point in your career as a football player you have a game that separates you from where you are and where you want to be. He said, "You have a great opportunity today."

He was right. Shaun Ellis was one of the best players in the country. I'm not saying I played a world-beater of a game, but I played pretty well against him. From that point on I felt I belonged. I knew I could play at this level.

The other game that stands out that year was when we lost to Georgia Tech in overtime [51–48]. That was the Jasper Sanks fumble that I don't think was a fumble. The whole play never made sense. They took the ball away from us, and I still don't get it. I will always be bitter about that game.

I thought expectations might be pretty high in 2000. When Coach [Jim] Donnan got up and said publicly that he had been waiting for a team like this all his life, I knew there was going to be pressure. But the truth is, when I looked at that team on paper, I thought we matched up well with anybody that we were going to play.

That team had the talent and it had the system. We just didn't put it all together every Saturday.

South Carolina [21–10] was really the eye-opener. I think all of us had bought into the hype about our team, but five turnovers later we realized that we weren't invincible after all.

I thought we had gotten it back together after we beat Tennessee [21–10] at home for the first time in ages, but we stumbled down the stretch. After we lost to Georgia Tech [27–15], the players were making a push to keep Coach Donnan around. He was a players' coach, and the guys really liked him.

But it didn't work. I was headed to the Butts-Mehre building for a meeting, and we were all pretty sure what it was about. A coaching change is never a great thing for the players, but it was going to happen to us.

All we could do was try to send that coaching staff out as winners when we went to Hawaii for the bowl game. That was a strange situation, knowing that none of those coaches would be back. At least we were able to beat Virginia [37–14] in Coach Donnan's last game.

You could tell early on that things were going to change under Coach [Mark] Richt. Coach Donnan's approach and Coach Richt's approach were very different. Coach Richt was a more hands-on coach, and he wanted things done his way every time.

Jon Stinchcomb proudly followed in the footsteps of his brother, Matt, as an All-America tackle for the Bulldogs.

It wasn't long after Coach Richt got to Georgia that we were introduced to mat drills, which was the off-season conditioning program that Coach Richt brought from Florida State. That was an eye-opening experience. The first thing that a new staff wants to do is show that they are completely in charge—that things are going to be done their way. They proved it with those mat drills, and we paid for it.

There were 10 sets of mat drills, and after we had gone through about one and a half, some of us were ready to hang it up. But the good thing was that after we did the 10th one, we looked around and realized we had made it through together as a team. I believe it brought us closer together as a team.

Whenever you have a new coaching staff, there comes a moment when everybody finally buys in to what they are selling. For the 2001 team, that moment came in Tennessee.

I mean, that stadium was really rocking, especially after Tennessee scored late on a screen pass to take the lead [24–20]. We got the ball back with less than a minute left, and to be honest with you, nobody in the huddle thought we were going to lose. It was like, "Okay, let's go score."

It all started with a quarterback like David Greene. Maybe it was because he was so young, but I don't think David was really aware of how serious a situation we were in. He basically said, "Let's go do it."

You don't make a big drive like that unless guys step up and make plays. And Randy McMichael stepped up big-time to put us in position to score with a couple of big catches. The play to Verron Haynes was one that we had run in practice a bunch of times. It was a great call by Coach Richt, and we caught them in the right defense to make it work.

I can say that game was the starting point for building the team that would win the SEC championship in 2002.

Early in the season every good team needs to define itself, and I think we did that when we came from behind to win at Alabama [27–25]. Alabama had a very good team, but when we fell behind we didn't panic. We ran our offense and put Billy Bennett into position to win the game.

The Florida game [a 20–13 loss] is still a burr under my saddle. Here was a time when we were confident that we were the better team, but we just let too many opportunities go by the wayside. It was really disheartening, and when we walked off that field in Jacksonville, I was worried that maybe we had just let the SEC championship slip away.

Whenever people ask me about the big play against Auburn, I figure they mean the fumble I recovered in the end zone for a touchdown in the third quarter. I'm kidding, of course.

I mentioned how cool David was in the Tennessee game the year before. It was the same thing that night at Auburn. Everything was on the line in that game. We were behind and facing fourth down at the 19-yard line, and Greene came into the huddle and said something like, "Okay, we need to make a play here. Make sure you give me enough time."

So he threw that ball up there, Michael Johnson just jumped up and grabbed it away from the guy, and we won. What a great play!

Coach Richt always talks about knocking the lid off the program and achieving big things. That's what we did in the SEC championship game. We knew we were going to win, and when we did it was like a huge weight had been lifted off our shoulders. We were carrying the weight of the past 20 years because it had been that long since Georgia had been able to win an SEC championship. We had a lot of fun that night.

I'm only a few years removed from it, but I know what a big deal it was to be a part of the team that finally brought a championship back to Georgia. And I know that the further removed I am from it, the more pride I will feel.

I came to Georgia because of its great tradition. I knew what Georgia represented, and I wanted to be a part of that. Hopefully my senior class left its mark on Georgia, and what better way to do it than with a championship? I know it is something that I am going to be proud of for the rest of my life.

Other Brother Combinations to Play at Georgia

The Dye brothers: Nat (1957–1958), Wayne (1954–1956), and Pat (1958–1960). Pat was an All-American who went on to become the head coach at Auburn in 1981.

The Kelly brothers: Bob (1978–1980) and Steve (1978–1981). Natives of Savannah, both were on Georgia's 1980 national championship team.

The Luckie triplets: Dustin, Mike, and Miles (1995–1999). They are thought to be the only triplets to sign with a major college football team.

The McPipkin brothers: Jim (1971–1973), Joe (1972), and Paul (1969–1971).

The Smiley brothers: Julian (1969–1970) and Ronnie (1972).

The Swinford brothers: Gene (1970–1972), Wayne (1962–1964).

The Weaver brothers: Eddie "Meat Cleaver" (1978–1981) and Mike (1981–1984).

The Wynn brothers: George (1989–1991) and William (1989–1990).

The Retired Jerseys

Only four men in the history of Georgia football have had their jersey number retired, never to be worn again:

Frank Sinkwich, Running Back, No. 21: Sinkwich became Georgia's first player to win the Heisman Trophy in 1942 when he led the Bulldogs to an 11–1 record and a spot in the Rose Bowl. His jersey was the first at Georgia to be retired, in 1943.

Charley Trippi, Running Back, No. 62: Trippi had a brilliant career interrupted by World War II but returned to Georgia in 1945 for the second half of the season. In 1946 he led Georgia to an 11–0 season and the SEC championship. His jersey was retired in 1947.

Theron Sapp, Running back, No. 40: Sapp was an All-SEC running back in 1958 but will always be known as "the Drought Breaker." Sapp's one-yard run for a touchdown in 1957 gave Georgia a 7–0 victory over Georgia Tech in Atlanta and broke the Bulldogs' eight-game losing streak to the hated Yellow Jackets. Georgia fans were so grateful that they retired his jersey in 1959.

Herschel Walker, Running Back, No. 34: Walker, the 1982 Heisman Trophy winner, is the most decorated football player in Georgia history. On September 2, 1985, Walker was joined by Sinkwich, Trippi, and Sapp as his jersey was retired during half-time ceremonies of the Georgia-Alabama game.

Bulldogs in Their Own Words

THERON SAPP

Running Back, 1956–1958

It's hard to believe that a one-yard run in one football game could change somebody's entire life, but that's exactly what happened to me after I scored and we beat Georgia Tech 7–0 in 1957. I'm 76 years old now, and I still get letters from people wanting autographs because of that one game.

And it almost never happened.

I had always been a Georgia fan growing up. Back then there was no television, so we listened to the Georgia Bulldogs or the Georgia Tech Yellow Jackets on the radio.

We moved to Macon when I was in the second grade, and my mother worked in Warner Robins at the air force base. I went to Lanier High for boys, which is now Central High School.

We had a pretty good team my senior year. We won the South Georgia championship and ended up playing Grady High in Atlanta for the state championship. Erskine Russell, who would someday be the defensive coordinator at Georgia, was the head coach. They beat us 9–6.

I kind of figured I was going to Georgia, but some other schools like Auburn, South Carolina, and Florida started paying attention to me, so I thought I would listen to what they had to say. I remember that it was the week before the state championship game, and I had gotten a big cut on my chin at practice. I had to go have it stitched up, and when I got home there was a bunch of recruiters waiting on me. It was the first day of recruiting. I know there were coaches from South Carolina, Florida, and Georgia there.

Coach Quinton Lumpkin, who was recruiting me for Georgia, met me in the driveway. He just looked at me and said, "You might as well choose to go to Georgia because your mama has already signed your grant-in-aid! But don't tell these other guys that. It will be our secret."

It turned out that Coach Lumpkin had gotten there early and done a selling job on my mom. So she made the decision for me. I guess you could say it was the right decision.

But my playing career at Georgia got off to a rocky start. I was in Atlanta where we were having practice for the Georgia High School all-star game. In the first scrimmage I got hit and knocked up in the air. When I came down, I hurt my neck. They took me to the hospital for X-rays. The doctor said nothing was broken so they let me go home, but I still couldn't move my head.

As it turned out, the doctor read the X-rays while they were still wet. I was on my way back to Macon when he looked at them again and noticed that I had three cracked vertebrae. They got in touch with me and told me to go to the hospital in Macon immediately.

At first they put me in traction for four or five days, and then they put me in an entire body cast from the waist up so that I could not move my head. When I was in the hospital, Coach [Wally] Butts and Coach Lumpkin came down to visit me. Coach Butts told me that even if I never played football again, I would still get my scholarship to go to Georgia. That was really something. He didn't have to do that. I told him not to worry. "When I get out of this body cast I will be playing football," I told him.

I started to sit out that fall and not go to school. I didn't want to walk around the campus in that body cast and have people ask me all those questions. But Coach Lumpkin convinced me to come and give it a try. He wanted me to go ahead and start blending in with the rest of the guys. I did it, but people were always asking me if I had been in a train wreck or a car wreck.

When I came back to school in 1955, they told me I had to get permission from my doctor to play again. My doctor in Macon wouldn't give it to me. Coach Butts told me that if I were his son, I probably wouldn't be playing. I told him I wasn't his son and I was going to give it a shot.

Theron Sapp scored the winning touchdown to beat Georgia Tech 7–0 in 1957. That broke Tech's eight-game winning streak and led to Sapp's jersey being retired.

I played on the B team in 1956, but in 1957 I started the first game of the year at fullback against Texas in Atlanta. After that I started 20 straight games.

We weren't in the best frame of mind when we played Georgia Tech in the last game of the 1957 season. We had only won two games that year. We had a chance to beat Auburn the week before but fumbled the ball at the 1-yard line and lost 6–0. Auburn went on to win the national championship.

It seemed like we were in every game that year, but we just didn't get the breaks to come our way. But we were up to play Georgia Tech. They had beaten us eight straight years, and we hadn't scored a touchdown against them in four years.

Driving over to Atlanta from Athens, I told Coach Butts, "I've got a good feeling that we're going to win this game. I couldn't sleep at all last night. I felt like a kid on the night before Christmas."

Coach Butts said, "Hell, Sapp, you think we're going to win them all. But I'll tell you this: we are going to play them hard and tough. That much I will promise you."

Well, Coach Butts was right. We did play them tough. And on Tech's first or second drive of the second half, I recovered a fumble around the 50-yard line. It was the field position we had been looking for, and we had to take advantage of it.

I can remember every single play of that drive. The big play was when we faced a third-and-12 around the 40-yard line. Charlie Britt hit Jimmy Orr for 13 yards and it gave us a first down at their 27-yard line. Now it was time to go to work.

I carried the ball six straight times down to the 1-yard line. On third down Charlie tried to sneak it in, but he got nothing because Tech put a nine-man line in.

On fourth down the play came in. Somebody said, "Coach Butts said give it to Sapp." I just remember saying, "Yeah, give it to me. Give it to me."

I ran off tackle, and the blocking was perfect. I fell into the end zone, and I wanted to jump up and start running out of the back of the end zone.

We still had a lot of football to play, but we hung on and won [7–0]. And when the game ended, I couldn't believe it. There was all this hugging and kissing. I couldn't get to the locker room. It was really crazy. It had been so long since Georgia had beaten Tech, and we were having such a tough year.

The next year, 1958, Tech was really laying for us. They had all those great players, like Maxie Baughan, but we beat them again [16–3]. I was named the Most Valuable Player in that game, too. In those two games against Georgia Tech I carried the ball 40 times for 194 yards.

It was after the 1958 game with Tech that some of the Georgia people started talking about retiring my number [40]. I didn't think I should have my jersey retired. That honor belonged to guys like Charley Trippi and Frank Sinkwich. But I wasn't going to tell those people no. They retired my jersey at the next spring game, and it was such an honor.

I guess everybody has their own story about Coach Butts, but mine is pretty funny. In 1958 we were playing The Citadel in Athens and beating them pretty good. It was the next-to-last game of the season, and I was chasing Billy Cannon of LSU for the rushing title in the SEC. Coach Butts took me out of the game when we got the big lead because we had Tech the next week and he didn't want me to get hurt.

Well, I wanted to catch Cannon, so when Coach Butts wasn't looking, I put myself back in the game. I told Britt that Coach Butts said give me the ball. I ran for about 15 yards on the next play, and Coach Butts looked up and started screaming, "What the hell is that?"

Coach Butts called timeout and jumped all over me, saying, "Sapp, go sit your butt on the bench and don't get up again unless I call you."

I never did catch Cannon. [Cannon won the SEC rushing title in 1958 with 682 yards. Sapp finished with 635.]

I got a chance to play some pro ball and was on the 1960 NFL championship team with the Philadelphia Eagles. But nothing compares to those five years at Georgia. I remember the panty raids and how Dean [William] Tate would call on the football players to protect the girls. That was a pretty good deal. There were trips to Daytona Beach on spring break. We would take the pigs from the university farm and have a barbecue. I made enough friendships to last a lifetime. I wouldn't trade those years for all the money in the world.

And the Georgia people gave me an honor that has stuck with me for my entire life. When you go to Georgia today, you'll see only four retired jerseys: Trippi, Sinkwich, Walker, and Sapp.

One time I was there and I heard somebody say, "Sapp? What did he do?"

I just told him, "Well, he was just somebody they liked."

Other Georgia Players You Should Know

Most of the players listed here were either All-America or All-SEC. But some of the players on this list distinguished themselves for their character and their contributions to the University of Georgia in other walks of life. By no means is this a definitive list, but if you are a Georgia fan, these are players you should know:

Peter Anderson, Center, (1983–1985): Anderson, a native of New Jersey, was the captain of the 1985 team. He was an All-American that season and became the first Georgia player to be named captain at mid-season.

Buck Belue, Quarterback, (1978–1981): Belue was one of the South's most highly recruited quarterbacks coming out of Valdosta High School. He came off the bench as a true freshman to lead Georgia to a 29–28 win over Georgia Tech in 1978. He was the quarterback on Georgia's 1980 national championship team. He led Georgia to SEC championships in 1980 and 1981. Today Belue has his own radio show in Atlanta.

MIKE BOBO, QUARTERBACK, (1994–1997): Bobo led Georgia to a 10–2 season in 1997 and a big upset of No. 6 Florida, 37–17, in Jacksonville. Today Bobo is the offensive coordinator for the Bulldogs.

EDMUND RAYMOND "ZEKE" BRATKOWSKI, QUARTERBACK, 1951–1953: Bratkowski was a three-time All-SEC quarterback who went on to play 14 seasons in the NFL. He was part of three NFL championship teams with the Green Bay Packers.

JOHN CARSON, END, 1950, 1952–1953: Carson was both an All-America football player and an All-America golfer for Georgia. He is one of only two Georgia athletes in history (Herschel Walker is the other) to be named All-America in two sports.

MIKE CASTRONIS, TACKLE, 1943–1945: "Coach Mike" was one of the most beloved players and coaches in the history of the University of Georgia. He was an All-SEC lineman from 1943 to 1945 and an All-American in 1945. He was a successful high school coach and then returned to Georgia in 1962 as an assistant coach.

MIKE CAVAN, QUARTERBACK, 1968–1970: Cavan was the SEC sophomore of the year in 1968 as he led Georgia to the conference championship. He served as an assistant to Vince Dooley and was the head coach at Valdosta State, East Tennessee State, and SMU. Today Cavan is back in Athens as a major gifts officer of the Georgia Bulldog Club.

EDGAR CHANDLER, OFFENSIVE GUARD, 1965–1967: A two-time All-American and one of the best offensive linemen that Georgia has ever produced. He played linebacker in the NFL because of his great speed. He died in 1992 after a long illness at the age of 46. He is a member of the Georgia Sports Hall of Fame.

GEORGE COLLINS, GUARD, 1975–1977: Collins was an All-America guard in 1977 and a member of Georgia's 1976 SEC championship team. He went on to become a successful high school coach.

COWBOY AND MOONPIE, GUARD AND TACKLE, 1974–1976: "Cowboy" was Joel Parrish and "Moonpie" was Mike Wilson, and together they formed one of the most dominating blocking tandems in Georgia football history. They anchored the offensive line that led Georgia to the 1976 SEC championship. Both were named All-Americans in 1976.

ART DECARLO, SAFETY, 1950–1952: DeCarlo was an All-SEC safety in 1952 and played on the Baltimore Colts NFL championship teams of 1958 and 1959.

DICKY CLARK, DEFENSIVE END, 1974–1976: Clark was a converted quarterback who became an All-SEC defensive end in 1976. He was the defensive captain of Georgia's 1976 SEC championship team. He was an assistant coach at Georgia for 15 seasons.

BOBBY ETTER, PLACE-KICKER, 1964–1966: Etter will always be remembered for his slight build and his touchdown run with a botched field goal attempt that gave Georgia a 14–7 win over Florida in 1964. Etter received his Ph.D. in mathematics from Rice University and is a professor at Sacramento State University. He is also a world-class bridge player.

FRED GIBSON, WIDE RECEIVER, 2001–2004: As a freshman in 2001, Gibson set a Georgia record with five 100-yard receiving games in a season. In 2001 Gibson had 201 yards receiving against Kentucky, which is still a Georgia record.

FREDDIE GILBERT, DEFENSIVE END, 1980–1983: Gilbert, considered to be one of the greatest pass rushers in Georgia history, was an All-America defensive end in 1983. He was captain of the 1983 team that went 10–1–1 and beat No. 2 Texas in the Cotton Bowl.

RAY GOFF, QUARTERBACK, 1973–1976: Goff was the SEC Player of the Year in 1976 when he led the Bulldogs to the SEC championship. A native of Moultrie, Georgia, Goff is the best option quarterback to ever play for the Bulldogs. He returned to Georgia as an assistant coach and later served as head coach from 1989 to 1995.

BILL GOLDBERG, DEFENSIVE TACKLE, 1986–1989: Goldberg was an All-SEC defensive tackle in 1988 and 1989 who went on to a highly successful career in professional wrestling.

DAVID GREENE, QUARTERBACK, 2001–2004. Green led Georgia to 42 victories as a starting quarterback, which was the NCAA record until Colt McCoy of Texas broke it with 45 wins in 2009. He remains Georgia's career leader in passing yardage, with 11,528 yards.

A.J. GREEN, WIDE RECEIVER, 2008–2010: A three-time All-SEC player and considered by many to be the best receiver in Georgia history. His junior season was cut short due to a four-game NCAA suspension. Still, Green caught 57 passes for 848 yards and nine touchdowns. He finished his career with 166 catches, 2,619 yards, and 23 touchdowns.

STEVE GREER, NOSE GUARD, 1967–1969: Greer was an All-America nose guard and the captain of Georgia's 1969 team. He returned to Georgia in 1979 as an assistant coach and was later named director of football operations.

GLYNN HARRISON, RUNNING BACK, 1973–1975: "Glidin' Glynn" Harrison was an All-SEC running back for the Bulldogs in 1975. He was captain of Georgia's Cotton Bowl team.

RODNEY HAMPTON, RUNNING BACK, 1987–1989: Vince Dooley called him "one of the most natural running backs I have ever seen." A rare recruit from Texas, Hampton led Georgia in rushing in 1989 with 1,059 yards. He finished his career with 2,668 yards, which is fifth on Georgia's all-time list.

GARRISON HEARST, RUNNING BACK, 1990–1992: Hearst is one of Georgia's greatest running backs. In 1992 Hearst finished third in the voting for the Heisman Trophy (behind Gino Torretta of Miami and Marshall Faulk of San Diego State) and won the Doak Walker Award, which goes to the nation's best running back. He played with the Arizona Cardinals, Cincinnati Bengals, San Francisco 49ers, and Denver Broncos.

PAT HODGSON, TIGHT END, 1963–1965: Hodgson was a three-time All-SEC selection for Georgia. He was an assistant coach for nine seasons for Vince Dooley.

LEN HAUSS, CENTER, 1961–1963: Hauss got relatively little recognition at Georgia because he played on some bad teams, but the native of Jesup, Georgia, went on to play 14 seasons with the Washington Redskins. He was All-Pro five times and is listed as one of the 70 greatest players in franchise history.

CLAUDE HIPPS, HALFBACK, 1944, 1949–1951: Hipps enrolled at Georgia and then spent four years in the Marines before returning to school in 1949. He was captain of the 1951 team when he was first-team All-SEC.

CRAIG HERTWIG, OFFENSIVE TACKLE, 1972–1974: Nicknamed "Sky" because of his 6′8″ frame, Hertwig was an All-America tackle in 1974.

ANDY JOHNSON, QUARTERBACK, 1971–1973: Johnson earned All-SEC honors as a sophomore in 1971 after leading Georgia to an 11–1 record. A star at Athens High School, Johnson was one of the most physically talented athletes to ever play at Georgia. He was also a starter on the Bulldogs' baseball team. He played nine years in the NFL and is a member of the Georgia Sports Hall of Fame.

RANDY JOHNSON, OFFENSIVE GUARD, 1973–1975: Johnson quit football for six weeks as a sophomore but then came back to become an All-America guard. He played professionally for the Seattle Seahawks and the Tampa Bay Bucs. He later became a high school teacher.

WAYNE JOHNSON, QUARTERBACK, 1985–1988: Johnson will always be remembered for leading UGA to an upset victory at Auburn in 1986 and for being the starting quarterback in Vince Dooley's final game, a 34–27 win over Michigan State in the Gator Bowl.

BILL KRUG, DEFENSIVE BACK, 1974–1977: A native of Suitland, Maryland, Krug became one of the most instinctive defensive players to ever suit up for the Bulldogs. He was a three-time All-SEC defensive back.

JOHN LASTINGER, QUARTERBACK, 1981–1983: Lastinger had a record of 20–2–1 in games that he started for Georgia during the 1982 and 1983 seasons. The 1982 team went undefeated in the regular season and played Penn State in the Sugar Bowl for the national championship. The 1983 team went 10–1–1 and faced No. 2 Texas in the Cotton Bowl. Lastinger's 17-yard touchdown run with 3:22 left gave Georgia a 10–9 victory.

TOMMY LAWHORNE, LINEBACKER, 1965–1967: Lawhorne was the ultimate overachiever as a football player and a student at Georgia. He was the valedictorian of the 1968 senior class and was a runner-up for the Rhodes Scholarship. He went on to attend medical school at Johns Hopkins. Today he is a surgeon living in Columbus, Georgia.

KENT LAWRENCE, RUNNING BACK/WIDE RECEIVER, 1966–1968: Lawrence was an All-SEC flanker in 1968 and a member of two

SEC championship teams. He went on to law school and became a state court judge in Clarke County, Georgia.

JOHN LITTLE, SAFETY, 1983–1986. A two-time All-American, Little was a former high school quarterback who converted to defense once he got to Georgia. Little replaced Hall of Famer Terry Hoage at the all-important rover position.

TOMMY LYONS, CENTER, 1968–1970: Lyons was an All-America center in 1969 and 1970. He earned his medical degree while playing for the Denver Broncos of the NFL. He is a member of the Georgia Sports Hall of Fame and the University of Georgia Circle of Honor. Today he is one of the nation's leading physicians in the field of obstetrics and gynecology.

HERB MAFFETT, END, 1927–1931: An All-America end in 1930 and the captain of Georgia's 1930 team, Maffett is a member of the Georgia Sports Hall of Fame.

RALPH "RED" MADDOX, GUARD, 1930–1931: One of the more interesting tales in Bulldogs history, Maddox last played for Georgia in 1931, but his status as an All-American was not uncovered until 32 years later. Georgia publicist Dan Magill discovered that Maddox had made the International News Service All-America team in 1930, but that the feat was never recorded. Maddox never knew of the honor because he was killed in World War II during the Normandy invasion.

WILLIE MCCLENDON, RUNNING BACK, 1976–1978: McClendon began his career at linebacker and moved to tailback. In 1978 McClendon ran for 1,312 yards, which broke the school record previously held by Frank Sinkwich, the 1942 Heisman Trophy winner. McClendon was captain of the 1978 team and was named the SEC Player of the Year. His son, Bryan, a former Georgia wide receiver, is now the running backs coach for the Bulldogs.

Kirby Moore, Quarterback, 1965–1967: Moore was the captain of Georgia's 1967 team but is best remembered as the quarterback on the famed "Flea Flicker" play (Moore to Hodgson to Taylor) that beat Alabama in 1965. He is an attorney in Macon.

Knowshon Moreno, Running Back, 2006–2008. Moreno was an All-American in 2008 when he ran for 1,400 yards and 16 touchdowns. He finished his career with 2,734 yards.

Kevin McLee, Running Back, 1974–1977: McLee, a native of Uniontown, Pennsylvania, was the SEC Rookie of the Year in 1975 and was the leading rusher on Georgia's 1976 SEC championship team. McLee died suddenly of a stroke on July 15, 2007. He was 52 years old.

Jimmy Orr, Wide Receiver, 1955–1957: Orr came to Georgia without a scholarship and went on to lead the SEC in receiving twice during his career. He had a successful pro career with the Pittsburgh Steelers and the Baltimore Colts.

George Patton, Defensive Tackle, 1964–1966: A three-time All-SEC player and an All-American in 1965 and 1966. He was captain of Georgia's 1966 SEC championship team.

Jimmy Payne, Defensive Tackle, 1979–1982: Payne was a three-time All-SEC player. He had 28 career sacks and 12 sacks in 1981. He died in 1998 at the age of 38.

David Pollack, Defensive End, 2001–2004: One of only two players in Georgia history (Herschel Walker is the other) to be named All-America three times. He was the SEC Player of the Year in 2002 as a sophomore. Pollack's NFL career was cut short by a neck injury.

George Poschner, End, 1939–1942: Poschner was an All-SEC end who went on to great distinction for his service in World War II. He received the Bronze Star, the Purple Heart, and the

Distinguished Service Cross. He is a member of the Georgia Sports Hall of Fame.

PRESTON RIDLEHUBER, QUARTERBACK, 1963–1965: Ridlehuber was the MVP of the 1964 Sun Bowl and the quarterback on Vince Dooley's first team at Georgia. He lives in St. Mary's, Florida.

MATT ROBINSON, QUARTERBACK, 1974–1976: Robinson was the passing quarterback (to Ray Goff's running quarterback) on Georgia's 1976 SEC championship team. He was the quarterback in the game for the famous "Appleby to Washington" play that beat Florida 10–7 in 1975. He went on to play professionally in the NFL and USFL. He lives in Jacksonville, Florida.

MIXON ROBINSON, DEFENSIVE END, 1969–1971: Robinson was an All-SEC defensive end in 1971 and went on to become a successful orthopedic surgeon in Athens.

REX ROBINSON, PLACE=KICKER, 1977–1980: Robinson was a two-time All-American and the kicker on Georgia's national championship team in 1980. In that season he kicked four field goals of more than 50 yards.

FRANK ROS, LINEBACKER, 1977–1980: Ros came to the United States from Spain when he was only six years old. He was the captain of Georgia's 1980 national championship team. Today he is a vice president at the Coca-Cola Company.

LEMAN "BUZY" ROSENBERG, DEFENSIVE BACK, 1970–1972: One of the best defensive backs and punt returners in Georgia history. He was All-SEC in 1970 and 1971. He still holds the Georgia record with 202 punt return yards in one game. In that win over Oregon State, Rosenberg returned two punts for touchdowns.

TROY SADOWSKI, TIGHT END, 1985–1988: Sadowski was an All-America tight end for Vince Dooley's last Georgia team in 1988. He played 10 years in the NFL.

JEFF SANCHEZ, SAFETY, 1982–1984: Sanchez came to Georgia from junior college in 1982 and became a two-time All-SEC safety. He finished second in the nation in interceptions in 1982 with nine.

HERB ST. JOHN, GUARD, 1944–1947: St. John was a three-time All-SEC guard and was named All-America in 1946.

LINDSAY SCOTT, WIDE RECEIVER, 1978–1981: Scott was on the receiving end of the single biggest play in Georgia history, the 93-yard pass from Buck Belue to beat Florida 26–21 in 1980. Scott was an All-SEC receiver in 1981 and was later drafted by the New Orleans Saints.

RICHARD SEYMOUR, DEFENSIVE TACKLE, 1997–2000: Seymour was one of the most dominating defensive linemen ever to play for Georgia. He was an All-America pick in 2000 who finished his career with 223 tackles.

ROYCE SMITH, OFFENSIVE GUARD, 1969–1971: Smith was an All-America guard in 1971 and a classic success story. He came to Georgia as a 190-pound lineman and through hard work in the weight room turned himself into a 6′2″, 250-pound All-American. Smith died suddenly in 2004 at the age of 54. More than 45 of his teammates came to Smith's funeral in Statesboro, Georgia.

THE SUCCESS STORY OF ROYCE SMITH

Royce Smith's story actually began as a ninth-grader at Groves High School in Garden City, Georgia, on the outskirts of Savannah. On the advice of his high school football coach, Jack Miller, Smith gave up basketball and completely dedicated himself to football.

Smith began lifting weights three hours a day because he wanted to be in the best physical shape possible for football. After his junior year at Groves High, Georgia assistant coach John Donaldson came to visit. Donaldson told Smith that Georgia had some interest in him.

"I couldn't believe it," Smith said at the time, as related through a Georgia sports information press release. "I couldn't figure out why. I knew I couldn't play college football, and I wondered why they were wasting their time on me."

But Miller told him he could play college football if he worked for it. Smith took him at his word.

"On Saturday nights my senior year I went down to the weight room and worked out," Smith said. "I didn't have time for anything but football. All I could think about was playing football for Georgia. It seemed like the next place to heaven to me."

Other than the early contact from Georgia, the University of Richmond was the only other school that had showed interest in Smith. But Donaldson and Georgia coach Vince Dooley still liked the way he played football, and Donaldson made the trip to Garden City to sign Smith.

He arrived in Athens weighing 190 pounds, and the Georgia coaches quickly determined the best chance for him to play would be at offensive guard. He recommitted himself to the weight room and rose to 6′3″, 250 pounds, but he could still run the 40-yard dash in 4.8 seconds—the fastest for a Georgia lineman. And he could bench press a then–Georgia record of 430 pounds. Smith was so dedicated to weight-lifting that at times the Georgia coaches had to force him to leave the weight room.

Royce Smith, who thought he wasn't good enough to play college football, became a three-year starter at guard for Georgia and in 1971 was an All-American. He received the Jacobs Award, which goes to the SEC's best blocker. He was drafted by the New Orleans Saints in the first round of the 1972 NFL Draft.

Smith died suddenly on January 22, 2004, at the age of 54.

Following are the reflections of Smith's daughter, Kaysie, and his son, Royce Jr., on what being a Georgia Bulldog meant to their father.

Kaysie Smith

I grew up with my dad and brother. I guess I was quite a bit of a tomboy, always trying to keep up with my brother. Since my father coached my brother's Little League football team, I was always there. That was the phase in my life when I wanted to be a football player.

Looking back on it now, it was probably because I wanted my father's attention. It was somewhere around that time that I realized my dad had named me after one of his college football coaches, John Kasay. I knew that playing football for Georgia must have been a very important part of his life.

I guess I was maybe five years old when my father took me to my first G-Day game. I can remember him and all of his old teammates actually playing in a game. I remember playing with UGA, the mascot, and watching Dad play while he wore No. 66. After the game my father came to the sideline and picked me up. He was hot and sweaty in his football pads, but I remember thinking how "cool" Dad was.

When my dad moved us to Claxton, Georgia, he became a football coach there as well. Everyone was impressed to have a Bulldog and NFL player as a football coach. I was 13 years old then, and my dream of being a football player had changed. I was now a cheerleader, so I still got to spend time with my father and my brother, who played on the team.

I think that football taught my father many lessons. He learned that dedication and hard work will take you wherever you want to go. Those fundamental values followed him all of his life. He became a schoolteacher. He was a father who loved his children and put our best interests close to his heart.

He was an avid cyclist who trained for months and accomplished many challenging bike rides. Not only did he succeed in numerous ways, but he took his knowledge of football and taught it to other young football players so they could fulfill their dreams.

My father was a wonderful man. He had a huge heart and would have done anything for anyone. He was a great father, and I cannot thank him enough for everything he taught me. As I write this, I imagine my father is riding his bike through the streets of heaven watching over my brother and me.

And I know in my heart that he loved Georgia, because Georgia gave him the opportunity to live out his dreams.

Royce Smith Jr.

My dad was one of the best to ever play at the University of Georgia. I say this because he did not have the raw talent that other players did. He earned everything he got.

One story that sticks out in my mind is about how committed my dad was to be the best he could be for the Georgia football team. He borrowed a key to the Georgia weight room from an assistant coach. After he finished the workout, he went to the store and had a copy made. This way he could work out without "permission."

My dad knew he had to work harder than anyone else to compete at that level of football. I really think he underestimated his talent, but it only made him work that much harder.

Coach Dooley caught him one day and told him to stop working out so much, because he did not want all that extra weight on my dad. Coach Dooley thought it would slow him down. That sounds funny today, but the training back in the late '60s did not incorporate much weight training.

But Dad kept working out because somehow he knew that the weights would only make him better. He still ran a 4.77 in the 40. That was pretty good for a lineman back then.

At my dad's funeral I had a chance to talk to a lot of his former teammates. I was shocked at how many of them showed up. He was the captain of the 1971 team, and I knew it was a great tribute to a great man. I could see the respect they had for their fallen leader. My dad was a born leader, and people were drawn to him. Dad was an All-American that same year, but he told me that being voted as the 1971 team captain was a greater honor than any personal award.

> I know my dad was proud of his accomplishments at Georgia. He was always a Bulldog at heart.

MATTHEW STAFFORD, QUARTERBACK, 2006–2008: One of the most physically gifted quarterbacks to play for the Bulldogs. Stafford was one of the nation's most highly recruited players out of Highland Park High School in Dallas, Texas. He spent three seasons at Georgia and left as the third-leading passer in school history, with 7,731 yards. He became the third player in school history to become the No. 1 pick in the NFL Draft. The other two were Charley Trippi (1947), and Harry Babcock (1953).

RICHARD TARDITS, DEFENSIVE END, 1985–1988: "The Blitz from Biarritz" and a native of France, Tardits came to Georgia for his education never having played American football. Georgia used his great athletic gifts at defensive end, where he set a school record with 29 career sacks. That record stood until it was broken by three-time All-American David Pollack in 2004. Today Tardits lives in France.

Bob Taylor, Running Back, 1963–1965: Taylor is remembered for scoring the winning touchdown on the "Flea Flicker" play to upset Alabama in 1965, but his career came to a sudden end later in the season when he suffered a broken leg against Florida State. He would never play football again.

Jimmy Vickers, End, 1957–1959: Vickers was an All-SEC end in 1959 and later returned as an assistant coach at Georgia from 1971 to 1976.

Bobby Walden, Halfback/Punter, 1957–1960: Known as the "Big Toe From Cairo," Walden played halfback and punted for Georgia's 1959 SEC championship team. He went on to become an All-Pro punter for the Pittsburgh Steelers and was a member of their Super Bowl teams in 1974 and 1975.

Hines Ward, Quarterback/Wide Receiver/Running Back, 1994–1997: A high school quarterback who came to Georgia and became one of the most versatile players in school history, Ward went on to an All-Pro career with the Pittsburgh Steelers, where he won two Super Bowls. Ward was the MVP of Super Bowl XL. Ward has proven to be just as versatile away from football, and in 2011 he won the *Dancing with the Stars* competition on ABC television.

Charlie Whittemore, Wide Receiver, 1968–1970: Whittemore led Georgia in receiving for three straight seasons and returned to Athens as an assistant coach for Vince Dooley.

Jim Wilson, Offensive Tackle, 1962–1964: Wilson was an All-America tackle on Vince Dooley's first team at Georgia in 1964. He went on to become a successful professional wrestler. He was inducted into the Georgia Sports Hall of Fame in 2001.

Chip Wisdom, Linebacker, 1969–1971: Wisdom was an All-SEC linebacker in 1971 and later was an assistant coach at Georgia for nine seasons. He was a three-year starter at linebacker for the Bulldogs.

Scott Woerner, Safety, 1977–1980: An All-American in 1980 when Georgia won the national championship, Woerner had 13 career interceptions.

Tim Worley, Running Back, 1985–1988: Worley was a consensus All-American in 1988 who also led the SEC in rushing that season with 1,216 yards.

Ben Zambiasi, Linebacker, 1974–1977: A small but very tough linebacker who recorded 467 career tackles as a three-year starter, Zambiasi (pronounced "Zam-Bee-Zee") went on to play for 14 seasons in the CFL. His 467 career tackles is still first on Georgia's all-time list.

Eric Zeier, Quarterback, 1991–1994: Zeier was one of the greatest quarterbacks in Georgia history. He became the starting quarterback as a true freshman in 1991 and when he left in 1994 had become Georgia's all-time leading passer, with 11,153 yards. Today he is still Georgia's No. 2 all-time passer behind David Greene.

chapter 7
THE COACHES *of* GEORGIA

EACH OF THE FIRST 14 MEN WHO SERVED as Georgia's head coach from 1892 to 1909 held the job for two years or less. Needless to say, coaching was not considered to be a long-term career choice in the early days of the sport.

As time went on and football became more important to the alumni, Georgia found some stability in the coaching ranks. W.A. Cunningham (1910–1919) was Georgia's first long-term coach, with 10 years on the job. Harry Mehre (1928–1937) also held the Georgia job for 10 years.

Georgia's longest period of stability at head coach came under Wallace Butts (22 years from 1939 to 1960) and Vince Dooley (25 years from 1964 to 1988). Dooley is Georgia's all-time winner, with 201 victories.

Georgia's current coach, Mark Richt (2001–present) is the third-longest-reigning coach as he is set to begin his 11th season in Athens.

In total, 25 different men have served as the head football coach at Georgia in its 120-year football history.

Mark Richt (2001–present)

by David Greene

I was a freshman in 2000 when Jim Donnan, who recruited me to Georgia, was let go and Mark Richt became our head coach.

Of course, I was a little apprehensive. There are always concerns with the unknown. You don't know what the new culture is going to be. You come to the University of Georgia because you are comfortable with the way things are. Now they were going to change.

But after a while I started to get excited about the arrival of Coach Richt. He had already coached two Heisman Trophy winners at Florida State (Charlie Ward in 1993 and Chris Weinke in 2000) and had had a lot of success as the offensive coordinator. I was going to work with somebody who really knew how to develop quarterbacks. I was 19 years old and hungry. I was ready to learn. I couldn't wait to get Coach Richt's playbook.

People talk about our win up at Tennessee in 2001 [Greene threw a six-yard touchdown pass with only five seconds left to give Georgia a 26–24 win in Knoxville] and how big it was. I just thought it was a great win for the program. I guess when you're young you don't know any better. I knew we hadn't won up there in a long time [since 1980], but it was my first trip to Knoxville and the first time Coach Richt had been up there too. He called the plays, and we executed them. It was a great day for Georgia.

That sort of got things started. We won the SEC championship in 2002 and played for it again in 2003. I was just proud to be a part of the group that got things turned around at Georgia and got us winning again.

The main thing you need to know about Coach Richt is that he is a great man. When I was a player, we had a student-teacher

Mark Richt, posing here with UGA VI, has won 96 games and two SEC championships since becoming head coach of Georgia in 2001.

relationship. Now I consider him to be a friend. I always look forward to seeing him and his family. I am very lucky to have played for Coach Richt.

In four years (2001–2004) as Georgia's starting quarterback, David Greene won 42 games, which was an NCAA record at the time.

In 10 seasons at Georgia, Mark Richt has won 96 games and two SEC championships. He is one of only seven coaches in NCAA Division I-A history to win 90 games in his first nine seasons as a head coach.

Jim Donnan (1996–2000)

Donnan became Georgia's coach under most unusual circumstances. On December 18, 1995, Glen Mason of Kansas was named Georgia's new head coach to replace Ray Goff. But only one week later, on Christmas Day, Mason decided he would remain at Kansas. In less than 24 hours Donnan was hired as head coach.

Donnan, who won a Division I-AA national championship at Marshall, won 40 games and took Georgia to four bowl games in his five seasons as head coach. His biggest win was a 37–17 victory over Florida in 1997.

Jim Donnan was Georgia's head coach from 1996 to 2000.

RAY GOFF (1989–1995)

by Eric Zeier

When Coach Goff recruited me to come to Georgia, I knew one thing right away: regardless of how many games we won, I would have a relationship with him for the rest of my life. Coach Goff made it clear from the very beginning that he felt a strong responsibility to his players, not only on the field but off the field.

Take away the wins and losses, which are important, but after that, the primary job of a coach is to take boys and turn them into men. And once guys stopped playing for him, that responsibility does not end for people like Coach Goff.

I can't tell you how many ways Coach Goff has supported me since I left Georgia. Last year I was inducted into the Circle of Honor [Georgia's highest award for former student-athletes], and Coach Goff showed up at the banquet to support me. He didn't have to do that. But those are the kinds of things that he does to show how much he cares for his former players, and that is why, when you talk to his players, you'll find out that they are extremely loyal to him.

Ray Goff, the SEC Player of the Year in 1976, became Georgia's head coach when Vince Dooley retired after the 1988 season.

The only regret I have is that I wish we could have won more games for him. But at the end of the day, after all the games have been played, what we are left with in life are the relationships that we build along the way. I have had a number of phenomenal coaches who have helped me in life, and Coach Goff is right at the top of the list. He is truly a good man.

Eric Zeier completed his career at Georgia with 11,153 passing yards, which is still the fourth-highest total in SEC history.

Goff, who was the quarterback on Georgia's 1976 SEC championship team, had a record of 46–34–1 in seven seasons as head coach.

Vince Dooley (1964–1988)

by Frank Ros

There are so many positive things that I could say about Coach Dooley. But the biggest compliment I can pay him is that I didn't fully appreciate his impact on my life until after I left Georgia.

I wasn't a highly recruited player, so I didn't really have a lot of contact with Coach Dooley until my first practice. But once I did meet him, one thing was perfectly clear: he was the man in charge.

My first impression was that with Coach Dooley, you did not first speak to him. You waited to be spoken to. He kept his distance, but he has his reasons and those reasons are not clear when you're young. When you get older, you understand why he did what he did.

Today you would compare Coach Dooley to the CEO of a major corporation. He had his executive team—the assistant coaches—who executed his strategy. He hired very good people to work for him, and he made it very clear what his expectations were of them.

After winning 201 games as Georgia's head coach (1964–1988), Vince Dooley went on to become one of the most successful administrators in the history of college athletics.

Then it was the job of the assistant coaches to convey those expectations to us and to teach us to execute Coach Dooley's plan.

There are so many memories with Coach Dooley during my time at Georgia. There was the incredible season of 1978—they called us the Wonder Dawgs because we won so many close games. Then we struggled in 1979 [a 6–5 season], and people wondered if Georgia and Coach Dooley would ever win another championship.

Those of us who were seniors on the 1980 national championship team have a bond that will never be broken. The thing that I will never forget is the locker room after we beat Notre

Dame to win the national championship. The players put Coach Dooley on their shoulders and just passed him around the room. I was shocked when it happened because we had never seen Coach Dooley let his guard down and enjoy a moment that much.

But at that moment I realized that he had reached the pinnacle of his profession. We had won every game and now there was not another game to play. He could relax and enjoy the moment with us without holding back. I will never forget it.

They say that the best teachers are the ones who are the toughest on you and demand more than you think you can give. They demand that you be the very best that you can be. And you don't fully appreciate the tough love until later in life.

That's the way I feel about Coach Dooley. I've taken the lessons I learned from Coach Dooley and used them in my business career. I am proud that I played for him.

Frank Ros was the captain of Georgia's 1980 national championship team. Today he is a vice president at the Coca-Cola Company.

Vince Dooley won 201 games, six SEC championships, and one national championship as Georgia's head coach. After retiring as coach in 1988, he served as Georgia's athletics director until 2004. In 1994 he was inducted into College Football Hall of Fame.

Johnny Griffith (1961–1963)
by Preston Ridlehuber

When Johnny Griffith took over for Wally Butts as head coach [in 1961], it was a very difficult time for Georgia.

Coach Griffith and Coach Mike Castronis recruited me in high school, so I got to know Coach Griffith as a very sincere and down-to-earth guy. But the reality was that he didn't have full control of the football team. Coach Butts still exercised a lot of control as the athletics director.

We had coaches arguing among themselves, and sometimes it didn't seem like anybody was in charge. We don't know what kind of coach Johnny Griffith could have been if he had had the authority. I guess we'll never know.

The thing you need to know about Coach Griffith was that he was a Georgia man through and through. And it just absolutely killed him the way things turned out. [Griffith posted records of 3–7, 3–4–3, and 4–5–1 in his three seasons as Georgia's head coach. After a 14–3 loss to Georgia Tech in 1963, Griffith resigned.)

It was just a bad situation. After the Tech game [in 1963] there were all kinds of rumors that Coach Griffith had been fired. I remember going to a team meeting and listening to Coach Griffith talk and tell us that he was leaving. As I was listening to him, I was thinking, *What in the world have I gotten myself into?*

But then one of the secretaries from the athletic department knocked on the door and told me and several other players to go down to the Continuing Education Center. When I asked her why, she told me that we were going to meet the new coach. I said, "You've got to be kidding me!" We had not gotten through saying good-bye to the old football coach!

So we went down to the Continuing Ed Center, and I saw one of the members of the athletic board that I knew. I asked him the name of the new coach. He said, "Vince Dooley." And I asked, "Who the hell is Vince Dooley?"

We would soon all find out. It was going to be a new day for Georgia football. It was the day that we said hello to Coach Dooley and good-bye to Johnny Griffith, a fine man who really never had a chance.

Johnny Griffith was a player on Georgia's 1946 SEC championship team. He was a Georgia assistant coach from 1956 to 1960 and took over the Georgia program from the legendary Wallace Butts on January 6, 1961. His biggest coaching victory was a 30–21 upset of Auburn in 1962. He resigned as coach in December of 1963 and went on to establish a successful construction business in Atlanta. He is a member of the Georgia Sports Hall of Fame.

Preston Ridlehuber was the MVP of the 1964 Sun Bowl and a member of Vince Dooley's first two teams at Georgia. Today he lives in St. Mary's, Florida.

James Wallace "Wally" Butts (1939–1960)

by Fran Tarkenton

Coach Butts was a hard man to know, and I can't say that I ever really knew him. But I can say this: the man was a genius when it came to the passing game. He gave me a base in the passing game that allowed me to learn from others in my career. I've often said that I got a master's degree in the passing game from Wally Butts at Georgia. Then I got a Ph.D. in the NFL from Norm Van Brocklin. When I got to the NFL, I was way ahead of the other quarterbacks when it came to the passing game, and that was because of Coach Butts.

Coach Butts and I were never close, but I remember that later in my career, when I was playing in New York, I attended the College Football Hall of Fame banquet in the city. I ran into Coach Butts at the dinner, and he looked at me and said, "I think you're the best quarterback in football today."

I have to tell you that it was the greatest football-related compliment that I have ever received. I don't think Coach Butts ever

Coach Wally Butts (center), quarterback Fran Tarkenton (left), and guard Pat Dye (right) led Georgia to the 1959 SEC championship.

thought I was going to be a great quarterback when I was at Georgia. For him to take the time to say that to me was pretty special.

Fran Tarkenton was an All-SEC quarterback at Georgia in 1959 and 1960. He played for 18 seasons in the NFL and participated in three Super Bowls.

Wallace Butts, "the Little Round Man," was Georgia's head coach from 1939 to 1960. He led Georgia to 140 victories and four SEC championships. After his coaching days, he served as Georgia's athletics director until 1963. He went on to have a highly successful career in the insurance business. He is in the College Football Hall of Fame, and the Butts-Mehre Heritage Hall on campus is named in his honor.

Bulldogs in Their Own Words

JOE TERESHINSKI SR.

END, 1942, 1945–1946

I grew up in the Wyoming Valley area of Pennsylvania, near Wilkes-Barre. About 20 to 30 miles away, Charley Trippi lived in the town of Pittston. He and I grew up the same way. Our fathers worked in the coal mines, and we both knew that football was our chance to get out. As fate would have it, Charley, two other guys from our area—Andy Dudish and Francis Riofsky—and I all went to Georgia together.

My contact with Georgia started with a football official named John Bryan. Mr. Bryan worked several of the games I played as a senior, and he took an interest in me. He then introduced me to Mr. Harold Ketron. Mr. Ketron was originally from Clarksdale, Georgia, up in the mountains. He was a captain on the Georgia football team of 1906 and owned the Coca-Cola bottling plant in Wilkes-Barre.

I wasn't very big in high school. The most I ever weighed was about 162 pounds, and I was afraid that my lack of size might keep some schools away. I remember the first time Coach Wally Butts came to my house for a recruiting visit. It was around Christmas, and he brought Coach Bill Hartman with him.

When they arrived, I was at the store running an errand for my father, and when I walked into the kitchen, my mom told me there were some coaches from Georgia there. I was afraid they would think I was too small, so I went into my room and put on two huge sweaters and then put a big basketball jacket over the top of it so I would look bigger.

I went into the living room and said hello to Coach Butts and Coach Hartman. After a while, Coach Butts asked, "Joe, what do you weigh?" I was going to tell the truth, but before I could say 162, Mr. Ketron, who was also there, jumped in and said 186. I didn't correct him.

When I got to Georgia, one of the first things they did was put me on a scale. Sure enough, it said 162. They asked me what happened, because my paperwork said I weighed 186. I told them I got sick and just couldn't put the weight back on.

I remember my first practice because it was very, very hot. Man, that Georgia sun was just beating me down!

In the first scrimmage they put me in at right end, and opposite of me was probably the best player that Georgia had at the time—Tommy Greene from Macon, Georgia. Tommy played defensive tackle and was about 6′3″ and 245 pounds. At right end I had to block him on every single play.

When the practice was over, Coach Butts walked up to me. He had been watching me from only about 10 or 15 yards away.

He said, "Joe, we were ready to send you to Georgia Military College [a prep school] to put some weight on you. But I watched you on every play during the scrimmage. Anybody who wants to play football as badly as you've shown me...well, you can stay here as long as you wish."

Well, that was really all I needed to build up my confidence. I also started eating the good food they served us at the dorm and started gaining some weight. I knew I was in the right place.

We all moved into the Milledge Annex, where the football players lived. It seemed like we had about 125 freshmen that year. I

Joe Tereshinski's sons (Joe Jr. and Wally) and grandson (Joe III) have all played football for Georgia.

will never forget the day when I heard somebody down the hall saying there were some "damn Yankees" living in the dorm.

Some guys finally walked into the room that I was sharing with Trippi. They were nice enough, but when they left, one of them said, loud enough for me to hear it, "I wonder how long it will be before he is packing his bag and heading back to Yankeeland?"

Well, of all those freshmen who came in with us, there were only about 14 or so left for the spring of our sophomore year. But I was still there and so was Trippi.

We had a great team in 1942, and I was the second-string right end to Van Davis. George Poschner, the great All-American, played the left end. Now, I played a lot of football, both college and pro, and I'm telling you that Davis and Poschner were the greatest set of ends I ever saw on one football team. Offense. Defense. Covering kicks. Everything. They could do it all. That's a helluva statement, I know, but I really believe it.

I went off to the service in 1943 and didn't make it back to Athens until the end of 1945. But I did get to play against Tulsa in the Oil Bowl. We played that game in Houston and won 20–6.

In 1946 we felt confident that we could have a pretty good football team, and we did. We went undefeated and then went to the Sugar Bowl to play North Carolina and their great back Charlie Justice.

My most vivid memory of that game is that I intercepted a pass and lateralled it back to Dick McPhee. The ball was thrown laterally, but it turned out to be a very disputed play. We won the game 20–10. [Georgia finished the season 11–0.] I was fortunate to have a really good game and make the all-time Sugar Bowl team for the 1940–1950 era. That was a great honor for me.

I know a lot of people have their own stories about Coach Butts. But the thing you need to know about Coach Butts is that he demanded that you give 100 percent of everything you had in practice, in the game, and in everything you did. And he could tell if you were not giving 100 percent. He would come right up to you and look you straight in the eye. If you were looking elsewhere, he would give you a forearm shiver and knock you to the ground.

He was an actor, too. I remember a game against Furman when we had a big lead at halftime. He was talking and got mad at somebody and kicked a pail of ice. I think it broke his toe, but he never showed it.

I admired Coach Butts. He was the greatest coach I ever played for—college or pro. And he would give you the shirt off his back.

Thanks to the great training I got from Coach Butts and ends coach J.V. Sikes, I was able to play eight years with the Washington Redskins. I coached another five before I started selling automobiles full-time. I was pretty successful at it; I think I sold about 11,000 cars in 50 years.

Everything that I was able to accomplish all goes back to Georgia. I have lived in Bethesda, Maryland, since 1947, and just about everybody I meet has some kind of connection or knows somebody with a connection to Georgia.

Georgia has meant everything to me. I remember growing up near the mines in Pennsylvania and hearing the sound of the ambulance as it raced toward another accident near the shaft. We called it the "Black Mariah" and every time it raced past, we prayed that nobody was dead.

Georgia allowed me to leave that life and start a new one. The best thing I can say about Georgia is that my sons—Wally and Joe—went to school there and played there, and my grandson—Joe III—was a quarterback there.

In the words of the song, Georgia is our alma mater and we have been true and loyal to thee.

Joe Tereshinski Sr. was an All-SEC end in 1946 and played on two SEC championship teams (1942, 1946). Both of his sons, Joe Jr. and Wally, played for Georgia in the '70s. His grandson, Joe Tereshinski III, was a quarterback for the Bulldogs from 2004 to 2006.

HARRY MEHRE (1928–1937)
by Bill Hartman Sr.

Back when I was coming along as a football player, everybody in the South thought that the way to be successful was to hire a coach from Notre Dame and let him come down here and do what Notre Dame was doing. In 1928 Georgia was looking for a coach to replace "Kid" Woodruff. Coach Woodruff had to look no further than his top assistant, Harry Mehre. Coach Mehre had come to Georgia in 1923 on the recommendation of Knute Rockne, the famous Notre Dame coach. That's how Harry Mehre came to Georgia and how he eventually became my coach.

There were a lot of great memories under Coach Mehre. In 1935 I was a sophomore, and we played against Alabama. They had a senior end by the name of Paul "Bear" Bryant.

In 1936 we went up to New York and played a Fordham team that was supposed to be headed for the Rose Bowl. They had an offensive line they called "the Seven Blocks of Granite." One of those blocks was a guy named Vince Lombardi. We tied them 7–7 and knocked them out of the Rose Bowl.

My funniest memory at Georgia involved Coach Mehre. It was the next-to-last game of the season, and we were playing at Georgia Tech. I remember that the score was tied 0–0 at the half. Coach Mehre was late getting out of the locker room and for some reason

Coach Harry Mehre (right) and halfback Cy Grant pose at Yankee Stadium in New York before a game between Georgia and New York University, November 1934.
Photo courtesy of AP Images

got into an argument with one of the stadium guards. He was still arguing with the guy when I ran the second-half kickoff back 93 yards for a touchdown. I thought we had won that game, but Tech came back with a late touchdown and tied it 6–6, and that's how it ended.

Coach Mehre was a colorful man. He left Georgia and went to Ole Miss, where he had some success. When he was done coaching, he came back to Georgia and became a football analyst for the *Atlanta Journal*. He had a great sense of humor.

Bill Hartman, an All-American at Georgia in 1937, was associated with the university from his freshman season in 1934 until the time of his death in 2006. He is a member of the College Football Hall of Fame.

Harry Mehre posted a record of 59–34–6 in his 10 seasons as Georgia's coach. He is most remembered as the coach of the Georgia team that dedicated Sanford Stadium with a 15–0 win over Yale in 1929. Mehre's teams beat Yale five straight times.

Other Coaches in Georgia History

Joel Hunt (1938)

Hunt came to Georgia to replace Harry Mehre and coached only one season, going 5–4–1. Hunt was replaced by his line coach, Wallace Butts. Hunt also coached at Wyoming and LSU.

George Cecil "Kid" Woodruff (1923–1927)

Woodruff's 1927 "Dream and Wonder Team" went 9–1 and almost went to the Rose Bowl. A captain and the star of Georgia's 1911 team, Woodruff came back to Georgia in 1923 and decided he wanted to install Knute Rockne's Notre Dame system. In order to do it, Woodruff brought in three of Rockne's best minds: Harry Mehre, Frank Thomas, and Jim Crowley. All three went on to become successful head coaches. Woodruff, who had already made his fortune in business, coached the Georgia team for a salary of $1 a year.

Herman J. Stegeman (1920–1922)

"Stege" played at the University of Chicago under Hall of Fame coach Amos Alonzo Stagg. After he graduated in 1919, the Army sent Stegeman to Athens to install a physical training program for the ROTC students at Georgia. He became an assistant coach to W.A. Cunningham for a season and then was head coach for three seasons, posting a record of 20–6–3. He also coached baseball, track, and basketball. He later became Georgia's athletics director

Georgia's Head Coaches, 1892–Present

Coach	Years	Record At UGA
Dr. Charles Herty	1892	1–1–0
Ernest Brown	1893	2–2–1
Robert Winston	1894	5–1–0
Glenn "Pop" Warner	1895–1896	7–4–0
Charles McCarthy	1897–1898	6–3–0
Gordon Saussy	1899	2–3–1
E.E. Jones	1900	2–4–0
Billy Reynolds	1901–1902	5–7–3
M.M. Dickinson	1903, 1905	4–9–0
Charles A. Barnard	1904	1–5–0
W.S. Whitney	1906–1907	6–7–2
Branch Bocock	1908	5–2–1
Frank Dobson, J. Coulter	1909	1–4–2
W.A. Cunningham	1910–1919	43–18–9
H.J. Stegeman	1920–1922	20–6–3
George Woodruff	1923–1927	30–16–1
Harry Mehre	1928–1937	59–34–6
Joel Hunt	1938	5–4–1
Wallace Butts	1939–1960	140–86–9
Johnny Griffith	1961–1963	10–16–4
Vince Dooley	1964–1988	201–77–10
Ray Goff	1989–1995	46–34–1
Jim Donnan	1996–2000	40–19–0
Mark Richt	2001–Present	96–34-0
Total		737–396–54

and dean of male students. Georgia's basketball facility, Stegeman Coliseum, is named in his honor.

W.A. Cunningham (1910–1916, 1919)

In Georgia's first 18 years of football, the school had 14 different head coaches. Georgia finally found the stability it wanted when William A. Cunningham became head coach in 1910. According to Mark Schlabach's book *Georgia Football Yesterday and Today*, Cunningham was coaching baseball at Gordon Military College when, during a game against Georgia, athletics director S.V. Sanford (who would later become UGA's president), scribbled a proposed contract on the back of an envelope. Sanford handed the envelope to Cunningham, who agreed to become Georgia's coach. Cunningham tutored under Vanderbilt's Hall of Fame coach Dan McGugin. Cunningham had seven winning teams in eight seasons as Georgia's head coach. (There were no teams in 1917 and 1918 because of World War I). Cunningham coached Bob McWhorter, who was Georgia's first All-America player. Cunningham entered the Army during World War I and then returned to coach in 1919. He reentered the Army in 1920 and eventually rose to the rank of general.

J. Coulter and Frank Dobson (1909)

Coulter, who had never been a head coach, was unable to get Georgia's offense going, so he hired a co-coach in Dobson, who had worked for John Heisman at Georgia Tech. Still, Georgia went 1–4–2.

Branch Bocock (1908)

Bocock, a Georgetown graduate, took over for the last three games of 1907 and then led Georgia to a 5–2–1 record in 1908.

He worked in the law offices of Judge Hamilton McWhorter in the morning and left in the afternoon to work with the Georgia football team.

W.S. "Bull" Whitney (1906–1907)

Whitney's 1906 team went 2–4–1. But he is remembered for using four or five illegal players, or "ringers," in the 1907 game with Georgia Tech. The charges came from Grantland Rice of the *Nashville Tennessean* newspaper. Whitney admitted using the illegal players and had to give up the football team to interim coach Branch Bocock, who coached the last three games of the season.

Charles A. Barnard (1904)

Barnard, who attended Harvard, coached the team in 1904 while M.M. Dickinson was away playing baseball. Georgia opened the season with a 52–0 win over Florida and then lost its last five games.

M.M. Dickinson (1903, 1905)

Dickinson transferred to Georgia from Mercer and played for the Bulldogs from 1900 to 1902. He was also the captain of the baseball team. He led the Georgia football team to a 3–4 record in 1903 and then took a year off to play professional baseball in 1904. He came back to Georgia as head coach in 1905, and Georgia went 1–5. All five losses were by shutouts.

Billy Reynolds (1901–1902)

Reynolds, a Princeton graduate, had coached at North Carolina for four seasons when he came to Athens. His first team was 1–5–2 but then Georgia improved to 4–2–1 in 1902.

Glenn "Pop" Warner was Georgia's head coach from 1895 to 1896. His 1896 team went 4–0.

E.E. Jones (1900)
Jones was also a Princeton graduate who went 2–4 in his only season. The Bulldogs were outscored 159–28 in those six games.

Gordon Saussy (1899)
Saussy was a former Cornell player who was only 26 years old when he took over as head coach. Georgia went 2–3–1 that season. Saussy later became the mayor of Savannah.

Charles McCarthy (1897–1898)
McCarthy, a graduate of Brown, was the coach in 1897 when football was almost banned at Georgia after the death of Richard "Von" Gammon in the last game of the season against Virginia. But the sport survived, and McCarthy also coached the 1898 team, which went 4–2.

Glenn "Pop" Warner (1895–1896)
Warner, who went on to become one of the most famous names in American football, was paid $34 a week to coach Georgia for 10 weeks in 1895. In 1896 he got a raise to $40 a week and led the Bulldogs, then known as the Red and Black, to a 4–0 season.

Robert Winston (1894)
Winston, a former rugby player who had coached at Yale, was Georgia's first "paid coach." His only team went 5–1.

Ernest Brown (1893)
Brown was a Georgia graduate student who volunteered to coach the Bulldogs in 1893. Brown played on the team, which went 2–2–1.

Dr. Charles Herty learned the game of football as a student at Johns Hopkins. He formed Georgia's first football team in 1892.

Dr. Charles Herty (1892)

Herty founded Georgia's first football team in 1892 after learning the game while receiving his Ph.D. at Johns Hopkins University. A Georgia graduate, Herty returned to his alma mater in 1891 as a member of the faculty. Georgia's first team went 1–1 with a 50–0 win over Mercer in Athens and a 10–0 loss to Auburn at Piedmont Park in Atlanta.

chapter 8

THAT CHAMPIONSHIP SEASON

DURING THE FIRST 88 YEARS OF ITS FOOTBALL HISTORY, Georgia came close many times to fielding a team that was an undefeated, undisputed, consensus national champion.

Georgia was in position to win the national championship in 1927 but lost the last regular season game against Georgia Tech 12–0 on a sloppy field in Atlanta. The Bulldogs appeared to be a lock in 1942 with the dream backfield of Frank Sinkwich and Charley Trippi. But the No. 1 Bulldogs lost to Auburn 27–13 in a stunning upset. Georgia was named national champion in six polls recognized by the NCAA, but the Associated Press, the most prestigious poll of the day, gave its national title to Ohio State.

The 1946 team went 11–0 behind Trippi, who finished second for the Heisman Trophy. But the pollsters, as they would always do back then, looked down their noses at the southern team and instead gave the national championship to Notre Dame, which was 8–0–1 with a tie against Army.

Vince Dooley's 1968 team was one of his very best. The Bulldogs, who had two future NFL superstars on defense (Bill Stanfill and Jake Scott), were 8–1–2 with ties against Tennessee (17–17) and Houston (10–10). That team finished No. 1 in the Litkenhous poll, but the national championship in the two major polls (AP and UPI) went to Ohio State.

When Dooley became Georgia's head coach for the 1964 season, having an undefeated, untied, and undisputed national championship team was one of his goals.

"When you become a head coach, you want to build a program that is consistently competitive for the conference championship," said Dooley. "But if your career is going to be complete, I think you need to have a team that is undefeated and wins the national championship. Yes, that was something I wanted our program to accomplish before we were done."

No one really expected that magical championship season to finally happen at the University of Georgia in 1980. The year before, Georgia had gone 6–5 with nonconference losses to Wake Forest (22–21), Clemson (12–7), South Carolina (27–20), and Virginia (31–0).

"Other than the Virginia and Auburn [a 33–13 loss] games we could have won the rest of them. We were a lot closer to being a good football team than people knew," said linebacker Frank Ros. "We were really just missing one piece of the puzzle."

Ros was right. Everything else was in place for Georgia to win and win big in 1980. Buck Belue, a junior, was an All-SEC quarterback. The receivers, Lindsay Scott and Amp Arnold, are two of the best ever at Georgia. There was a veteran offensive line and an opportunistic defense that had seven seniors.

The missing piece of the puzzle was a top-flight running back. That piece was put into place on Easter Sunday, 1980, when Herschel Walker of Wrightsville, Georgia, signed to play for the Bulldogs.

The rest, as they say, is history. In a season filled with drama and some moments that will be forever frozen in time, Georgia finished the regular season 11–0 and then beat Notre Dame 17–10 in the Sugar Bowl to win the national championship.

The 1980 season would launch the most successful four-year stretch ever at Georgia, as from 1980 to 1983 the Bulldogs went 43–4–1 with three SEC championships and one national championship.

Here is a look back at the 12 games that made up the most significant season in Georgia football history followed by accounts from those who were there.

Game 1: Georgia 16, Tennessee 15

SEPTEMBER 6 IN KNOXVILLE, TENNESSEE: Tennessee took a 15–0 lead on a 36-yard touchdown pass from Volunteers quarterback Jeff Olszewski with 4:02 left in the third quarter. But Georgia got a safety after a muffed Tennessee punt, and then freshman running back Herschel Walker immediately made his presence felt when he was finally inserted into the game. Walker ran over safety Bill Bates for a 16-yard touchdown and then scored again from nine yards out to give Georgia a one-point lead with 11:16 left. Tennessee had a chance to win when the Vols drove inside the Georgia 10-yard line in the final minutes. But Georgia forced a fumble from UT running back Glenn Ford, and the Bulldogs recovered to seal the victory.

Game 2: Georgia 42, Texas A&M 0

SEPTEMBER 13 IN ATHENS: Walker made his home debut a memorable one with 145 yards on 21 carries, including an electrifying 76-yard touchdown run in the third quarter. "It was the first time we had seen his real speed," said Larry Munson, the legendary radio voice of the Bulldogs. "I'm looking around the press box and wondering, *My God! Did everybody just see what I just saw? What in the world do we have here?*"

Game 3: Georgia 20, Clemson 16

SEPTEMBER 20 IN ATHENS: Herschel Walker ran for 121 yards on 23 carries, but this will always be known as "the Scott Woerner game." Georgia's All-America defensive back returned a punt 67 yards for a touchdown and returned an interception 98 yards to set up another Georgia score. At halftime Georgia had run only 11 offensive plays but led 14–10 because of Woerner. In the second half, Rex Robinson kicked two field goals for Georgia and Obed Ariri kicked two field goals for Clemson. With Georgia holding onto a four-point lead, Clemson had a chance to win the game as the Tigers drove inside Georgia's 10-yard line with a couple minutes left. But on second down Mike Gasque's pass was tipped by Frank Ros and intercepted by Jeff Hipp to preserve the victory.

Game 4: Georgia 34, TCU 3

SEPTEMBER 27 IN ATHENS: Herschel Walker's 41-yard run set up Georgia's first touchdown of the day, and the Bulldogs rolled to 334 yards rushing to beat the Horned Frogs and go 4–0. Walker only had nine carries for 69 yards in the game after tweaking his ankle in the first quarter at the end of that 41-yard run. Leading 20–3 at halftime, Georgia scored a pair of touchdowns in 1:06 in the fourth quarter to put the game away. Rex Robinson kicked two field goals and four PATs to become Georgia's all-time scorer.

Game 5: Georgia 28, Ole Miss 21

OCTOBER 11 IN ATHENS: Running back Carnie Norris of Spartanburg, South Carolina, took up the workload for Herschel Walker (who was still hobbled by a bad ankle) and ran for 150 yards on 15 carries to beat Ole Miss. Georgia appeared to be in position for a blowout when Norris scored a touchdown on a one-yard run to give Georgia a 17–0 lead with 44 seconds left in the first half. Georgia actually had a chance to go up 24–0 because the Bulldogs got the ball right back with an interception by Jeff Hipp. But Belue threw an ill-advised pass to linebacker James Otis, who returned it 32 yards for an Ole Miss touchdown with only seven seconds left before the intermission. Now Georgia was in a dogfight for four quarters. Ole Miss scored with 1:42 left to come within a touchdown, 28–21, but could not recover the onside kick.

Game 6: Georgia 41, Vanderbilt 0

OCTOBER 18 IN ATHENS: Playing its fifth straight game at home, Georgia got a school-record 283 yards rushing from Walker to totally dominate Vanderbilt. Walker broke Charley Trippi's single-game rushing record (239 yards) that had stood for 35 years. After nursing a bad ankle for two straight games, Walker had touchdown runs of 60 (on his first carry of the game), 48, and 53 yards. On the Thursday before the game, Coach Vince Dooley, his wife Barbara, and son Derek were involved in a traffic accident in Athens. Barbara Dooley was hospitalized with multiple broken ribs and eventually had to have her spleen removed. Vince Dooley suffered a broken nose, concussion, and a busted lip that required 11 stitches. But when the game began, he was on the Georgia sideline.

Game 7: Georgia 27, Kentucky 0

OCTOBER 25 IN LEXINGTON, KENTUCKY: After five straight home games, Georgia finally had to go back on the road and posted an easy win over the Wildcats at Commonwealth Stadium. After his record-setting performance the week before, Walker was more workmanlike, gaining 131 yards on 31 carries. Georgia led 13–0 at halftime and 20–0 at the end of the third quarter. Early in the fourth quarter, Amp Arnold caught a 91-yard touchdown pass from Buck Belue, which is still the third-longest scoring pass in school history.

Game 8: Georgia 13, South Carolina 10

NOVEMBER 1 IN ATHENS: The showdown was set: Herschel Walker versus George Rogers. Georgia fans were convinced that Walker was the best running back in college football. South Carolina fans believed that Rogers, a native of Duluth, Georgia, was on his way to becoming the first Heisman Trophy winner in school history. Early in the game, Rex Robinson missed a 22-yard field goal, but then the All-American came right back and made a 57-yarder, the longest of his career and the fourth-longest in Georgia history, to give the Bulldogs a 3–0 lead that stood up until halftime. Later in the game Robinson made a 51-yard field goal. But this game will always be remembered for two plays: one by Walker and one by Rogers. In the third quarter, Walker burst off right tackle and, despite the fact that several South Carolina defenders had the angle on him, Walker outran them all for a 76-yard touchdown. Vince Dooley would later call it "one of the greatest runs I've ever seen." With Georgia clinging to a three-point lead late in the game, South Carolina drove to the Bulldogs' 17-yard line. The worst the Gamecocks could do, it appeared, was tie the game. But Rogers fumbled after a hit by Dale Carver, and Tim Parks recovered to preserve the win. Walker won his individual battle with Rogers, rushing for 219 yards on 43 carries. Rogers had 168 yards on 35 carries. Rogers still won the Heisman Trophy.

Bulldogs in Their Own Words

REX ROBINSON

KICKER, 1977–1980

One of the reasons I decided to go to Georgia was that under Coach Dooley the kicker wasn't just "the kicker." He was considered to be a very important part of the team. The way Coach Dooley managed a game, the kicker had a chance to become a star if he produced. I was fortunate in that I was put into some very important situations, and I feel like I did produce.

And today it's been more than 30 years since I kicked my last field goal for Georgia, but people will still walk up to me and say, "Are you *the* Rex Robinson?" A bunch of my coworkers think it's so funny that they have nicknamed me "The." That people still remember me after all those years still blows me away.

It's funny, but I was playing on the junior varsity team in high school when somebody first noticed that I could kick. I kicked a 51-yard field goal in a junior varsity game. The word sort of got around, and the next thing I knew Don McCellan of Channel 2 [in Atlanta] was out at practice with a camera crew. He came out there to verify that I could do it. It took me four tries, but I did it for him.

That next summer, before my junior year at Marietta High School, I met Peter Rajecki, who was a former Georgia kicker. He went to Sprayberry High School to do his off-season training. He was playing in the World League at the time. He showed me a lot of things that helped me improve—like taking three steps back from the ball and then two across to set up for the kick. I will never forget that.

Now, when I was a senior in high school, a lot of colleges wanted you to walk on, because they didn't want to use a full scholarship on a kicker. But I got offers from three—Memphis State, Georgia Tech, and Georgia. Georgia Tech seemed too close, and Memphis was too far away. Georgia seemed just right. They had just won an SEC championship in 1976, and Coach Dooley had a reputation for having four-year kickers. Allan Leavitt was finishing up his four years as a starting kicker, so the situation seemed perfect for me.

What does the book say? "It was the best of times. It was the worst of times." Well, my freshman year in 1977 was the worst of times for me.

Expectations were high on that team after winning the championship the year before. Instead, we gave Coach Dooley his only losing season [5–6] in his entire time at Georgia. I certainly didn't do my part, making only 10 of 20 field goals. I would watch the game film and could see the entire team sag when we drove the ball down into position and I missed the field goal. They were so let down.

But that was also the turning point for me. I set some very high goals for the next season and came to camp in the best shape of my life. The coaches were really surprised to see this old tubby guy actually show up in shape. A lot of the guys on the team that year had the same resolve.

In 1978 people called us the "Wonder Dawgs" because we won so many close games. I just think it was a group of guys who really hated losing the year before and who were going to do whatever it took to win. And after we won a few close games, we felt confident we were going to find a way to get it done.

When you're a kicker, you sort of remember things a little differently. I remember the first game against Baylor and their great linebacker, Mike Singletary. He made a tackle on our sideline, and for the first time, I saw the eyes that everybody would later talk about when he was with the Bears. That was scary.

I remember Lindsay [Scott] running the second-half kickoff back against LSU, which got us going for another close win [24–17], at Baton Rouge.

Of course, people still like to talk about the last-second field goal to beat Kentucky [17–16] in 1978. It's amazing. Hardly a day goes by when I don't meet somebody who was either there or listened to Larry Munson call it on the radio.

It's funny, the things you remember about certain games. I remember that I had missed a couple of field goals early in the game that could have made things easy on us. And I remember that when the score was 16–14, Kentucky missed a field goal that would have given them a five-point lead and made the last few minutes of that game totally different.

We got the ball back with 4:03 left, and immediately I realized that the game was going to come down to a field goal. We were getting big chunks of yardage, but I knew that when we got close, Coach Dooley was not going to take any chances. That's exactly what happened. We got down around their 10-yard line and called timeout with just a few seconds left.

Now, I tell young kickers today that they can't control all the noise and stuff going on around them, but they can control their own routine. It's like a pre-shot routine in golf. So I was going through my set routine when Kentucky called timeout to "ice" me.

It's a good thing they did, because Tim Morrison, who was supposed to be in the game, was kneeling on the sideline praying. Coach Dooley always likes to tell the story of leaning down to tell Tim, "Your prayers have just been answered. Kentucky called timeout."

Charlie Fales was the snapper, and Mike Garrett was the holder. I had complete confidence in them. It wasn't the greatest kick in

Rex Robinson, one in a long line of All-America kickers at Georgia, was a member of the Bulldogs' 1980 national championship team.

the world, but it was good, and the whole field was just pandemonium. They would deny this today, but some of the guys told me they loved me. Guys who had never spoken 10 words to me in two years were suddenly jumping up and down on top of me.

It was the first time in my career that I had ever kicked a field goal to win a game. And it felt great.

The only other great memory I have of that year is the Georgia Tech game, where we came back from 20–0 to beat them 29–28. Drew Hill ran back a kickoff about 100 yards against us to give them the lead. I dove and got a hand on his thigh pad, but I just didn't get there quick enough. The only good part of that play was that I took out a couple of Tech coaches when I dove at their sideline.

I never have been able to figure out what happened to us in 1979. I think we all felt pretty good about that team, but then we lost the opener to Wake Forest [22–21] and things just went downhill after that.

Everything seemed different going into the summer workouts of 1980. I started keeping a diary of what I heard and saw during those workouts. I just remember that it all started to click, even the little things like how we did our warm-up exercises. I remember writing that everything just seemed to be on point.

I believe we would all agree that the main thing missing from the 1979 team was a marquee running back. We had had Willie McClendon in 1978. We thought Herschel Walker might be it, but we had no idea how that was going to turn out.

Everybody says they knew Herschel was great after the first game against Tennessee [a 16–15 Georgia win]. For me it was the first home game against Texas A&M, when I saw him break off his first long run. I had never seen anybody that size who could run that fast. I knew we had something pretty special.

When that year started, I just wanted us to win the SEC championship. After all, I had never won any kind of athletic championship before, and I figured it was a realistic goal. But we just kept winning, and around the time of the Vanderbilt game I started thinking that we could win them all. In fact, we had a pep rally before that Vanderbilt game, and I said something about it then.

I guess the game that I'm most proud of that year was when we beat South Carolina 13–10. The two teams seemed evenly matched. They had George Rogers. We had Herschel. I thought it might come down to kicking.

I missed an easy 22-yard field goal early in the game, and I was pretty upset by that. By my senior year I didn't expect to make a mistake like that. All I did was miss my alignment on the kick.

One thing I had learned how to do was forget about bad kicks, so when we had a chance to kick a 57-yarder later in the game, I was confident I could do it. Coach Dooley could tell I was confident, and he let me kick it. I made that one and then made a 51-yarder in the second half. I think that year I made four field goals that were over 50 yards. That was a great day and a great win for us.

People ask me all the time what I was doing when Lindsay Scott scored the miracle touchdown against Florida. The truth is, I really didn't see him score, because when Lindsay got to midfield I started running to the end of the bench to get my tee, thinking he'd get tackled and I'd have to kick a field goal to win the game. By the time I got my tee he was in the end zone and being mobbed. We didn't kick the extra point because we went for two.

That was a great plane ride home from Jacksonville to Atlanta. We had learned earlier that Georgia Tech had tied Notre Dame and that we'd be No. 1 in the next polls. We would get a shot at the national championship if we could just beat Auburn and Georgia Tech, which we did.

The play I get asked about from the Sugar Bowl is the kickoff that the Notre Dame guys forgot to field. We knew going into the game that one of their kickoff guys, Jim Stone, was considerably better than the other one. So my job was just to kick high and away from Stone. The two guys just didn't communicate, and they both ran away from the ball. Bob Kelly got down there and got on the ball, and we got an easy touchdown. After the game some of the sportswriters actually asked me if we did it on purpose. Erk [Russell] called it "the longest onside kick in history." But it was one of those plays that showed that it was our day.

What happened on the field right after the game was just incredible. It only took a few seconds before that field was covered in red. What was so weird was that I saw a lot of people I knew, and we were having a great time. It took me quite a while to get to the locker room because the celebration was still going strong.

It's been 30 years since I played my last game at Georgia, but today little kids come up to me and know who I am. Their dads introduce them to me, and they know what jersey number I wore. It's kind of mind-blowing to me that after all this time a kid would even care to know about something like that.

My wife is from Michigan, and when we met I didn't make a big deal about the fact that I played at Georgia. Now she is working in Atlanta and teaching with people who make a big deal about it when they find out we're married. She thinks it's really funny.

But that's one of the many things that make Georgia special. When you're 18 years old, you have no idea that the decision of where you are going to school will shape the rest of your life. The Georgia people become your family, and once you wear that uniform, they never forget you. And the friendships I made at Georgia are the ones I'll have forever. I know a lot of other guys have probably said this, but it was the most important four years of my life.

Rex Robinson was an All-America place-kicker in 1979 and 1980. Today Robinson lives in Atlanta, Georgia, where he works for a sporting goods manufacturer.

Game 9: Georgia 26, Florida 21

NOVEMBER 8 IN JACKSONVILLE, FLORIDA: At 8–0, Georgia was ranked No. 2 in the nation when it arrived at the Gator Bowl for its annual showdown with Florida. The year before, the Gators had gone 0–10–1 in their first season under Charley Pell. In 1980 they were 6–1, ranked No. 20, with their only loss to LSU, 24–7. Thanks to a 72-yard touchdown run by Walker and a 13-yard touchdown pass from Belue to fullback Ronnie Stewart, Georgia led 14–10 at the half. Georgia stretched the lead to 20–10 going into the fourth quarter on a pair of short field goals by Robinson. But Florida fought back with a touchdown and a two-point conversion to bring the Gators to within two, 20–18, early in the fourth quarter. Then Florida drove to the Georgia 24-yard line, and Brian Clark kicked a 40-yard field goal to give the Gators a 21–20 lead with only 6:52 left.

Georgia's hopes and dreams for the season appeared to be dashed when Florida punted the ball out of bounds at the Georgia 7-yard line with only 1:20 remaining. Georgia's first two plays from there were incomplete passes, setting up a big third-down play. The play, Left 76, was designed to get the ball down the field and keep the drive alive. Georgia wide receiver Lindsay Scott caught the ball near his 25-yard line, turned to go upfield, and suddenly found a clear path to the end zone. He outran the Florida defense, touching off a wild celebration in Jacksonville. When Georgia finally got to its locker room after the miracle play, the players learned that Georgia Tech had tied No. 1 Notre Dame 3–3 in Atlanta. The next day Georgia would move to No. 1 in the polls and "Belue to Scott" would become the single most significant play in Georgia football history.

Bulldogs in Their Own Words

LINDSAY SCOTT

WIDE RECEIVER, 1978–1981

It's funny, but when you're young you have no idea how a few seconds on a football field in Jacksonville, Florida, will change your life. You have to grow older and get a little perspective to realize the real impact of something like the touchdown play that beat Florida in 1980.

It's not something I talk about every day, but I don't mind if other people want to ask me about it. I'm flattered that they still remember because it was more than 20 years ago.

When I look back on my time at Georgia, I like to remember just hanging out with my teammates in the locker room. I like to remember getting ready for the games and the celebration after a game when we won. I like to remember the friendships that I made then that are so important to me today. For me, that was the real joy of my four years at Georgia. That's what being a Bulldog is all about.

When I was a senior at Wayne County High School in Jesup, I was looking around outside the state. I wanted to go somewhere where I could get the opportunity to get the ball on a regular basis. My high school coach, John Donaldson, was a Georgia man, and I think he figured out that I would score a touchdown every four times I touched the ball. So he put together all kinds of ways for me to get the ball. That was the only drawback when I thought about Georgia, because they had a great history of running the ball—three yards and a cloud of dust, you know.

My dad really liked the Tennessee offense. Coach Johnny Majors had come to Tennessee, and they were known for sending a lot of great receivers to the NFL. But my mom really wanted me to go to Georgia because she wanted to come see me play. I had an older brother, Dennis, who went to Virginia Tech, and there was just no way that we could get up to Blacksburg to see him play very often.

The other thing was that I had developed a bond with Coach Mike Cavan. That made all the difference in the world. When Georgia signed Buck Belue at quarterback, I was convinced they would open up the offense because Buck was a great passer. So I decided to stay at home and go to Georgia.

I'll never forget my freshman year, in 1978. I expected to play early, and by the LSU game, I was a starter. I was able to run the second-half kickoff back for a touchdown, and we went on to win that game [24–17] over there in Baton Rouge. I wish I could explain what it felt like to do that in front of those 90,000 people. It was really something, and I believe that's when people started to notice what I could do. You always wonder as a young player if you can compete at this level. That's when I was sure that I could.

Later on that year we beat Georgia Tech [29–28] in the wildest game I've ever been a part of. Buck came off the bench and brought us from behind to win that game. I know that was a big moment for him.

That was a good team for a lot of reasons, but the guy I looked up to was Willie McClendon, our running back. We played against a lot of good running backs, but nobody ran harder than Willie. I really looked to him for my inspiration.

I wish I knew what happened in 1979 [when Georgia went 6–5]. We lost a lot of good players, like Willie, and that was a team that really needed to grow up. We were talented but still very young. That was such a weird year; we started by losing to Wake Forest [22–21]. We lost all of our nonconference games but kept winning the conference games until we got to Auburn, who beat us pretty good [33–13]. But if we had beaten Auburn, we could have gone to the Sugar Bowl with a 7–4 record. That was really strange.

I'll never forget something that Coach Wayne McDuffie said during that time. Coach McDuffie once told us that we were happy winning on a regional level when we should be thinking on a national level. He believed that Georgia had everything it needed to compete for the national championship. Now, nothing was broke at Georgia, but he thought that we should be thinking bigger. I think our class listened to him. We thought we could do something big.

[In the spring of 1980, Lindsay Scott lost his football scholarship for one year after an altercation with an athletic department official, but was allowed to stay with the team and pay his own way to school. In late summer, he was involved in an automobile accident that left him with a concussion and several dislocated bones in his foot. One of the doctors told Scott's mother that he would never play football again.]

After the accident I did sit around for a while and wonder "why me?" But the honest answer was that I had never had to face any real adversity in my life. Things had always rocked along pretty well for me.

The fact is, I had to grow up a little bit. I'm sure that at some point every college kid goes through what I went through. It's just not all over the papers the next day. But that's part of being a college football player at a place like Georgia. I had forgotten who I was supposed to represent. I wasn't just representing myself. I was representing my family and my school. I had to learn that.

Yes, a doctor told my mother I would never play again, but that was a joke because I knew I was coming back. I didn't care how hard I had to work. I know my mother was afraid for me, but she never questioned me when I said I was going back and that I was going to play. She never asked me not to play. She knew deep down inside that I was going to be all right.

It took a while before I felt right again. The foot healed up fine, but it took me a while to get my equilibrium completely back. I don't think I ever felt completely right until we got to Jacksonville to play Florida.

We weren't throwing the ball very much, but I understood why. Herschel Walker had come on as a freshman and had been an incredible running back. And with a player like that, you knew Coach Dooley was going to keep giving him the ball.

But you know how it is when you're a receiver—you want to catch the ball. It's funny now, but back then an article came out where a reporter asked some of us receivers if we wished we were throwing the ball more. Well, what would you expect us to say? Of course! What receiver doesn't want to catch the ball more?

But the article made it sound like we were unhappy with the way the offense was being run. Well, if you know Coach Dooley, you know that wasn't going to work. He pulled us aside the next day and politely told us what he thought. That was the last time we talked about that issue.

When we got to Jacksonville, I had not caught a touchdown pass all season. We had played nine games, and I was shut out. We were winning, and I was happy about that, but catching a touchdown pass does wonders for your confidence. You feel like you're an important part of the offense. And to be perfectly honest about it, I needed something good to happen to me. With everything that had gone wrong in my life—losing my scholarship and the accident—I just needed something to go my way for a change.

Lindsay Scott's 93-yard catch and run for a touchdown against Florida in 1980 launched the Bulldogs into a national championship season.

I really thought we were going to put Florida away. We jumped on top of them early, but all of a sudden they jumped ahead of us 21–20. After all we had been through together, I just didn't see how we were going to let this thing slip away. And when they kicked the ball out of bounds at the 8-yard line, things didn't look good.

I remember that in the huddle Nat Hudson wouldn't let anybody get down. We knew what we had to do. We had an All-America kicker in Rex Robinson. We just had to get it close enough to give Rex a shot.

The first two plays were really frustrating. Buck lost a yard scrambling on the first play, and on the second play they took me out of the game. I was thinking, *What the hell are you doing! You brought me here to make plays. We talked about it! And with the game on the line I'm on the sideline!* I just didn't understand.

But I was put back in the game on third down, and Coach [George] Haffner called Left 76. All we wanted to do was get a first down and keep the drive alive.

My job was to go down and do a little curl pattern. I didn't know what was going on behind the line of scrimmage. All I knew was that Buck got me the ball, and when I caught it, I knew I had the first down.

But at that moment my mind went back to something that John Donaldson had taught me in high school. He always said, "Don't fall; keep on running after you catch the ball." So when I caught the ball and felt myself going down, I put my hand on the ground to steady myself and kept running. Once I caught my balance, I saw a guy go down, and then I saw an opening.

When I started running, my first thought was that I could get us into field goal range. After about 10 more yards it dawned on me, *Hell, I can take this thing to the house.*

I have no idea who was behind me or how close they were, but I knew I was fast enough to outrun them if I just didn't fall down. And the second I got to the end zone it seemed like the whole world came down on top of me. Everybody called it a miracle. To me, it was the greatest feeling in the world. It was the shot in the arm that I really needed.

Like I said before, I didn't understand the magnitude of that play for a long, long time. It began to sink in a little after we won the national championship. If we hadn't beaten Florida [26–21] that day then we probably never would have gotten the chance to play Notre Dame in the Sugar Bowl.

That team was really special. We had that big play against Florida, but guys had been making big plays like that all year. Every week it was somebody different. I can't begin to tell you how many plays Scott Woerner made during the course of that season. It was incredible.

The fact that we're still talking about that play more than 30 years later tells me that it is something special. But it was just one great moment in the four years that I spent at Georgia—the best four years of my life.

At Georgia I had the opportunity to play ball, travel, and meet friends who would stick with me the rest of my life. I had a chance to be with a group of guys who could say that we were the best team in college football. Not a lot of people get to say that.

The entire Georgia experience affected the way I think about life. Sure, I've had to regroup a couple of times in my life. And when I did, I would go back to the lessons I learned at Georgia from Coach Dooley. When things get tough, you always go back and pull those lessons out of the closet. That's because they work.

For me, going to Georgia was a once-in-a-lifetime experience. There has never been anything else like it.

Lindsay Scott was an All-SEC receiver in 1981. He was later drafted by the New Orleans Saints. Today Scott lives in Valdosta, Georgia, where he works for a trucking firm.

Game 10: Georgia 31, Auburn 21

NOVEMBER 15 IN AUBURN, ALABAMA: After the wild celebration in Jacksonville, it was only natural that Georgia would come out flat the following week at Auburn. Georgia went into that game ranked No. 1 and was heavily favored to win and clinch the SEC championship. Auburn was 5–4, but was 0–4 in the SEC. Coach Doug Barfield, who had taken over when the legendary Ralph "Shug" Jordan retired after the 1975 season, was on his way out. Still, Auburn jumped out to a 7–0 lead on 34-yard touchdown pass from Charles Thomas to Byron Franklin. Auburn still led 7–3 when the game turned in Georgia's favor. Greg Bell, a native of Birmingham, broke through the Auburn defense to block a punt. Defensive end Freddie Gilbert picked up the loose ball and ran 27 yards for a touchdown to make it 10–7. Georgia got another touchdown on the last play of the first half when Belue threw a one-yard pass to Norris Brown. Auburn assistant coach Paul Davis stormed onto the field, protesting that the clock had run out before Belue took the final snap. Davis and Auburn were assessed a 15-yard penalty for unsportsmanlike conduct. It meant that Georgia would kick off to start the second half from the Auburn 45-yard line. Coach Vince Dooley called for an onside kick, and Georgia recovered. Georgia turned that opportunity into another touchdown to go up 24–7. Auburn tacked on a couple of fourth quarter scores, but Georgia won to give Dooley his fourth SEC championship. Ironically, all four of those titles had been clinched with wins at Auburn, Dooley's alma mater.

Game 11: Georgia 38, Georgia Tech 20

NOVEMBER 29 IN ATHENS: It was one of the toughest tickets ever for a home game in Athens. There was so much going on for this final Saturday of the 1980 regular season. First of all, there was a two-week buildup for the game because the Bulldogs had been idle the previous Saturday. Georgia had already been invited to play in the Sugar Bowl against Notre Dame, and a win over Tech meant that the Bulldogs would arrive in New Orleans with a chance to win the national championship. Herschel Walker entered the game within striking distance of the NCAA rushing record for a freshman set by Pittsburgh's Tony Dorsett in 1973. Georgia had the opportunity to complete its first undefeated regular season since 1946. And if that wasn't enough, it would be the last game before Georgia would begin a huge expansion to Sanford Stadium. That meant this was the final game for the famed track people who sat on the railroad tracks and watched on the east end of the stadium. Georgia Tech was 1–8–1 in its first season under Coach Bill Curry, but the Yellow Jackets saw this as an opportunity to end Georgia's national championship dreams. Georgia, however, jumped out to a 17–0 lead. Walker put the game away with a 65-yard touchdown run in the fourth quarter that broke Dorsett's record. He ended the game with 205 yards on 25 carries and finished the regular season with 1,616 yards on 274 carries.

Game 12: Georgia 17, Notre Dame 10

JANUARY 1, 1981, IN NEW ORLEANS AT THE SUGAR BOWL: Despite Georgia's undefeated team and No. 1 ranking, the Bulldogs were an underdog against No. 7 Notre Dame (9–1–1) at the Sugar Bowl. Notre Dame, coached by Dan Devine, had risen to No. 1 that season before being tied by Georgia Tech (3–3) on November 8. The Irish were No. 2 on December 6 when they lost on the road at USC 20–3 in the last game of the regular season. The experts all picked Notre Dame because of its superior size and strength and because

Georgia's Scott Woerner (19) grabs a pass intended for Notre Dame's Pete Holohan (31) during the 1981 Sugar Bowl. *Photo courtesy of AP Images*

most of them thought Georgia was very lucky just to be in this position. But Georgia, as it had done so many times in 1980, found one more way to win.

The game did not start well for Georgia.

Notre Dame went up 3–0 on a field goal by Harry Oliver. Then, on Georgia's second offensive play, Herschel Walker took a hard shot to his left shoulder. Walker left the field, and trainer Warren

Morris told Dooley that the shoulder had been dislocated. "Warren told me that Herschel was done," Dooley recalled.

But Walker wasn't done. He insisted that the doctors pop the shoulder back into place. It was the first of many unforgettable moments that day for Georgia.

Notre Dame was in position to make it 6–0 when Harry Oliver lined up to kick another field goal. But freshman defensive back Terry Hoage, who was added to the Sugar Bowl traveling roster after he showed he could block kicks in practice, blocked the Notre Dame field-goal attempt. A few plays later, Rex Robinson kicked a 46-yard field goal to tie the game.

On the ensuing kickoff, the two Notre Dame return men became confused and allowed the ball to bounce near their own goal line. Bob Kelly recovered the ball for Georgia at the Notre Dame 1-yard line, and Walker dove over the top for the score to make it 10–3.

Then Notre Dame fumbled at its own 22-yard line, and Chris Welton recovered. Three plays later, Walker scored from three yards out and it was 17–3. The Georgia defense then made the lead stand up as Scott Woerner intercepted two Notre Dame passes. The second Woerner interception came with only 2:56 left, and Georgia was able to run out the clock. As the final seconds ticked off the clock, the playing field at the Super Dome became a sea of red as Georgia fans began a celebration that would last well into the night.

After separating his shoulder on the second offensive play of the game, Herschel Walker finished with 150 yards on 36 carries.

The next day Georgia was declared national champions in all the major polls.

Bulldogs in Their Own Words

"I will always remember the sea of red that flooded the Superdome floor when the game was over. One of the really great thrills in coaching is to be in the locker room after a great win. The players picked me up and passed me around the room. It was really fun. I don't remember a lot about what went on that night after the game, but I knew I had to get up early the next morning and keep a commitment I had made with Loran Smith. Barbara said she woke up in the middle of the night, and I was in bed with my clothes still on, my sideline pass still attached to my sweater, and a smile on my face." —Vince Dooley, head coach, 1964–1988

"The 1980 team was as close a group of guys as I've ever been around. I will never forget the final seconds of the win against Notre Dame. I had had my son, Jay, bring down a box of cigars in case we won. What I wanted to do was get all of the defensive players together and enjoy one last cigar together when the game was over. As it turned out, we had to run for our lives just to get off that field. But we got to enjoy those cigars together inside. What a year!" —Erk Russell, defensive coordinator, 1964–1980

"I've always thought it was ironic that I was a freshman in 1977—the only losing season that Coach Dooley ever had. When we were seniors in 1980, that same group of guys would help him win the national championship. I remember that in the spring of 1980, Coach Dooley brought in a motivational speaker. He began talking about the elements that make up a winner. He asked us when the national championship would be decided. We said January 1, 1981. So he told us to write that date down on an index card and attach it to our bathroom mirrors so that we would look at it every day. I still have that card." —Frank Ros, linebacker, 1977–1980, captain of the 1980 national championship team

"I've been asked many times what I thought of Herschel Walker when he arrived at our practice before the 1980 season. I would have to say that early on I was not impressed. Herschel just didn't do anything in practice to make him stand out. I had played with Willie McClendon, and to me he set the standard for what a running back should be. But then came that day against South Carolina when [Walker] ran a lead draw. I watched Herschel run up the sideline toward the bridge. I saw the safety man pick his angle to make the tackle, but when the safety got there, Herschel was gone! At that point I remember saying to myself, *Our buddy here might be serious.* From then on it was obvious to me and everybody else that he was something special." —Eddie "Meat Cleaver" Weaver, defensive tackle, 1978–1981

"I remember that around the South Carolina game I began to think that the 1980 season might be special. Lewis Grizzard was at my house for dinner, and we began to talk about doing a book. We had the Herschel angle, and the chance to do something special about a young man from my hometown [Wrightsville] just seemed like something really exciting. We figured that Georgia needed to win the SEC championship to make the book viable. And that didn't look too good until Belue got it to Scott down in Jacksonville. That whole season was an incredible time that none of us will ever forget." —Loran Smith, longtime sideline reporter

department of athletics
p.o. box 1472

the university of georgia
athens, georgia 30613

July 7, 1980

Gentlemen: (and Linemen)

The football season of '80 will be my seventeenth as a Georgia Bulldog. During this time there have been many thrilling Saturdays of competition, each with it's individual memories, because each game has it's own personality.

There are two Saturday traditions and experiences which have remained basically the same throughout the years for me and I would like to share them with you.

The first one concerns THE RAILROAD TRACK CROWD. These are my people because they love the 'Dogs almost as much as I do. Oh, I know they do some crazy things - like turn over our opponent's busses sometimes and now and then they throw one another down the bank and into the street below. But they stamp out Kudzu and they pull for us to win and that ain't bad.

If you can get off the bus to the cheers of THE RAILROAD TRACK CROWD and walk down those steps to the dressing room and not be inspired to play football as best you possibly can, something important is missing beneath the Georgia jersey you wear. It is impossible not to be inspired. They choke me up!

The season of 1980 will be the last for THE RAILROAD TRACK CROWD. A great Georgia tradition will have passed with the new addition to our stadium. The view from the tracks will be no more.

Your team will be the last Georgia Team to be greeted and cheered by THE RAILROAD TRACK CROWD. Wouldn't it be fitting if their last team was also the best Georgia Team ever. Think about it!

Another Saturday tradition which has meant so much to me over the years can be stated very simply: "THERE AIN'T NOTHING LIKE BEING A BULLDOG ON SATURDAY NIGHT - - - - - AFTER WINNING A FOOTBALL GAME". I mean like whipping Tennessee's ass to start with, then ten more and then another one.

This is the Game Plan. We have no alternate plan.

Sincerely,

Coach Russell

Erskine Russell
Assistant Head Football Coach

ER:nn

P. S. Run!

AN EQUAL OPPORTUNITY/AFFIRMATIVE ACTION EMPLOYER

In July of 1980, before Georgia would begin its national championship season, Bulldog defensive coordinator Erk Russell wrote this letter to the Georgia players. This plan became a reality. Georgia went 12–0 and won the 1980 National championship.

for the Georgia radio broadcasts and executive secretary of the Georgia Bulldog Club. His book, cowritten with Lewis Grizzard, *Glory! Glory!* chronicles Georgia's 1980 championship season.

"When Lindsay [Scott] scored on this incredible, incredible play [against Florida], I remembered something I learned a long time ago from the great announcers: just shut up and let the crowd tell the story. So I just let the crowd noise go on for a while. There wasn't much else to do, because in all this craziness, I looked around and my radio booth was empty. Everybody had run out into the hall to celebrate. I also remember that while Lindsay was running, I was trying to jump out of my chair, but I couldn't because the table was across my thighs. Every time I tried to jump up and fell back, my chair collapsed a little more. By the time the play was over, the thing had folded up like an accordion." —Larry Munson, the voice of the Georgia Bulldogs, 1966–2008

"If I had left Georgia, I would have missed out on that great 1980 season. I would have missed out on watching Herschel Walker do the little things that made him great. I remember day after day walking down the hall 30 minutes before the players' meeting, and there was Herschel, already dressed and ready to go. Man, that guy was special. I would have hated to miss that." —John Kasay, guard, 1964–1966. Kasay was Georgia's longtime strength and conditioning coach and still helps the school in that capacity today.

"I was a player and then I was a coach for a long time. And I can tell you that I've never seen a group of guys closer than our team in 1980. When you go through something like that together, it bonds you forever. I wouldn't trade anything for my memories of 1980. It was a helluva year." —Hugh Nall, center, 1977–1980

chapter 9 CHAMPIONS *and* TEAMS THAT COULD WALK *with* CHAMPIONS

IN 120 YEARS OF COLLEGE FOOTBALL, Georgia has had a number of great teams. Some won championships. Others came close—painfully close, in fact, and have earned the right to be mentioned along with the champions.

Georgia was a charter member of the Southeastern Conference when it was founded in 1933. It is, without question, the best conference in all of college football and enters the 2011 season having posted five consecutive national championships won by four different teams (Alabama, Auburn, Florida, and LSU).

In almost 80 years of SEC membership, Georgia has won 12 conference championships (1942, 1946, 1948, 1959, 1966, 1968, 1976, 1980, 1981, 1982, 2002, and 2005).

Here is a look at those teams and several others that will always hold a special place in the hearts of Bulldogs everywhere.

1927: THE "DREAM AND WONDER" TEAM

George "Kid" Woodruff was a captain and star quarterback at Georgia in 1911 and went on to make a fortune in private business.

In 1923 Woodruff returned to Georgia as head coach and volunteered to take a salary of only $1 per year. Woodruff knew that the most innovative football was being played by Knute Rockne at Notre Dame, so he hired several Rockne disciples—Harry Mehre, Jim Crowley, and Frank Thomas—to install the famed Notre Dame box offense.

The 1927 Georgia team was the culmination of Woodruff's work. That team, captained by end Chick Shiver, won its first nine games, including the school's first-ever win over Yale (14–10), a national power at the time. Georgia was so good that six of those nine wins came by shutouts, and only Yale scored more than seven points. Georgia was a unanimous No. 1 and needed only a win over Georgia Tech on December 3 to earn a trip to the Rose Bowl. But overnight rains turned Grant Field into a quagmire, and there were rumors that Georgia Tech watered the field even further to slow down Georgia's speed. Georgia Tech won the game 12–0, and Georgia's season abruptly ended. Woodruff was said to be so despondent over the loss that he stepped down as coach and turned the team over to Mehre.

1942: A Loss to Auburn Spoils Perfection

Without question, the 1942 team was the best Georgia had fielded since starting the sport in 1892. It had that year's Heisman Trophy winner in fullback Frank Sinkwich. It had the best sophomore running back in the country in Charley Trippi. It was the fourth team that Wallace Butts had put together in Athens, and it was loaded.

The Bulldogs appeared headed for an undisputed national championship when they were 9–0 and ranked No. 1. But on November 21 in Columbus, Georgia was upset by unranked

Auburn 27–13. The game is considered by many Bulldogs to be the worst loss in school history.

Georgia bounced back the following week to beat undefeated Georgia Tech 34–0 in Athens to win its first-ever SEC championship and earn a trip to the Rose Bowl to play UCLA. The Bulldogs won their first and only trip to the Rose Bowl 9–0 on Trippi's 115 yards rushing.

In those days voting for the national championship took place before the bowl games. Six different polls recognized by the NCAA voted Georgia No. 1, and so the school recognizes the 1942 team as a consensus national champion. Ohio State was declared national champion in the Associated Press media poll, the most prestigious poll of the day.

1946: Trippi Leads Georgia to 11–0 Season

After winning the SEC championship, Rose Bowl, and national championship in 1942, Georgia looked like it was ready to have a very good run as one of college football's elite teams. But before the 1943 season rolled around, many of Georgia's better players, including the great Trippi, had enlisted or had been drafted into the armed services.

Trippi served two years and at the midway point of the 1945 season he and many other Georgia players began returning to the campus. Georgia won the last five games of the 1945 season which simply set the stage for 1946, when Georgia went 10–0 in the regular season and won the SEC championship. Georgia dominated the competition, winning every game by 14 points or more.

Trippi would finish second in the Heisman Trophy voting [to Army's Glenn Davis], and Georgia would lose out on the AP national championship to Notre Dame. Still, the Bulldogs were invited to play North Carolina and their star, Charlie "Choo Choo" Justice, in the Sugar Bowl. Georgia won 20–10 to cap a perfect season. Even though Notre Dame won the national championship in most polls, Georgia was voted No. 1 in the Williamson Poll.

1948: Dawgs Win Third SEC Championship in Seven Years

After the undefeated team of 1946, Georgia took a step back and finished 7–4–1 in 1947.

So Georgia entered the 1948 season really uncertain about what would happen next. But Georgia did have a senior quarterback in Johnny Rauch, who had started every single game since he had walked onto the campus. They also had a good junior tailback in Billy Henderson.

Georgia lost only one regular season game, a nonconference showdown with North Carolina in Athens, 21–14. After that, the Bulldogs rolled to a 9–1 regular season and received an invitation to the Orange Bowl to play Texas. Among the players on that Texas team was Tom Landry, who would go on to fame as the head coach of the Dallas Cowboys.

Bulldogs in Their Own Words

BILLY HENDERSON

Halfback, 1946–1949

Growing up in Macon, Georgia, I had a lot of choices when it came time to go to college. But after I saw Charley Trippi play for the first time, I knew exactly what I wanted to do. I wanted to be a Georgia Bulldog.

In 1945 my high school coach, John Davis, took us to the Georgia-LSU game in Athens. Charley had just gotten out of the service and was going to play his first game in several years. I remember that Georgia didn't do too well that day [losing 32–0]. I read in the papers the next day that some of Georgia's linemen were so impressed with Charley that they started watching him and didn't take time to block. That's how good he was.

Later on that year I was a guest on the Georgia Tech sideline when they played Georgia. What I remember most is a bunch of Tech tacklers trying to get Charley Trippi, and him lowering his shoulder and just getting around them. I was hooked. I knew I was going to Georgia.

I remember getting off the bus in Athens in 1946 to start my freshman year. We didn't have doting parents back then. My daddy died when I was eight years old, and my mother had four kids to raise. I pretty much knew that when I got to Georgia that would be it. There would be no going back. I was on my own.

A buddy of mine and I walked to the Milledge Annex, where the football players lived. When we walked in, Weyman Sellers, whom I would later coach with, was doing pushups, and somebody was counting for him. When that guy started counting, "85, 86, 87," I turned to my buddy and said, "I think we better go back home." That's when I knew there were already some great athletes there and that things were going to be a lot different from what I was used to in high school.

I learned early on that Coach Wallace Butts would always make an example of one freshman to let everybody else know how things were going to be. That year he chose me.

I shall never forget it. I did something wrong during practice, and he asked me to come over and speak to him. While Coach Butts was talking to me, I reached down to tie my shoe. The next thing I knew I was flat on my back. He came up under me and knocked me down.

Coach Butts was fanatical about looking you in the eye when he talked to you. And if you didn't look him in the eye or if you were not paying full attention to him, he would let you know it.

I remember an episode one time in the locker room at halftime of a game. During that time he expected every eye to be on him. I was sitting next to Gene Chandler, who was trying to get some mud off of his cleats. Next thing I knew, Coach Butts sprinted at Gene and was all over him. He didn't care who you were—he expected your attention and your respect.

Psychologically, Coach Butts knew how to keep his team a little on edge. He never wanted us to get overconfident. One time we were up 40 or 50 to nothing against Furman, and he came into the locker room and kicked the potbellied stove. But we didn't let up and won that game 70–7.

But there was another time in 1947 when Coach Butts tried something like that and it didn't work. We had just beaten LSU and things were going pretty good for our team. *Life* magazine came to campus to take a team picture. There was something about it that Coach Butts just didn't like, and when the picture was over, he gave us a few choice words and told us to go put our practice gear on. We weren't supposed to practice that day, but we stayed out there until after dark.

That Saturday we went to Kentucky, and they wore us out 26–0. Talk about leaving your game on the practice field! That Kentucky team, by the way, was coached by Paul "Bear" Bryant.

Billy Henderson left UGA and went on to become one of the most successful coaches in Georgia high school history.

Coach Butts taught me a lot about coaching, and the lessons I learned from him I used as a coach for more than 45 years.

I was a freshman at Georgia in 1946 and had the privilege of playing on a great, undefeated team. My job was to be a backup to Charley Trippi. That was a great honor, given the respect I had for him.

I remember playing the Sugar Bowl in New Orleans against North Carolina and the great Charlie "Choo Choo" Justice. We won [20–10], and when the game was over and we were in the locker room getting cleaned up, a bunch of the guys started putting on their ties. They said they were going to a place called Bourbon Street.

That wasn't for me. I got on a train, went back to Macon, and married my high school sweetheart, Fosky. We moved into an apartment in Athens.

We had another good team in 1948 and went down to play Texas in the Orange Bowl. I remember learning the Texas fight song really well that day because they beat us pretty badly [41–28].

The 1949 season was really tough [4–6–1]. About the only real memory I have of that season is losing to Georgia Tech 7–6. Bob Durand missed an extra point when we scored the first touchdown, which turned out to be the difference in the game. I don't think Bob went back to Athens. I think he went straight home to Pennsylvania after that. It was a tough, tough loss.

My goal since I was a little boy was to someday play major league baseball. I played a couple years of minor league baseball after I left Georgia in 1950. But by the summer of 1952, I was impatient. I had a young son and decided I couldn't wait on the major league dream to come true. So I got into coaching. Other than going to Georgia, it was the best decision I ever made.

I made a bunch of stops along the way but finally made it back to Athens almost 40 years ago. I became the head coach at Clarke Central High School, and it was a job I truly loved. We have been in Athens ever since.

The best way to explain how I feel about Georgia is to tell you a story about my son, Johnny, who would later play for the Bulldogs.

When I was coaching in Macon, we would bring a group of kids to Georgia each season to watch the Bulldogs play. Johnny was about 10 or 11 years old and would always like to break away from the crowd and go around the Georgia dressing room. That day when the second half started, I looked around and there was no Johnny. I thought, *What in the world am I going to tell his mother?*

Two or three minutes later Johnny came back screaming at the top of his voice, "Dad, Dad! I just touched Kirby Moore!" Kirby, of course, was Georgia's quarterback at the time.

At that moment, I think Johnny knew that he wanted to someday play for Georgia and be a part of that great tradition. And I remembered that I had felt the same way when I saw Charley Trippi play in 1945. That's how the great Georgia tradition gets passed on from generation to generation.

Being a Bulldog means being unafraid to take on the best competition in the world. And what you learn at Georgia, win or lose, in those four years will help you no matter what you choose as a profession. I wouldn't take anything in the world for that experience.

Billy Henderson left Georgia and went on to become one of the state's most successful high school football coaches, winning three state championships. His son, Johnny, played on Georgia's SEC championship team in 1976.

1959: Tarkenton Leads Dawgs Back to SEC Championship

After the success of 1948, Georgia went 10 years without winning an SEC championship, and the Bulldogs faithful were really starting to get restless. In fact, Georgia entered the 1959 campaign with losing records in five of the past six seasons.

"The 1958 team [which went 4–6] was very talented, but it wasn't a team," said Pat Dye, an All-America guard. "If you go back and look at the statistics, I'll bet we were better than just

THEY SAID IT

"I often get asked if I was nervous or if I understood how important that moment was in Georgia history. The honest answer is that when you're young, you never realize the seriousness of the moment. You never really understand the magnitude of such a play—unless you lose." —Fran Tarkenton, quarterback, 1958–1960

about every team we played. But we made too many mistakes. That team had no business going 4–6."

But the 1959 team had Dye and two very good quarterbacks—Fran Tarkenton and Charlie Britt.

The only time Georgia stumbled all season was in a nonconference game at South Carolina, where the Bulldogs fell 30–14.

"They just beat the hell out of us and nobody could explain why," said Tarkenton. "It was a wake-up call for that team, and we played well the rest of the year."

But Georgia needed a stroke of creativity from Tarkenton in order to win the SEC championship. Trailing Auburn 13–7 in the closing moments of a game in Athens, Tarkenton kneeled down and literally drew up a play in the dirt.

"Francis just looked at us and said, 'We are going to win the game,'" said Dye.

Tarkenton's impromptu play worked as he threw a 13-yard pass to Bill Herron for the touchdown. Georgia won 14–13 to give Coach Wallace Butts his fourth—and last—SEC championship as the head coach of the Bulldogs. Butts stepped down from his post after the 1960 season.

Bulldogs in Their Own Words

BOBBY WALDEN

HALFBACK AND PUNTER, 1957–1960

As a senior in high school, I was as sure as anything I was headed to Tennessee.

Johnny Majors was the starter up there at halfback, which was a running and passing position in their offense. That was the position that I played, and I could see myself fitting right in that position and taking over for him.

But things changed after I broke my leg. Tennessee backed off and didn't show me any more interest. I was kind of scared because I really didn't know what was going to happen to me. I never thought that much about getting a college scholarship until I was a senior, but I hated to think that I was going to be so close and lose it.

Then one day a letter came in the mail from Coach Wally Butts over at Georgia. They had offered me a scholarship, too, but knew I was looking hard at Tennessee. In his letter, Coach Butts said his scholarship offer was still good, and it would stay good, even if I never played a down of college football.

Well, that was it. That would be the first of many good things that Coach Butts would do for me in my life. I had been given a second chance, and I really wanted to make the most of it.

Now, that was a tough time to be going to Georgia. We hadn't been to a bowl game in six or seven years. We had lost eight straight games to Georgia Tech, and that is never a good thing. Coach Butts was starting to feel the heat.

But as players, we were pretty much removed from that kind of stuff. It wasn't like it is now, where everybody knows what's

Punter Bobby Walden (39), seen here with coach Charley Trippi, went on to play for two Super Bowl championship teams with the Pittsburgh Steelers.

going on, or at the very least they are speculating about it on TV or radio.

I had a lot of fun playing freshman ball in 1957 because I came in with a pretty strong freshman class. Francis Tarkenton was in that group. So was Pat Dye. I'm not going to say that we always beat the varsity when we scrimmaged them, but we certainly held our own. They never ran over us.

We only played three or four freshman games, but at the end of the year we played Georgia Tech in the Scottish Rite game, and that was something really special. Obviously, none of us had ever played in front of that many people before. And the day before, they took us in to see the kids in the hospital; it is something I will never forget.

There's not a whole lot you can say about the 1958 season. We had some pretty good players, like Theron Sapp, who was a senior, but we just couldn't get anything going. [Georgia posted a 4–6 record in 1958.]

I was happy that in 1959 we were able to win another SEC championship for Coach Butts. It had been a long time for him, and he deserved it.

But that championship didn't come easy. We had only one slip-up in the season, when we lost at South Carolina [30–14] in a game that I still can't explain. We just weren't ready to play, and they kicked our butts.

We were able to win the rest of them, thanks to some heroics by Francis.

We were trailing Auburn 13–7, but got the ball back late after Pat Dye recovered a fumble. People often joke that Francis was drawing up plays in the dirt, but that's exactly what happened. He was always changing plays to give the defense a look that they had not seen before, and that's what he did on this play.

It was fourth down and something like 13 yards to go, and this would be our last chance. Francis told me to go down and across the field to my right so that the majority of the defense would come with me. He was right. After I had run my route, I looked over and there was Bill Herron catching the ball for a touchdown. The crowd went absolutely nuts, and we won the game 14–13. You have to give Tarkenton credit—the man knew how to play under pressure.

After we beat Tech [21–14], we finished the season by beating Missouri [14–0] in the Orange Bowl. Georgia football was back on top, where it was supposed to be, but we didn't stay there for long.

We lost some good players from that 1959 team, and we just didn't seem to have enough to get back to the top. We lost to Alabama in the first game [21–6] and then went to Southern California and lost way out there [10–3]. Then things seemed to kind of unravel. At least we beat Tech [7–6]. My senior class could say that we beat Tech four straight years, and that was important.

We had no idea that Coach Butts was going to be removed after that season. I was really sad to see it because I had a great deal of respect for that man. I was scared to death of him when I got to Georgia, but at the same time I loved him. He was a tough guy to play for, but if he told you he was going to do something, he did it. You could count on it. He was tough on the field, but off the field he did so many kind things for people that you never heard about.

When they accused him of working with Bear Bryant to fix a game, I thought that was the most ridiculous thing I had ever heard. It made me extremely mad.

As it turned out, I was a pretty lucky guy. I played up in Canada for a couple of years, and after their season, I stopped by Minnesota to see Francis, who was with the Vikings. He talked Norm Van Brocklin into signing me, and that began my NFL career. After Van Brocklin got fired, the new coach, Bud Grant, traded me to the Pittsburgh Steelers in 1968. It turned out to be the greatest thing that ever happened to me.

After a couple of years with the Steelers, I thought I was going to quit and just hang it up. But then they hired Chuck Noll, who was a great guy. I ended up staying with the Steelers until 1977 and kicked on a couple of Super Bowl teams. That's not too bad for a little boy from Cairo, Georgia.

It's funny: I've been out of football for over 30 years, and today I still get two or three letters a week from fans. They usually want something signed for their collection. It's nice to be remembered, so I always try to write them back.

But it all began at Georgia, where I learned all the lessons about growing up that I probably wouldn't have learned for a long time if I had stayed at home. One of the main things Coach Butts always told us was, "Don't give up. Keep digging and digging and trying, no matter what."

That, and all the friendships I made at Georgia, helped me adjust to professional life. You can't put a money value on that. I've always said that my four years at Georgia were the best of my life, and I still feel that way.

Bobby Walden, "the Big Toe from Cairo," was an All-SEC halfback in 1958 and went on to become an All-Pro punter for the Pittsburgh Steelers. He played on Pittsburgh's Super Bowl champion teams in 1975 and 1976.

1965: Injuries Wreck What Could Have Been Dream Season

Georgia posted a 7–3–1 record and went to the Sun Bowl in 1964, Vince Dooley's first year as head coach. And when Georgia opened the 1965 season with an 18–17 win over Alabama, the defending national champions, Bulldog Nation started getting excited.

Two weeks later, when Georgia went to Michigan and beat the defending Rose Bowl champions 15–7 in a huge upset, the Bulldogs looked like a team more than capable of winning the SEC championship.

But everything changed on October 16 when Georgia went to Florida State and lost 10–3. In that game, running back Bob Taylor, who had scored the winning touchdown against Alabama, suffered a severely broken leg. He would never play football again.

The injuries then began to pile up and Georgia stumbled to a 6–4 season.

They said it: "That team was good enough to win the SEC championship but then Bob got hurt. He never recovered and neither did our team." —Bobby Etter, place-kicker, 1964–1966.

"I've heard people say that our season turned bad because I got hurt. I don't believe that. We had a lot of guys who could take my place, but we had a lot of injuries other than mine. I sure wish that team could have stayed healthy. We might have been able to win the SEC championship." —Bob Taylor, running back, 1963–1965

Bulldogs in Their Own Words

TOMMY LAWHORNE

Linebacker, 1965–1967

Early in my life I was taught that one of the secrets of success was to take the opportunities you had and apply yourself to them as much as you possibly could. You should never put any limits on yourself because of where you are from or what your background might be.

Given my background, I probably shouldn't have been a successful college football player. My high school team was 1–9, and I was not a highly recruited athlete. I grew up in tiny Sylvester, Georgia, and some might say that I shouldn't have been able to go from there to one of the top medical schools in the country.

But thanks to the University of Georgia, I was able to do both of those things.

I always loved Georgia growing up, and I had already committed to go to Georgia in the fall of 1963 when Coach [Vince] Dooley was hired. I never thought about changing my mind.

But that first fall in 1964 was a very long one for me. I took about 17 hours that first quarter because I pretty much knew that I wanted to go to medical school. There were lots of labs and lots of extra studying to do.

Freshmen didn't play back then, and we were kind of fodder for the varsity. I'd finish up practice about 7:00 PM, have to hustle to eat, and then get to the library where I would stay all night. There were a couple of times when I said to myself, *I don't know if I can do this.* I wanted to do both, but if it came down to a decision, I was going to let football go.

But I loved the game and just wanted to play. So I kept plugging along and finally got through that first fall, but it was no fun, I can tell you that.

The following spring practice I went to my position coach, John Donaldson. We called him "Hubba, Hubba" because that was one of his favorite sayings. I was a quarterback in high school, but they moved me to wingback. I was the No. 3 wingback, and it really didn't look like I was going to get a chance to play. I sure didn't want to get redshirted, because I knew I wasn't going to stay more than four years because of medical school.

So in the summer of 1965 I decided to get serious about working out. I ran every day, and before the summer was over, I put on about 20 pounds of muscle and got up to about 205. I was ready.

About 10 days before our first game with Alabama one of our best linebackers got hurt, so they asked me to play linebacker. They put me into a scrimmage on the Saturday before the game, and I had a pretty good day. The next thing I knew, the coaches were telling me that I was going to start against Alabama. I was scared to death.

But Coach Erk Russell, our defensive coordinator, knew what to do. To me he is the greatest motivator who has ever lived. Coach Russell came up and put his arm around my shoulder. He was chewing on his cigar. He said, "Tommy, you're going to start Saturday against the national champions. You're starting at linebacker, and I don't know of anybody in the world I would rather have starting for me than you."

Well, of course he was lying, but after that I was really jacked up to play. If my grandmother had been wearing an Alabama helmet, I would have said, "Look out, Granny, here it comes."

We probably didn't have any business beating Alabama that day [18–17]. They were the defending national champions. We had about 20 really good football players. They had about 50. But the game was on national television, so we got a few more rest breaks than in a normal game. I just remember how good it felt to win a game that big.

That 1965 team started 4–0, and early in the year we were good enough to play with anybody in the country. But like I said, we didn't have any depth. Bob Taylor got hurt down in Tallahassee, and we had a hard time getting it back together.

Tommy Lawhorne was the valedictorian of the 1968 senior class at Georgia.

The 1966 team was a very good one. I was a junior, but I remember we had some very strong seniors, like George Patton. We also had some very talented sophomores, like Bill Stanfill and Billy Payne. What I remember most is the only game we lost, which was to Miami, 7–6. We missed a couple of chances to kick field goals, and I believe the boy who scored Miami's touchdown was from College Park, Georgia.

That was my junior year, and I missed some games due to injury. I went ahead and applied to medical school and got accepted. I was thinking about leaving for med school early and not playing as a senior in 1967. But we had a lot of guys coming back off that 1966 team, and I thought we had a chance to win another championship. I decided I really wanted to be a part of it.

I really don't know why, but that 1967 team just didn't play as hungry as we did the year before.

My most vivid memory is a painful one. We went to Houston and played on a Friday night. I was running a fever of about 104 because I had an abscess on my tailbone. I was really miserable. On the night before the game, Dr. Butch Mulherin asked me if I wanted him to drain that thing, and I told him I had to get some relief.

So Lee Daniel grabbed one of my arms and Billy Payne grabbed the other to hold me still. Somebody else grabbed my legs. Dr. Mulherin sprayed some ethyl chloride on that thing and proceeded to go to work. I couldn't go to the movie with the team that night, but the next day I felt great. They made me a little donut to protect that area, and I went out and had one of my best games of the season.

Unfortunately, we lost the game 15–14 when Paul Gipson scored the winning touchdown. Larry Kohn and I got our signals crossed, and we both took the same guy on the play, so Gipson went in untouched for the score.

We finished the season 7–3 and went to the Liberty Bowl, but I didn't go with the team to Memphis. I stayed in Atlanta for the final interviews for the Rhodes Scholarship. After the interviews, I flew on a private plane and got to the stadium in time to put on my uniform, warm up a little, and then play the game.

It was not a great day. Earlier in the afternoon I found out that I didn't win the Rhodes Scholarship. Then I went out to play my last game for Georgia, and we lost to North Carolina State 14–7.

Still, good things were ahead. I was honored to be named valedictorian of the senior class at Georgia. It was something special to give the valedictory address at graduation.

I went on to medical school at Johns Hopkins, where there were a lot of students from Ivy League schools. I took pride in knowing that I was as well prepared as any of them for medical school.

I spent 10 years at Johns Hopkins, gave a few to Uncle Sam, and then came back to Columbus, Georgia, to practice my craft.

Those four years at Georgia made several major impacts on my life. The greatest impact was meeting a little girl from Jonesboro named Susan. She is the mother of my children and my best friend.

The second impact: it was Georgia that spurred me on to be the best I could be. It took me from a little rural town in Georgia to one of the most prestigious medical institutions in the world.

And finally, Georgia gave me friendships that have lasted forever. Playing football together is like going through boot camp together. You never forget those guys. I still talk to one teammate about three times a week. Guys like Bruce Yawn and Jack Davis will always be with me.

At Georgia you go from wanting to be an adult to actually having to become an adult. It was the best possible training I could have had. That's why Georgia will always be a special place to me.

Dr. Tommy Lawhorne was the valedictorian of the 1968 senior class at the University of Georgia. He attended medical school at Johns Hopkins. Today he has his own surgical practice in Columbus, Georgia.

1966: Dooley's First SEC Championship

Despite the disappointment of 1965, there was a lot of optimism as the 1966 season approached.

There was a core of good senior players like defensive tackle George Patton, an All-American, but there were a bunch of really talented sophomores like defensive tackle Bill Stanfill, tailback Kent Lawrence, and tight end Billy Payne.

Georgia jumped out to a 4–0 record and then had to make a trip to Miami for a nonconference game. The Bulldogs lost 7–6, and it felt eerily like the previous year's trip to Florida State. After that loss in Tallahassee, the 1965 season fell apart. But 1966 would be different.

Georgia won the rest of its games and clinched the first of Dooley's six SEC championships with a 21–13 win at Auburn. The Bulldogs went on to beat SMU in the Cotton Bowl to finish the season 10–1.

Bulldogs in Their Own Words

GEORGE PATTON

DEFENSIVE TACKLE, 1964–1966

I grew up in Tuscumbia, Alabama, where I was a quarterback trying to follow in the footsteps of my two brothers. [Patton's brother, Jim, played on Alabama's 1961 national championship team.] I was a slow quarterback with a strong arm, who could throw it a long way. Back then, though, everybody ran the ball all the time, so there weren't a whole lot of teams looking for a quarterback with no foot speed.

My brothers helped me look around to see if I could maybe get a partial scholarship. Alabama wanted me to play center, and Ole Miss wanted me to play tackle. But I was hardheaded—I thought I could still play quarterback.

There were a couple of guys who lived near me who were Georgia supporters, and I found out that they sent some film over to the coaching staff in Athens. Next thing I knew, Georgia sent over Spec Towns and Bobby Towns to talk to me and my teammate Vance Evans. They were really after Vance because he was a good player.

They invited us over to Georgia to look around. We met coach [Johnny] Griffith. We talked, and before Vance and I left, we got scholarship offers. Vance said he liked Georgia. Nobody else was recruiting me, so it was kind of a no-brainer. That's how I ended up at Georgia.

When I got to Georgia in the fall of 1962, I was at least the No. 6 quarterback on the depth chart. I was on the freshman team in 1962, and in 1963 I was redshirted and basically played quarterback on the B-team. I don't think the coaches had any idea what to do with me. I didn't know if I was ever going to get on the field.

But in the spring of 1964 Coach Dooley came. He and his staff started moving players around to different positions, trying to get the best athletes on the field. They tried me at end but quickly found out that I had hands of stone.

Then one day Coach Dooley said, "What about defensive tackle?" That decision would change my football life.

They put me in at defensive tackle, and I immediately did well. Everybody was lean and quick back in those days, and teams depended more on speed than on size. I found that being a former quarterback helped me anticipate the play, and being a good athlete allowed me to slide through all those big linemen trying to block me and make the play. It wasn't long before I realized I had found a home.

A lot of stories have been told about Coach Dooley's first year at Georgia in 1964. He and that coaching staff did a lot of really good things to help us win. The biggest thing they did, I think, was see things in players that other coaches didn't see. I didn't know that I could be a good defensive tackle, but they did.

When we went to Alabama in 1964, Coach Dooley's first game, I was convinced we were going to win. They had us so well prepared. Well, Alabama clobbered us [31–3] and showed us what a good team really was. But Coach Dooley convinced us that if we kept working, we could be a good team. He made some adjustments, and that team got better as the year went along.

The next year, when Alabama came to our place, we were ready. Coach Dooley told us that if we played hard, we could play with anybody. I was lucky enough to pick off a tipped pass and run it back for a touchdown. [Patton intercepted a Steve Sloan pass, which was tipped by Jiggy Smaha, and ran it 55 yards to give Georgia a 10–0 lead.]

I never knew the flea-flicker pass against Alabama was coming. I just remember standing on the sideline and looking up when Pat [Hodgson] pitched the ball back to Bob Taylor. I thought, *Where in the world did that come from?*

But I knew the answer. It came from the imagination of Coach Dooley, who had made our guys work on that play earlier in the week. Then we went for two and made it to win 18–17. For an Alabama boy, that was mighty sweet.

My other great memory of 1965 is when we went to Michigan and played up there in front of 100,000 people. I remember being in the tunnel with all those people yelling and screaming at us. We really wondered what we were getting into.

When we won the game [15–7], it really made those people get quiet. I remember Edgar Chandler, our great offensive tackle, blocking their big All-America defensive tackle [William Yearby]. When that game was over, Edgar was just beat to death. He was bloody. I thought Edgar was just great that day.

George Patton was a high school quarterback who became an All-America defensive tackle for the Bulldogs.

I really thought that team was good enough to win the SEC, but down at Florida State two weeks later, Bob Taylor, our great running back, broke his leg. That was a killer for our team, and I think we lost four of the next six games to finish 6–4.

In 1966 we knew we were going to have a pretty good team. There were a lot of seniors, like me, who had been through the wars. And we had some really talented sophomores like Bill Stanfill and Billy Payne.

We were 4–0 when we went down to Miami and lost 7–6 in a game we really should have won. The year before we were 4–0 when we lost to Florida State, and that started a downhill slide. I could tell Coach Dooley was concerned that the same thing might happen again.

The following Monday we were practicing in Stegeman Hall because it was raining, and Coach Dooley took me up into the stands to talk. He said, "George, we're not going to allow this to happen again, are we?"

I promised him that this team was not going to fall apart. We had too many good players.

We kept winning, and we made it down to Auburn, where a win would give us the SEC championship. We played a lousy first half and were behind 13–0. We got close to their end zone a couple of times and fumbled. I was sure that Coach Dooley was going to chew us out at halftime.

But all he did was say, "We've made all the mistakes we can make, so let's turn it around."

And that's exactly what we did. The seniors took over that game at halftime and inspired the sophomores to step it up. We came back and won [21–13] and gave Coach Dooley his first SEC championship. That was a great day.

The thing I still get asked about the most is playing quarterback at the end of the Cotton Bowl. I didn't know it was going to happen. After we beat Georgia Tech, I read in the paper that Coach Dooley had considered it but didn't do it. I never thought about it again.

We were beating SMU pretty good in the Cotton Bowl, and after the last defensive series, Coach Dooley grabbed my jersey as I was coming off the field. "George, go back in there and play quarterback," he told me. I thought he was kidding. He was not.

I got in the huddle and told the guys that they were going to let me play quarterback. Everybody just smiled. I hadn't taken a snap from center in three years, so I decided to get into the shotgun. I told the receivers to run as far and as fast as they could and I was going to throw it.

Well, we did that for three plays, and fortunately I just overthrew my guys and nobody intercepted it. I think the SMU players thought we were making fun of them, because on fourth down I ran the ball, and a bunch of those guys jumped on me and started hitting me with their fists in the pileup. I tried to tell them that the team was honoring me by allowing me to play quarterback one last time. Later that night we had a banquet and got it straightened out.

That was a long time ago, but hardly a day goes by that I don't talk to somebody who saw it on television or who was at the game.

It's hard to imagine what my life would have been like if I hadn't gotten the opportunity to play at Georgia. It's one of those things that seem to impact you every day of your life. No matter where I go, there is somebody who saw me play or went to school with me. All those friends and contacts have opened so many doors for me.

Today, I still go back to the games, and people remember me. And the guys who you played with become your extended family. We're close because it was really beating the odds for our group of guys to win a championship.

In my life I went from thinking I wouldn't even get a college scholarship to being an All-American. It is hard to believe when I look back on it. But it was Georgia that gave me the opportunity to succeed.

George Patton, a three-time All-SEC player, was captain of Georgia's 1966 SEC championship team. He was an All-American in 1965 and 1966. Today Patton lives in Lilburn, Georgia.

Bulldogs in Their Own Words

KENT LAWRENCE

FLANKER, 1966–1968

How I got to Georgia is a pretty unusual story. I grew up near Clemson, South Carolina. My older brother went to Clemson. My younger brother ended up going to Clemson. My high school idol growing up was Jimmy Howard, the son of Frank Howard, Clemson's legendary football coach.

I played some of my little league football games at Memorial Stadium in Clemson. So everything I experienced when I was growing up said that I should probably go to Clemson.

Truth be told, I was really looking hard at Tennessee. I was being recruited for both football and track, and back then Tennessee had the premier college track program in the country. Tennessee was also recruiting a great sprinter by the name of Richmond Flowers from Alabama to play football and run track. Richmond and I were two of the top high school sprinters in the country, and I finally met him when we ran against each other in the Florida Relays.

Richmond and I got to know each other. Chuck Rhoe, the Tennessee track coach, made it clear that he wanted both of us. I had a good visit to Tennessee, and it was reasonably close to home. Doug Dickey was the football coach, and I liked and respected him. So at that point I was probably leaning to Tennessee.

But right after that I made my first visit to Georgia, and a funny story goes with that visit.

The visit was on a Saturday, and the night before we had played Greer High School in the state playoffs. They had a player named Steve Greer who was a legend in South Carolina high school football. Steve was a great, great player.

Well, we beat them, and as the final seconds wound down, I looked across the line and saw Steve. Now, I had never met him before, but he was screaming at us because he was really upset because his team was about to lose. Well, I decided to give a little bit of it right back to him. As soon as the game was over, I think he started looking for me, but I ducked into the locker room.

The next morning we were in Athens, and when we arrived, Coach [Frank] Inman took me and my parents upstairs to meet Coach Dooley. As soon as we walked in the door Coach Dooley said, "Well, I guess you know these people."

It was Steve Greer and his parents.

After that, Steve and I got to be good friends, and we started going on recruiting visits together. We decided at the same time that we were both going to Georgia. And that brings me to another interesting story.

Steve and I went on our last recruiting visit together down to Florida. Steve Woodward, who was Greer's teammate, went with us. They flew us down on a Thursday night, and we weren't there long before we decided that we really didn't like it. So we got a car Friday night and started driving home.

We stopped in Macon and bought an Atlanta paper. In the paper was a story about how Georgia was signing all these great players and putting together a super recruiting class. The signing period had just started. So we got back in the car and started driving again.

Kent Lawrence, one of the fastest men ever to play at Georgia, became a judge in Athens.

I'm not sure how it happened, but somewhere between Macon and Athens the three of us all decided that we were going to Georgia. We all liked it there, and Coach Dooley had really impressed me and my parents. It was about 1:00 in the morning when we got to Athens, so we stopped at a Gulf station outside of town and called Coach Inman's house.

Mrs. Inman answered the phone and said, "Where in the world are you guys?" She said Coach Inman and Coach [Sam] Mrvos were already in Greer looking for us. She said they had already signed three other South Carolina players—Pat Rodrique and Steve Farnsworth from Greenville and Wayne Byrd from Florence.

So we called Greer's house, and sure enough Coach Inman and Coach Mrvos were there. So we kept driving, and they dropped me off at Clemson and went on to Greer's house. They signed Greer and Woodward at about 4:30 in the morning. Then they came to my house and signed me at 6:30 in the morning. And that's how the top six players in the state of South Carolina ended up going to Georgia in 1965.

We played freshman ball back in those days, but I hardly got into the games at all. I played some against Georgia Tech in the Scottish Rite game and had a reasonably good game. I think that caught the eye of some of the varsity coaches.

My sophomore season, in 1966, I was second-team tailback to Randy Wheeler, who was a senior, going into the first game with Mississippi State. Unfortunately, Randy got injured in the first quarter and never completely recovered. It was my first game, and we won [20–17]. You never forget that.

The next week we went up to Roanoke to play Virginia Military Institute, and I had some decent plays there. [Lawrence returned a kickoff 87 yards for a touchdown against VMI in a 43–7 win.] Then I just kind of built from that.

What I remember most about the 1966 season, of course, is giving Coach Dooley his first SEC championship. He had only been at Georgia three years, but every year the program got better and better. We beat Georgia Tech when they were undefeated and headed toward the Orange Bowl. And we beat Florida in the year that Steve Spurrier won the Heisman Trophy. All in all you'd have to say that was a pretty great year, and that team was as close as any team I've ever been on.

It's hard to say what happened in 1967. That team just never jelled. Richard Trapp of Florida made a long run against us, and they beat us. Things just never seemed to click.

Some people say that the 1968 Georgia team was as talented as any team we've had. I don't know that I would argue with that. Any team that has Jake Scott and Bill Stanfill has to be good. And we had some new young talent, like Mike Cavan at quarterback and Dennis Hughes at tight end.

We had a couple of ties against Tennessee and Houston, but we went undefeated and won another SEC championship. We ended up going to the Sugar Bowl and playing Arkansas, and that day, on offense at least, we just didn't play well at all and got beat [16–2]. I did not play well because I was seeing some defenses I had not seen all season. It was a tough way to go out.

I tried pro football for a while. I enjoyed traveling and meeting people, but it was a business. I was probably a bit naïve, but it just didn't give me the satisfaction I got from my college experience or my high school experience.

So I came back to Athens and got into law enforcement. I worked for the district attorney's office as a special investigator and then became the chief of police in Clarke County at the tender age of 25. Then I decided I wanted to go to law school. In 1985 I got the opportunity to be a judge, and I've been doing it ever since.

There is really no way to measure what I've gotten from playing football at the University of Georgia. It taught me discipline. It taught me about work ethic. It taught me about the team concept and a commitment to the task at hand. All those lessons have carried over into my professional life.

And what I'm doing now allows me to give back to a community that has given so much to me. Georgia gave me the opportunity to leave home and go to college. It gave me a chance to make personal relationships that are still a big part of my life today. Georgia opened doors for me that otherwise never would have been open.

I look at the University of Georgia as a family. In 1965 Georgia invited me to be a part of its family. I have been grateful ever since.

Kent Lawrence was an All-SEC flanker in 1968 and was later inducted into the Cotton Bowl Hall of Fame. He went on to become a state court judge in Clarke County, Georgia.

Bulldogs in Their Own Words

BILLY PAYNE

Tight End/Defensive End, 1966–1968

I often tell people that I probably had the easiest job of anybody who has ever played at Georgia.

As a sophomore, I was a tight end playing next to Edgar Chandler, the great All-America tackle. Edgar was so good that he would block everybody in his area and leave the leftovers for me.

As a senior, I was a defensive end and played next to Bill Stanfill, who won the Outland Trophy at defensive tackle. Bill would occupy all the blockers and leave me free to make a play now and then. And if I messed up, I had Jake Scott, another All-American, behind me at safety. It's hard not to be good when you have that many great players around you. What an experience that was!

Because my dad [Porter Payne] was a great player at Georgia, I guess people always assumed that's where I would go to school. I remember going with my dad when he was an official and worked Georgia's scrimmages. I would sit in Coach [Wally] Butts' lap and do all the things a young kid could do at practice.

But when you're young and pretty cocky, you think you need to make your own way. I went through the whole recruiting process to the very end. I went through a stretch in my own mind when I was looking at anywhere but Georgia. I have to give credit to my dad—he never said he wanted me to go to Georgia. He was going to let me make up my own mind.

So I went just about everywhere on recruiting visits. The two schools that really attracted me were Florida and Auburn. Part of the reason was that the two guys who recruited me for those respective schools were friends and former teammates of my dad's—Rabbit Smith at Florida and Buck Bradberry at Auburn.

Buck was a wonderful man and really had a way of making the kids he was recruiting feel important. I grew very attached to him. I think I was very close to going to Auburn, but at the end of the day I had to sit down and evaluate the situation.

The truth was I had grown up totally associated with Georgia. Finally, I had to admit to myself that that was where my heart was.

The freshman class of 1965 was Coach [Vince] Dooley's first full recruiting class, and it was very good. In fact, there was a lot of talk early on about how good that class was. I remember the coaches put us in a scrimmage against the varsity a week before they opened up with Alabama—and we kicked their butts in that scrimmage. Our defense stopped the varsity every time. I thoroughly enjoyed playing freshman ball.

When we were sophomores, in 1966, we thought we had a chance to be a pretty good team. There were a lot of seniors who had come up through the ranks combined with a bunch of talented sophomores like Stanfill and Scott. Plus, Coach Dooley and his staff taught the fundamentals in such a way as to allow average players to be very good on Saturday. It was obvious that the Georgia program was taking a step forward and doing it very quickly.

We made a lot of great memories in 1966. The only game we lost was down at Miami [7–6]. But what I remember most about that game is that my backup at tight end—a guy named Wayne Ingle from Conyers, Georgia—broke his neck on the opening kickoff. Then they came to me and said I had to cover kickoffs for the rest of the game.

Of course who can ever forget us kicking [Steve] Spurrier's butt the year he won the Heisman Trophy! [Georgia won the game in Jacksonville 27–10.] It was one of those days where everything was clicking. If you go back and look at that film, you'll see that between George Patton and Bill Stanfill, Spurrier never had a chance to set up all day. It was total domination by those two guys. Stanfill put it in a different gear that day.

To this day I can't explain why we didn't have a better year in 1967 [when Georgia went 7–4]. I remember going to the Astrodome to play Houston, who had one of the greatest sets of running backs I had ever seen. They were so fast we were all left looking around and wondering, *What is this?*

We played that game on AstroTurf, and early in the game I got the crap knocked out of me and hit my head on that hard turf. It really rang my bell, and for several series I was just standing around because I didn't know where I was. Finally, Edgar Chandler started screaming at me to wake up. I told him I couldn't remember the play.

He screamed at me, "Dammit, Billy! We've only got three plays! Just block the guy in front of you!"

Before the 1968 season, Coach Dooley brought me into his office for one of his "talks."

He said, "Billy, you're one of the best all-around players that I've ever had at Georgia."

Then he paused.

"But you're not particularly outstanding at anything." He meant it as a compliment, I think.

That was Coach Dooley's way of telling me that he wanted me to move from tight end to defensive end. There were a couple of good reasons for this. We had been hit hard at defensive end by graduation. Also we had a good young guy at tight end named Dennis Hughes who was better than me. I was a team player and just wanted to play, so I made the move.

Like I said earlier, when I made that move I found myself next to Bill Stanfill with Jake Scott behind me. How can it get any better than that?

I think the 1968 Georgia team was one of the most balanced that Coach Dooley ever had. We went undefeated during the regular season but had a couple ties to Tennessee and Houston.

The Tennessee game [17–17] should never have been a tie. My old Atlanta neighbor Bubba Wyche was the quarterback of that team, and I got to sack him a couple of times. But Tennessee trapped a pass in the end zone that was ruled complete. We should have won that football game.

I guess we were lucky to tie Houston [10–10]. Like the year before, they were running all up and down the field. Coach [Erk] Russell was giving us hell for getting blocked. Shoot, even if we didn't get blocked, we couldn't outrun them to the corner.

Still, we had a chance to tie the game late with a field goal. I'll never forget when our kicker, Jim McCullough, was getting ready to go on the field for the kick. Coach Dooley grabbed him by the

Billy Payne (right), pictured here as a baby with his father in 1948 and again when he became a player in 1968 (above), brought the 1996 Summer Olympics to Atlanta.

helmet and said, "You've been on scholarship for three years, and it's time for you to earn it! Now get in there and make that kick!"

We were horrified, thinking it would make Jim nervous. But he made the kick, and we tied the game.

A lot has been made of our trip to the Sugar Bowl, where we lost to Arkansas [16–2]. I just remember that we talked Coach Dooley into going down there several days earlier than normal as a reward to the seniors. About 80 percent of our top 22 players were married, and we were able to take our wives.

On that trip we had about $100 per diem that would allow us to charge food to the hotel room. We would go out to these official banquets and then come back late at night and order fudge sundaes and shrimp cocktails until the money ran out. I think all of us gained about five pounds that week.

Sure, I hated losing my last game because we didn't play very well, but in no way did that take away from the incredible experience I had at Georgia. I went back and coached with Coach Dooley for a couple of years while I went through law school. Coach Dooley put me on as a graduate assistant, and that really helped Martha and me through those lean early years.

I can honestly say that my four years as a football player at Georgia had a very significant impact on my life. I came from a disciplined family, and my dad was always persistent in saying that you have to earn your own way. He also always said that no matter how good you think you are, there is always somebody better. The only way that you can compete with those people is to work harder than they do.

That was the philosophy I took to Georgia, and I built on it with what I learned by playing for Coach Dooley. I picked up a lot of life's lessons while watching the way that Coach Dooley coached the game. My dad was right and Coach Dooley was right: those who make the greatest sacrifices and work the hardest are going to have the greatest successes in life...athletically and otherwise.

Those lessons are still with me today.

Billy Payne was an All-SEC defensive end in 1968. A graduate of the UGA law school, Payne went on to become the president and CEO of the 1996 Olympic Games in Atlanta. He became chairman of the Augusta National Golf Club in 2006.

1968: A Championship Team Fit to Be Tied

An argument can be made that the 1968 team was one of Vince Dooley's best. A total of 10 Bulldogs made one of the All-SEC teams. There were two All-Americans on the defense (Bill Stanfill and Jake Scott) who would go on to have stellar pro careers. Flanker Kent Lawrence was a senior and one of the fastest men in college football. Quarterback Mike Cavan would become the SEC Sophomore of the Year.

The 1968 Georgia team would go on to win its second SEC championship in three years but not without two of the more famous tie games in Bulldogs history.

Georgia opened the season at Tennessee in a nationally televised game. The game marked the first ever in the SEC to be played on an artificial surface.

But what really hurt Georgia in that game at Tennessee was that the Bulldogs led 17–9 only to have the Volunteers score with no time left in the game and then make a two-point conversion to tie 17–17.

"They scored on what should have been an incomplete pass," Dooley said. "The ball bounced on the turf and back into the [Tennessee] receiver's hands. Some ties feel like a win. Some ties feel like a loss. That one felt like a loss."

Later in the year, Jim McCullough had to kick a field goal in the final seconds to give Georgia a 10–10 against Houston in Athens.

"Houston was averaging 410 yards a game, an incredible number back then," said Dooley. "Erk Russell, our defensive coordinator, told his unit during practice: 'Nobody is going to have 400 yards against us.'

"Erk was right. Houston had 532. That tie felt like a win."

But Georgia beat Auburn 17–3 to clinch another SEC championship. Georgia lost to Arkansas in the Sugar Bowl but was still declared national champions in the Litkenhous poll.

Bulldogs in Their Own Words

MIKE CAVAN

QUARTERBACK, 1968–1970

Not a whole lot of people know this, but as a senior in high school, I actually gave a verbal commitment to Coach [Bear] Bryant at Alabama. I wanted to go there and be the next Joe Namath. Coach Bryant looked at me and said, "Son, you will never leave the state. Your daddy won't allow it. The governor won't allow it." I told Coach Bryant not to worry about anything. Hey, I was 18 years old and thought I could do anything.

Coach Bryant was right, of course. I went to Georgia, and it was the best decision I ever made...or I should say...had made for me.

When I told my daddy [Jim] I was going to Alabama, he didn't get mad, he just said, "No." Now, back then, when your daddy said you weren't going to do something, you didn't do it. This was in December of 1966, when you could sign early, so I just bowed my neck up a little and said, "Fine, I'm not going anywhere." And he said, "Fine, but you're not going to Alabama."

I went through Christmas break and through January, and I didn't sign with anybody. Then it dawned on me that Daddy was not going to budge on this particular issue. So I signed with Georgia. Daddy was right. But then again, he was just about always right.

Daddy and I had a different kind of relationship in high school. Not only was he my daddy, but he was also my head football coach. I knew he wanted at least one of his three sons to play at Georgia. My older brother, Jim Jr., went to Georgia Tech, because Georgia was kind of down when he was a senior. My other brother, Pete, was seven or eight years younger than me, and we didn't know if he would be a football player or not. So when it came to going to Georgia, I guess I was the chosen one in the family.

By the way, Pete did turn out to be a very good football player. He went to Alabama. His son [David] played for Alabama.

It's tough being the son of a head coach, and Jim Cavan was a very good coach. He started me at quarterback in my very first game as a freshman at Robert E. Lee Institute in Thomaston. And that brought about its own set of problems.

I remember my first year at Georgia I was sitting around the dorm with David McKnight, Brad Johnson, and Jake Scott, and we were talking about playing in high school. When I said I started at quarterback as a freshman, McKnight said, "What kind of a dumb coach would start a true freshman at quarterback?"

I said, "My dad."

But Dad and I went through some difficult times together. Because I was a freshman, he felt he had to be really hard on me or the other players wouldn't respect me. In fact, it got so bad that I went to my mom a couple of times and talked about quitting. She said no. She said there were reasons behind this and that I was too young to understand.

Mike Cavan was the SEC Sophomore of the Year and led the Bulldogs to the 1968 SEC championship.

Of course when I got older and became a coach myself, I did understand. He had to be tougher on me. But things got better later on, and we had some great times together. He died in 1983, and I still miss him a whole lot.

The 1960s were a great time to be at Georgia. I really enjoyed my freedom. I was playing freshman ball in 1967, and back then we thought that was a really big deal. At first I didn't handle my freedom all that well because, with nobody around telling me what to do, I let my schoolwork slide. I hung myself out there pretty good in the fall quarter, and then somebody got on me. I was okay after that.

In the spring of 1968 I got a chance to compete for the quarterback job. I was going against Paul Gilbert, who was from right here in Athens and a tremendous athlete. Coming out of the spring, Paul was a little ahead of me, and he should have been. I wondered if they were going to redshirt me.

But early in the first preseason scrimmage, Paul tore up his knee, and it was obvious that he was going to be out for a while. I knew then that I was going to have the opportunity to move up.

Coach Dooley is really smart. He knew it would not be the smart thing to let me start the first game against Tennessee. He let me come into the game and get used to it. We had Tennessee beat on the artificial turf in Knoxville, but they came back and tied us 17–17.

Donnie Hampton started the next week against Clemson, but I came in and had a really good game, and we won [31–13]. Then the following week at South Carolina, Donnie started again but threw an interception on the first play of the game.

Coach Dooley put me in, and I responded by throwing five interceptions in the first half!

At halftime coach Dooley came up to me and said, "How do you feel?"

I just said, "Coach Dooley, it can't get much worse."

Then he said, "I agree." And he stuck with me.

We came back and won the game [21–20]. I was the starter after that.

I think the 1968 Georgia team was a great, great football team. The guys were really close, and we had a lot of great football players. Jake Scott and Bill Stanfill could have played in any era. They were that good. We had guys like Dennis Hughes at tight end, Kent Lawrence at flanker, and Brad Johnson, who was the best blocking back I have ever seen. Charlie Whittemore was a great receiver. Tommy Lyons, our center, had a really good professional career.

That team averaged almost 200 yards in rushing and 200 yards in passing per game. That kind of offense was unheard of back then!

We went undefeated with a couple of ties, and we beat Auburn to win the SEC championship. We ended up going to the Sugar Bowl. I've heard the stories that some of our guys were upset that we didn't go to the Orange Bowl. We just figured that the Sugar Bowl was willing to take us before the Auburn game, win or lose, and Coach Dooley had a tough decision to make. Once I got to be a coach and an administrator, I really understood how tough those decisions are.

I've heard people say that we really didn't care about the game against Arkansas. I don't believe that for a minute. The fact is, Arkansas just lined up and whipped our butts.

And let's get the record straight on one other thing. There have been rumors all these years that me, Brad Johnson, and Jake Scott were out on Bourbon Street at 4:00 in the morning before the game. I can't speak for Brad or Jake, but I was in my room with my roommate, Billy Brice.

Besides, something like that would not have bothered Jake. He was so far ahead of everybody else as a football player.

It's funny. The 1968 SEC championship was the second in three years for Georgia. Those of us in the program then thought we were invincible. We thought it would go on like that forever. In

1969 we found out we were wrong when we went 5–5–1. It was just as bad in 1970 when I was a senior [5–5].

I learned a lot in those two years. They were tough, but they were probably good for me in the long run because they made me grow up. I learned about people. I learned about fans. I learned about the importance of having a veteran offensive line.

I learned that the quarterback gets too much praise when a team wins and too much criticism when they lose. But that's the way it is with quarterbacks, and if you want to play the position at this level, you'd better get used to it.

I was not used to losing. In high school we had always won. It was hell for those two years because everybody was looking at the team and saying it was my fault. I didn't play well, I'll admit it. But we lost a lot of great players after the 1968 season.

Those last two years made me pretty bitter. I was bitter at everybody—at Georgia, at the fans, at Coach Dooley. But you learn. I got away from football for a couple of years and realized that it was just life. I just got caught in a bad cycle. I'm happy to say that I put it to rest years ago.

After two years in the real estate business in Athens, I kept feeling myself being pulled back to the game. I wanted to be involved in football again. I asked Coach Dooley if I could come back as a graduate assistant. He let me come back and hired me full-time two years later. I stayed at Georgia for 13 years, and I was able to stay in coaching for a total of 29 years. Now I'm back in the development office at Georgia, and I love being back in Athens.

I feel like I'm lucky because I've been given a chance to repay Georgia for everything that it has given me. I was away from Athens for 16 years, but when I came back it was like I had never left. The friends you make and the relationships you build at Georgia last a lifetime. They are always with you.

And when you get right down to it, that is what it really means to be a Georgia Bulldog. I had a chance to play on a championship team, and today I'm still close to a lot of guys on that team. Being a student at Georgia means you are part of this incredible family for the rest of your life. It is a bond with a great university that nobody can ever take away.

I guess Daddy knew that all along.

Mike Cavan was the SEC Sophomore of the Year in 1968 after leading the Bulldogs to the SEC championship. He was an assistant coach at Georgia and later head coach at Valdosta State, East Tennessee State, and SMU.

Bulldogs in Their Own Words

TOMMY LYONS

CENTER, 1968–1970

When I look back on my life, it is amazing, all the twists and turns that occurred to make me end up at Georgia.

I grew up in Atlanta, and really the only thing pulling me to Georgia was my good friend, Bruce Kemp, who was also my across-the-street neighbor. He went to Georgia a year ahead of me.

My dad went to Georgia Tech to play football, and when I was a kid we went to Tech games all the time. They had been sending me tickets and sideline passes for years, but when it came time for recruiting, they really didn't do much. I don't know if they just assumed I was going to Tech or not. Back then people said that if Bobby Dodd comes to see you, then it's a done deal—you're going to Tech. I just didn't feel that way.

I looked all around, and actually I was being recruited well by Tennessee. But the coach who was recruiting me for Tennessee was killed in an automobile accident that fall. [On October 18, 1965, Tennessee assistant coaches Bill Majors, Charley Rash, and Bob Jones were killed when their car collided with a train in West Knoxville.]

After that the next recruiter from Tennessee was Vince Gibson. He was an older, down-home guy—just the opposite of the younger guys who had been recruiting me. Tennessee was a hot program back then, but after that it sort of fell by the wayside.

That's how I ended up at Georgia, which has been a really positive thing in my life.

I started at Georgia playing offensive and defensive end, but I wasn't really getting on the field. I played freshman ball in 1966, which was fun. We couldn't play on the varsity, so we would dress up and sit in the stands for home games and act like regular students. I liked it.

I got redshirted in 1967, and at the time I thought it was pretty crappy. The only really fun thing I got to do was make the trip to the Liberty Bowl with the varsity. Tommy Lawhorne, a senior, was my roommate, and that trip was something special. I'll always remember it because Tommy had to stay in Georgia to interview for the Rhodes Scholarship and come to Memphis later than the rest of the team. He was a brilliant guy who was going to be the valedictorian of the senior class and go on to medical school.

I remember when he walked back in after the trip, the first thing he said was, "I'm not going to get it."

I was floored. I believe the Rhodes was at that time one-third scholarship, one-third leadership, and one-third athletics. Well, Tommy was the captain of the football team, an All-SEC linebacker, the president of the senior class, and he was going to be the valedictorian. How does he not get that award? I guess the judging panel had never heard a guy from Sylvester, Georgia, talk.

It was the spring of 1968 when one of the coaches came to me and said that there was one position open—at center. He said if I wanted it, they would put me there and see if I could keep it. After two years of basically doing nothing, I just wanted to get on the field. I would stay in that position for the next three years.

The 1968 team at Georgia had to be one of the most balanced teams that Coach Dooley ever had. That team was so good offensively that we made it our goal to run at least 85 to 88 plays a game. To do that, the center had to get the huddle together quickly, get up to the ball, and snap it. It was my job to keep that offense moving fast, because if we ran under 80 plays in the game the coaches wouldn't be very happy with me.

Along those lines, my most embarrassing moment at Georgia came in a game against Kentucky. I rushed up to the line, and when I got there I noticed the ball was wet. When that happens the lead official is supposed to get you a new ball. Instead he said, "Turn it over." I did and it was wet on that side, too. I told him I wanted a dry ball, and he said, "Snap it anyway." When I didn't, we got a delay-of-game penalty, and I was furious.

Well, not too long after that, we ran a running play, and I came near that official. I never touched him, but I did sort of swipe my elbow in his direction. They penalized me 15 yards and threw me out of the game. I went off and, needless to say, Coach Dooley was not happy with me at all.

We played some incredible teams that year. Houston came to Athens with a bunch of studs. We were lucky to tie them [10–10]. That team was so good that they had a guy named Riley Odoms who just brought in the plays and then left the huddle!

Riley Odoms turned out to be one of the best tight ends to ever play the game.

We played Tennessee on that AstroTurf in Knoxville when it was incredibly hot. I think the line on that game was Georgia plus 36. I'm not a betting man, but I knew that Tennessee was not 36 points better than us. They tied us [17–17], but we should have beat them.

At the end of the year they told us that we had a choice between the Sugar Bowl and the Orange Bowl. They laid it all out for us. I didn't think there was any doubt. Everybody I talked to wanted to go to the Orange Bowl and enjoy Miami. We voted, but then they announced that we had chosen the Sugar Bowl. We just looked around and scratched our heads and said, "What?"

It was obviously one of those things where a deal had been made. I'm sure it was a better financial package. Sure, some guys were really mad, but that's not why we lost to Arkansas in the Sugar Bowl. We just didn't play very well, and they were better than they were ranked.

In 1969 we really thought we were going to make another run at the SEC championship. We started 5–1, and then the bottom just fell out. A bunch of people got hurt. I got hurt against Tennessee. We lost three out of the next four and tied the other one.

Then we went to the Sun Bowl to play Nebraska. I had hurt my knee late in the year, so I was in a cast and couldn't play. Well, Nebraska had an All-America nose tackle named Ken Geddes, who was big and as quick as a cat. And he would play right on top of the center. The guy who replaced me—Mike Lopatka—had a habit that when he snapped the ball, his head would dip. That was all Geddes needed. He was in our backfield all day. That was a long day and pretty painful to watch. [Georgia lost to Nebraska 45–6.]

To be perfectly honest about it, in 1970 we just weren't that good. Mike Cavan and Paul Gilbert shared the quarterback job, and that didn't seem to be a perfect situation. We finished 5–5. They asked us if we wanted to go to a bowl game, and we said no. We had had enough.

But we did have one great moment when we went down to Auburn. Nobody gave us a chance to win that game. Auburn had Pat Sullivan and Terry Beasley, and the game was going to be on national television. Back then that was a pretty big deal.

I remember we had our little walkthrough practice down there on the day before the game. It was like the Keystone Kops. We couldn't do anything right. I remember thinking that we were going to get killed.

But something changed on the day of the game. On one side of the locker room were the offensive players, with the defense on the other side. I think a set of lockers was between the two groups.

Frank Inman, the offensive coordinator, was talking to us while Erk Russell was on the other side of the room talking to the defense. Well, Coach Inman was not the most inspiring guy in the world. Suddenly I looked around the room and discovered that all of us on offense were listening to Erk. Coach Inman, to his credit, realized what was going on and stopped talking, and we all listened to Erk, who could fire up the boys like nobody else.

They didn't need to open the door to the locker room. We just went out and blistered them from the start. They were never in the game. It was a great win [31–17]. I just wish we hadn't lost to Tech in the last game, which is always awful.

I guess I am one of the lucky ones. I got a chance to play pro football for a number of years and get my medical degree at the same time. I had been playing football my whole life, and I was curious to know if I could mix it up with the big boys. At Denver

After a successful pro career, Tommy Lyons went on to become one of the nation's leading doctors in the field of obstetrics.

I was in the right place at the right time. In the NFL, once they find an offensive lineman who can get the job done, it's hard for a young guy to beat him out.

Then, after football, I was able to move into another phase of my life that I really enjoy. Not a lot of guys have been able to say that, I know.

A lot of nice things have happened to me in my life, and I have to say that playing football at Georgia was one of the major things that affected me. As a kid growing up in the South, I worshipped the guys who played. And to eventually become one of them was a dream come true.

The amazing thing was that when I moved back to Athens from Denver it was like I had never left. The people, then and now, treat you with the same kindness and generosity as they did when you played ball.

Georgia is a great university that certainly prepared me for anything I wanted to do from an academic standpoint. I think there are six or eight guys I played with who are now doctors.

Today, I'm basically a surgeon and, for some patients, the last stop for their problems. At those times you sit in the operating room and you realize there is no one you can call. It's just you.

That's one of the lessons that football at Georgia taught me. I feel like the Georgia people are my extended family. I'm grateful for the opportunity that they provided me. And let's don't forget, it was fun, too. I really had a great time.

Dr. Tom Lyons was an All-America center in 1969 and 1970. He earned his medical degree while playing for the Denver Broncos of the NFL. He received the NCAA Silver Anniversary Award for distinguished achievement in 1996. He is a member of the Georgia Sports Hall of Fame and the University of Georgia Circle of Honor. Today he is one of the nation's leading physicians in the field of obstetrics and gynecology.

1971: Andy Johnson Leads Dawgs to 11–1 Record

After winning the SEC championship in 1968, Georgia struggled for two straight years in 1969 (5–5–1) and 1970 (5–5).

But in 1971 Georgia once again had a winning blend of solid seniors and super sophomores.

Georgia had a veteran offensive line, led by Tom Nash, Royce Smith, Kendall Keith, and John Jennings—all seniors. There were seven senior starters on defense, including Mixon Robinson, Chuck Heard, and All-SEC linebacker Chip Wisdom.

But the fresh young talent came in the form of sophomore quarterback Andy Johnson from Athens, one of the South's most highly recruited players, and running back Jimmy Poulos, "the Greek Streak."

The 1971 Georgia team won its first nine games (four by shutouts) and will always be remembered for two unforgettable games in November. On November 13 Georgia was ranked No. 7 when it hosted undefeated Auburn, which was ranked No. 5. Auburn was led by one of the nation's best passing combinations in quarterback Pat Sullivan and wide receiver Terry Beasley. Georgia had no answer for Sullivan that day as Auburn won 35–20. Sullivan used his four-touchdown performance against Georgia to clinch the Heisman Trophy.

"I said it then and I still say it today," said Dooley. "On that day Pat Sullivan was a super player having a super day. I still think it is a game that we could have won."

But 12 days later, on Thanksgiving Night, Georgia won a game at Georgia Tech that took the sting out of the loss to Auburn. Trailing 21–17 at Grant Field, Georgia regained possession with only 1:29 left at its own 35-yard line. Facing a fourth-and-10 with less than a minute left, Johnson hit tight end Mike Greene to keep the drive alive. From the 1-yard line Poulos dove over the top of the Georgia Tech defense with only 14 seconds left for a 28–24 victory.

For finishing the season 10–1 Georgia was invited to the Gator Bowl to play North Carolina, which was coached by Vince Dooley's younger brother, Bill. Big brother won 7–3.

Bulldogs in Their Own Words

TOM NASH

Offensive Tackle, 1969–1971

Because my dad was an All-American at Georgia, some people believe that I basically had no choice but to go to Georgia. The truth is I had lots of choices. Daddy told me that it was my decision and that I should make it.

I looked pretty closely at Georgia, Georgia Tech, and Auburn. I did not look at Alabama because Bear Bryant once said that if an offensive lineman had any teeth, then he was probably blocking too high.

Like I said, Daddy didn't try to steer me in any particular direction, but I do remember us going to a Georgia–Georgia Tech game in Atlanta. We were guests of Georgia Tech and sitting up in their press box. And while the game was going on, Daddy was ever-so-quietly singing "Glory, Glory to Old Georgia" under his breath. He couldn't help himself.

Seriously, he would have supported my decision no matter what it was. But everything in my life at that time pointed toward my going to Georgia.

Coach Dooley was nice enough to do some of the recruiting himself, and he and I developed a very good relationship. Ultimately I decided that given what I wanted to do—which was practice law in the state of Georgia—going to Georgia would seem like a pretty good choice.

When he thought I might be getting full of myself, my daddy always used to say, "Remember, there is always a bigger cat than Tom."

When I got to Georgia in the fall of 1968, I knew exactly what he was talking about.

When you get to college as a football player, all of a sudden you realize that everybody is just as big as you are, and everybody is just as fast as you are. You really need to step it up a notch if you're going to compete.

My freshman year was especially tough. The varsity was out there winning an SEC championship while the freshman coaches were trying to find out how many of us could really play. The competition was at a whole different level. What I found out was that some of the guys with the biggest names weren't always the best football players.

I was lucky enough to become a starter at tackle in 1969. We basically had a sophomore offensive line, but we had a lot of other really good players. After winning the championship the year before, the expectations were pretty high, but we had lost a lot at the skill positions from 1968. Our youth caught up with us, and we really struggled going down the stretch of that season [and finished 5–5–1].

The 1970 season really wasn't any better [5–5]. The only real highlight was that we went down to Auburn and beat them [31–17] when we really weren't supposed to. It's hard to explain

Tom Nash followed in the footsteps of his father, Tom Sr., who was also an All-American at Georgia.

those two years. We just had a bunch of tough losses, and our inexperience really seemed to hurt us.

But it all came together in 1971, except for that one afternoon when we played Auburn in Sanford Stadium. [Georgia was 9–0 and ranked No. 7 when it played No. 6 Auburn, also 9–0, at Sanford Stadium on November 13. Auburn won the game 35–20.]

I often think that if we had played that game in Auburn, we might have won. The excitement level was so high that everybody was way past the point of being mentally prepared. It was the most exciting event I have ever been involved in...even though we lost it.

The great thing that year was that we finally beat Tech over there on Thanksgiving night. The thing I remember most is that when we were behind with about two minutes left, Andy Johnson came in the huddle and said, "We're going to score." And everybody believed him.

People still talk a lot about the fourth-down pass from Andy to Mike Greene that kept that last drive alive. Many years later we had a reunion of that team, and Coach John Kasay said, "Yeah, we had a quarterback who can't throw and called a pass to a tight end who can't catch. And it worked!" Everybody in the room broke up.

That play worked, and once we got close, I knew we were going to score the touchdown. That was the thing I really appreciated about our offense. When we got close to the goal line, we could say, "Okay, here we come." I think everybody in the stadium knew where that play was going. We got Jimmy Poulos just enough room to get him over the top to win the game [28–24].

The main thing I remember about that night, however, is that my father had a heart attack during the game. He had to go to the hospital, but he recovered from that one.

After my last game, I played in the Senior Bowl and then got drafted in the last round by Philadelphia. They said they drafted me so late because they knew I wanted to go to law school. Pro ball didn't work out, so I worked for a law firm for one year and then went to law school at Georgia.

I'm really one of the lucky ones. Not only did I get to play football at Georgia and go to law school there, but I have been able to have an almost continuous relationship with the university by serving on the athletic board. And the more you're around Georgia, the more you appreciate what a special place it truly is.

The friendships I made at Georgia have been with me my entire life. My daughter, Jessica, went to law school at Virginia, and she has made professional connections with people who went to law school with me. Those kinds of relationships are a lifetime blessing, and that's what Georgia gave to me.

I'm glad my daddy let me make my own decision to come to Georgia. It turned out to be the best one I've ever made.

Tom Nash was a three-year starter at tackle and was an All-SEC selection in 1970 and 1971. Today, he is an attorney in Savannah.

Bulldogs in Their Own Words

MIXON ROBINSON

DEFENSIVE END, 1969–1971

I guess if I should thank anybody that I went to Georgia, it would be my buddy, Bob McDavid. When I was a senior at Lanier High in Macon, Bob and I would go on recruiting visits together.

By the time we hit the road, I pretty much had made up my mind that I was going to Alabama, Duke, or Georgia.

Bob and I went to Alabama, and man, it was 100 percent football all the time. I was an okay high school player, but nothing great. I thought that might be a bit too much for me.

Then Bob and I went to Duke, and I kind of liked it. I had a brother at Harvard and a sister at Vanderbilt, so it would be kind of in line with what they were doing academically. The guys were pretty nice.

So Bob and I were flying home—it was my first big jet flight—and I told him I might want to go to school at Duke.

He said I was crazy—that I'd never have any fun because I would be studying all the time. He said, "You need to think real hard about that."

Well, Bob must have told the Georgia coaches, because a couple of days later Coach [Erk] Russell called. So did Coach John Donaldson, who was recruiting me. Let me tell you what—Coach Donaldson was a helluva recruiter.

So I started thinking about it, and I decided to play at Georgia. My daddy was a big Georgia football fan, and I think one of his biggest thrills was being able to drive up on Saturday and watch me play. I already had a brother, Don, playing at Tech, so Dad had some weekends when he could watch two games.

At that point I didn't know for sure if I wanted to go into medicine, but I knew I could get a good education at Georgia. They were always talking about Tommy Lawhorne, who became the valedictorian of the 1968 senior class. He was going on to medical school at Johns Hopkins. Besides, my future wife was going to school there, so there were many things pulling me toward Georgia.

I will never forget my freshman season in 1968. We had a freshman coach named Dick Wood who was one of the meanest, most ruthless guys I've ever been around. He ran off a ton of players, and he tried to run me off. Back then they could afford to have more injuries because they signed so many players. Once we made it through freshman year, though, everything got easier.

My sophomore year I was a backup tight end, and I played in about half the games. It didn't turn out to be a very good year.

Our 1969 team started 3–0, and we were No. 5 in the country when we went down to Jackson to play Ole Miss and Archie

Manning. We knocked Manning out of the game and were sure we were going to win. But they bandaged him back up, and he came out in the middle of the third quarter and beat us 25–17. Let me say this: people talk about Archie's boys, Peyton and Eli, and how good they are. The boys are nice players, but they are not better than their daddy. Archie Manning could throw and run, and he could carry an entire team.

Then in the spring of 1970, I got moved to defensive end. Coach Russell could see something in me that I didn't see. The first thing he did was put me on the goal-line defense. He lined up behind the offensive end and said, "I want you to get here as fast as you can."

That was the one thing I could really do—get to a spot in a hurry—so I started playing goal-line defense. I got to play both ways most of the year.

The 1970 season may have been the most difficult time ever for Coach Dooley at Georgia. I think we lost three of our first four games, and going back to the season before, we had a stretch where we were 1–7–1.

I was still playing defense when halfway through the season all the tight ends went down, and I moved back there. John Kasay became my personal coach, and he worked me really hard.

I wasn't a very good tight end, but I did have a moment that almost turned into something special. In 1970 we were leading Florida 17–10 and were driving to their goal. I caught a pass near the goal line and stumbled just short of a touchdown. If I had gotten into the end zone, we might have won the game, but on the next play Jack Youngblood forced a fumble and recovered it. Florida beat us 24–17.

The only wonderful memory from 1970 was when we went down to Auburn and beat Pat Sullivan and Terry Beasley. We had no business beating that team, but our locker room was as

Mixon Robinson was an All-SEC defensive end in 1971 and became a successful orthopedic surgeon in Athens.

emotional a place as I've ever been around. Erk gave his usual speech, and then a guy named Ronnie Rogers, who was a senior guard, gave one of the most emotional speeches I've ever heard. Then we went out and beat those guys bad.

Thank God for 1971. I got moved to defense and stayed there. I loved it because we had a really good defense. We had four shutouts, and in five other games we gave up one touchdown or less. The only bad game we had was against Auburn, and they beat us pretty good in Athens [35–20]. Still, that year made my career at Georgia. I will never forget being on that team.

The other reason I'm glad I went to Georgia is that I got to meet Dr. Butch Mulherin, our orthopedic surgeon. Once I met him and watched him work, I knew what I wanted to do with my life. And I knew that I would always want to live in Athens.

So in that sense I'm one of the lucky ones. Not only did I get to play at Georgia, but I now live in Athens and still get to work with the football players of today. I get to be around a university and a town I really love.

If I had gone to Duke, I probably wouldn't have married my wife. I probably wouldn't have gotten into medical school. I might have wound up being a football coach. Now that would have been interesting.

When I got out of medical school, it helped that I had played football at Georgia. People had a connection with me, and I had a connection with them. Those kinds of relationships have been a big part of my life and my career.

Going to Georgia and being a Bulldog have been a very important part of my life. I can never give back to Georgia everything it has given me.

Dr. Mixon Robinson was an All-SEC defensive end in 1971. Today, he is an orthopedic surgeon living in Athens.

Bulldogs in Their Own Words

BUZY ROSENBERG

Defensive Back, 1970–1972

College football was so different back in 1969 when I was a freshman at Georgia. Today, people follow recruiting so closely that they know basically what every kid can do by the time he arrives on campus. When I was a freshman, I'm not sure anybody knew what I could do—including me.

I wasn't tall and I wasn't all that fast, but I was quick and I could jump. I think I caught the coaches' attention one day when they were asking players to jump up and touch the crossbar of the goal posts. The fact that I could do it at 5′9″ sort of made them notice me.

Then one day before my sophomore season, the team was practicing punt returns. Coach Jim Pyburn was leading the drills, so I asked him to let me try running back a punt.

"Do you really think you can run back a punt?" he asked. I just smiled and told him I'd like to try.

While the ball was in the air, I looked over at Coach Pyburn and said, "Hey, Coach, this one's for you." I took it back about 70 yards. That's how I became a punt returner.

My sophomore season started out with a bang—the first punt I touched against Tulane I took back 68 yards for a touchdown. It was an important moment for me, because until you get out there, you really don't know if you can play with the big boys or not.

Unfortunately, we lost the game [17–14]. That would be the beginning of a very strange year. We finished 5–5 with a team I thought had a chance to be much better. But we did make one

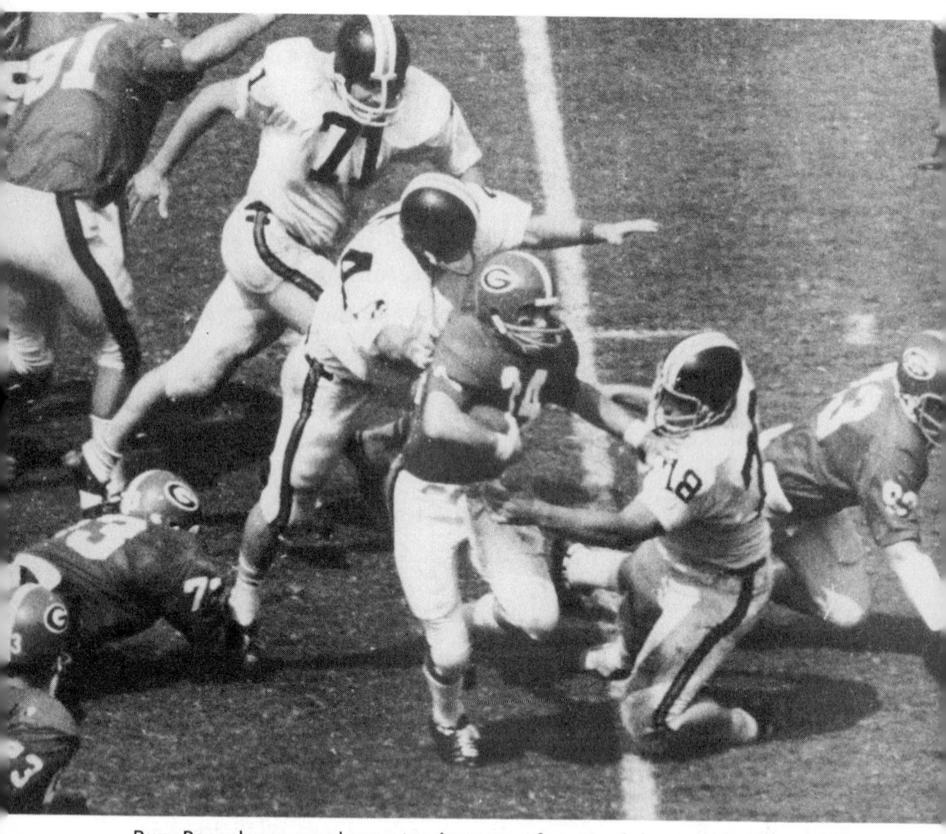

Buzy Rosenberg, seen here returning a punt for a touchdown against Oregon State in 1971, was small in stature but became one of Georgia's best defensive backs.

great memory when we went over to Auburn and beat one of the best teams in the nation [31–17].

Nobody gave us a chance to beat Auburn, who had the great Pat Sullivan and Terry Beasley. And I would be less than honest if I didn't admit that I had my doubts as well. Usually in my pregame prayer I just asked God not to let anybody get hurt and for my team to be able to compete. On the day of the Auburn game, I asked for the same thing, but I added, "And please, God, don't let us get beat by more than 21 points and don't let me get embarrassed."

I don't know if they were overconfident. I think they had only lost one game and were ranked in the top 10. [Auburn was 7–1 and ranked No. 6 when it played Georgia on November 14, 1970.] But we played the game of our lives and beat those guys.

A year later Auburn got their revenge. In 1971 we were undefeated and had a chance to play for the national championship when Auburn came to Athens and beat us [35–20]. Pat Sullivan had a super day, and because of it he won the Heisman Trophy. That day was one of the greatest college atmospheres I've ever been a part of. I just wish we had played better.

I'll bet if you talk to the guys who played in 1970 and 1971, they'll tell you that one of their greatest thrills at Georgia was beating Auburn in 1970. They'll also tell you that losing to Auburn in 1971 was one of their greatest disappointments.

I still get asked about the Oregon State game, which was the first game of the 1971 season. Before the game I told Larry West, who was my designated little brother on the team, that I felt really good. I said, "Larry, when I score today I'm going to throw up my hands, and you'll know that I'm waving to you." [On September 11, 1971, Buzy Rosenberg set a Georgia record when he returned five punts for 202 yards and two touchdowns in a 56–25 win over Oregon State. That record still stands.]

It was just one of those days that you wish could go on forever, because everything was working.

That 1971 team was really good. We played 12 games, and in nine of them we gave up seven points or less. If we hadn't lost to Auburn, then we probably would have played Nebraska in the Orange Bowl for the national championship. I'm not saying we would have beaten them, because that was one of the best Nebraska teams ever, but I would have loved to have gotten that chance.

We came back to beat Georgia Tech. Andy Johnson played the game of his life and led us down the field. And Jimmy Poulos who, for my money, was one of the best running backs we've ever had at Georgia, went over the top.

There is not a lot positive I can say about my senior year, in 1972. I had torn ligaments in my right foot in the Gator Bowl in the previous season, and I didn't completely recover. We lost a lot of good players off that 1971 team, and we just couldn't seem to get it together. We were 7–4, which is not a bad year, but I had hoped that we would make one more run at an SEC championship.

After my football career was over, I came back to Georgia and went to graduate school for a year. I also worked with the freshmen on the football team. That's how I got to know guys like Bill Krug, who would go on to become a great player.

The only regret I have is that sometimes I wish I had stayed with coaching, because I love working with young people who want to learn. I apply the lessons I learned as a player at Georgia to my life every day.

I remember the motivation of Erk Russell. Coach Russell was a man's man; an honest man; a trustworthy man. He was willing to give you 100 percent of everything he had, and we were willing to do the same for him.

I knew I wasn't the fastest guy in the world, but Coach Russell would look at me and say, "I don't care, Rosenberg. As far as I'm concerned you're the fastest man on the field." And you know what, after that I believed I was the fastest man on the field. And because of that I think I outran some people I shouldn't have.

I still use a lot of Coach Dooley's sayings today in my business life. When I face a tough situation that I don't quite know how to handle, I think about how Coach Dooley would deal with it.

To play football at Georgia was absolutely an honor for me. Many of the friendships I made in those four years are still with me today. You have a very special relationship with people who fought with you down in the trenches.

I don't consider myself a former Georgia Bulldog. Once you are a Bulldog you remain one the rest of your life. That is something that never changes.

Buzy Rosenberg was an All-SEC defensive back in 1970 and 1971. He still holds the Georgia record for punt return yardage in a single game for returning five punts for 202 yards and two touchdowns in a 1971 game against Oregon State. Today Rosenberg works for a beverage distributor in Jacksonville, Florida.

1976: Goff Leads Georgia to SEC Championship

The "Junkyard Dawgs" of 1975 won nine games and went to the Cotton Bowl. And with a veteran offensive line returning plus a pair of talented quarterbacks in Ray Goff and Matt Robinson, Georgia was pretty optimistic that it could contend for the SEC championship as the 1976 season began.

That offensive line featured two players who would become All-Americans (Joel Parrish and Mike Wilson, who became known as "Cowboy and Moonpie") and another (George Collins) who would be an All-American in 1977.

There were three unforgettable games in 1976.

THEY SAID IT

"I'm an old guy now but I still get goose bumps when I think of the Alabama game in 1976. The game was great. The party after the game was even better." —Bill Krug, defensive back, 1974–1976

On October 2, Alabama came to Athens for a game the town had been buzzing about since the previous spring.

"As a player, assistant coach, and head coach I've been in Athens a lot of years," said Goff, who was Georgia's head coach from 1989 to 1995. "I had never seen Athens the way it was on that day for Alabama. And it has not been like that since."

Georgia won 21–0, and the traffic in Athens was so bad that the police just shut down Milledge Avenue.

On November 6 in Jacksonville, Georgia trailed 27–13 at halftime and 27–20 in the third quarter. Sensing that Georgia was taking control of the game, Florida coach Doug Dickey elected to go for it on fourth down at his own 29-yard line. It didn't work. Georgia got the ball and quickly tied the game 27–27. Goff scored five touchdowns in the game (three running, two passing), and Georgia won 41–27.

After clinching the SEC championship with a 28–0 win at Auburn on November 13, Georgia immediately accepted a bid to play No. 1 Pittsburgh in the Sugar Bowl. But it appeared that before it got to New Orleans, Georgia was going to be tied by Georgia Tech in Athens. The score was tied at 10–10 when Goff fumbled with about four minutes left. But Georgia got the ball right back, and Allan Leavitt kicked a field goal with just seconds remaining to give Georgia a 13–10 win and a 10–1 record.

Georgia was ranked No. 4 and had an outside shot at the national championship when it played Pittsburgh and Tony

Dorsett in the Sugar Bowl on New Year's Day. It was no contest. Pittsburgh won 27–3 and captured the national title.

1981: Georgia Wins Its Second Straight SEC Championship

In terms of sheer talent, there are many who believe that Georgia's 1981 team was better than the one that won the national championship the year before. Ten Bulldogs made one of the All-SEC teams. Herschel Walker was a sophomore. The Bulldogs had a senior quarterback in Buck Belue and two of the best defensive linemen in school history—Jimmy Payne and Eddie "Meat Cleaver" Weaver. Georgia replaced an All-America kicker (Rex Robinson) with a freshman (Kevin Butler) who would go on to become the first kicker ever chosen to the College Football Hall of Fame.

"The 1981 team could do everything," said Dooley. "We had a senior quarterback in Buck Belue. We had the best running back in the country [Herschel Walker]. The defense was stout and talented. The team was capable of winning it all again."

But two difficult games—one in September and one on January 1, 1982, kept the Bulldogs from winning their second straight national championship.

On September 19 at Clemson, Georgia had nine—that's right, nine—turnovers in a 13–3 loss at Death Valley. Clemson would go undefeated and win the national championship.

Georgia then won eight straight games and beat Auburn 24–13 to clinch its second straight SEC championship. The Bulldogs were in position to beat Pittsburgh, leading the Panthers 20–17 with only 35 seconds left. But the Panthers' great quarterback, Dan Marino, threw a 33-yard touchdown pass to John Brown to give Pittsburgh the 24–20 victory. Georgia finished the season 10–2.

Bulldogs in Their Own Words

FREDDIE GILBERT

Defensive End, 1980–1983

I really don't know what I expected to happen when I came to Georgia in 1980. Georgia was coming off a really tough season [6–5] in 1979, so I thought there might be an opportunity to play pretty early. At least that's what I was hoping for. I had no idea that our freshman class would leave Georgia in 1983 with the best four-year record [43–4–1] in school history.

To tell the truth, I thought I was headed to Auburn after high school. I really liked it, and I felt that I would fit in pretty well there. I was also looking hard at Tennessee, Florida, and Florida State. But I really thought I was leaning toward Auburn.

Then I visited Georgia. It was such a great campus, and my mom fell in love with it. It was pretty close to home because we lived in Griffin, and I knew my parents could get there easily.

Then Coach Dooley got personally involved in my recruiting, and that was impressive. Plus, there were a lot of guys on my visit, like Eddie Weaver, who looked out for me and made me feel welcome. Later on, when Coach Dooley came to my home, it kind of closed the deal. I was going to be a Bulldog.

Now, we had won a state championship in high school, so I knew what winning was about. But it's kind of hard to go from a state championship game, where there were about 3,000 people, to your first college game, which was at Tennessee with 90,000 people.

I knew from my recruiting visit that Tennessee had a big stadium, but once you see all those people, it's kind of overwhelming.

It's hard to describe what it feels like to be a freshman and to win a national championship in your first college season. That was a truly special team. We had a bunch of really solid seniors and some talented young guys, like Herschel Walker. All season long the coaches told us to work hard and prepare, and then the game time would be fun. They were right. That team was always prepared, and every week we found a way to win. I had never been a part of something like that.

Some guys said they were surprised by what Herschel did that season. I wasn't. I had run track against him, and I knew how fast he was for a man his size. He was an amazing athlete and made the things he could do look effortless.

What I wondered about was whether or not he could be just as fast when he put on pads. He was.

I was lucky because I got to play a pretty good bit in the Sugar Bowl against Notre Dame as the backup to Pat McShea. I remember that when that game got tight at the end, Coach [Erk] Russell kept telling us, "Just do it one more time." What he meant was that we were going to have to keep Notre Dame from scoring for the rest of the game if we wanted to win. I remember turning to Jimmy Payne and saying, "How many times is Coach Russell going to say that?" But Coach Russell was right. We kept stopping them one more time until we had won the game 17–10.

I want to give a lot of the credit for that win to Coach John Kasay, our strength and conditioning coach. One thing we knew going into the game was that we would be ready to play for 60 minutes. We knew that we could run with anybody in the country because of the work Coach Kasay did.

Some people disagree with me, but I thought the 1981 team was better than the team in 1980. We could do a lot more things, but we didn't get as many breaks. A bunch of those young players—Herschel, Terry Hoage, Clarence Kay—really started coming into their own.

Freddie Gilbert was one of the greatest pass rushers ever to play at Georgia.

That team was good enough to go undefeated, but we had a bad day at Clemson [13–3], and we ran into an offense we just couldn't stop against Pittsburgh in the Sugar Bowl. I was really impressed with Pittsburgh's offensive line. I don't think we touched

Dan Marino the entire day. We had them beat but gave up a big play at the end and lost [24–20].

We should have won the national championship in 1982, but Penn State made one more big play than we did in the Sugar Bowl [a 27–23 loss by Georgia].

Despite all those wins the first three years, I am most proud of our 1983 season, when I was captain. We lost Herschel, who turned pro early, and people were talking about what a disaster it was going to be. I couldn't believe that attitude. Sure, Herschel was a great player, but we still had a lot of really good football players.

So we all got together and decided we were going to shock the world. We challenged everybody on that team to step up to the plate and take up the slack. And that's exactly what that team did.

We almost won another SEC championship, but Auburn had Bo [Jackson], and they were a little bit too good for us. Auburn won the championship, but I'll tell you what, those guys knew they had been in a game.

And when we decided to go to the Cotton Bowl, nobody gave us a shot. Texas was No. 2, and their fans wanted to know why they weren't playing a higher-ranked team. They thought they had us from the get-go.

But now everybody knows what happened. Our defense kept it close, and then the offense finally got a break. Old [John] Lastinger used to get all kinds of grief at quarterback, but he got the ball in the end zone that day, and we won 10–9.

Man, was that sweet. We knocked Texas out of the national championship, and they couldn't believe it. For the next few days I loved it when people would ask, "What time is it in Texas?"

Ten to nine, baby. That was the perfect way for that group of seniors to go out.

My group has a lot to be proud of. To lose only four games in four years is something that has never been done at Georgia.

For now, when the Georgia fans are asked about the glory days, they always say 1980 to 1983. You gotta like that no matter how old you get.

There is not a thing I would change about my four years at Georgia. There were so many people who helped me. Eddie Weaver took me under his wing and taught me the attitude you had to have to play at this level. I got to play for Coach Russell for a year, and I'll never forget that. Coach [Steve] Greer and Coach [Bill] Lewis knew how to get the very best out of us. As I got older I realized that's what coaches and teachers are supposed to do.

Georgia was where I learned to be a football player, but it is also where I finally grew up. I learned that in life everybody is going to have ups and downs, and when the downs come you have to fight through them. You can't quit. Yeah, I had to learn some hard lessons, because I can be stubborn. But I did learn, and those things made me a better person.

All I know is that it's been almost 30 years since I played, and I can still walk into a crowded room and somebody will say, "Hey, there's Freddie Gilbert. He played football for Georgia." That's still pretty neat.

Freddie Gilbert was an All-America defensive end in 1983 and a two-time All-SEC performer. He was captain of the Bulldogs' 1983 team, which went 10–1–1. He played for the Denver Broncos before returning to Athens, Georgia, and entering private business.

1982: Dawgs Come Up Short in Sugar Bowl

In many ways, Georgia really didn't look like a national championship contender in 1982. Yes, the Bulldogs had Herschel Walker, the best running back in college football. But they had lost quarterback Buck Belue, and his replacement, John Lastinger, had never started a game. But after two years of backing up Belue, Lastinger was ready.

"I figured it was my time," Lastinger said. "But all I read in the newspapers was that we had signed this all-world freshman named Jamie Harris. All the stories said, 'Look for Lastinger to play early but look for Harris to take over by midseason.' I was thinking, *Damn boys, I've been through a lot. I'm not going to just give up.*"

Lastinger didn't give up. In fact, he led Georgia to an 11–0 season and a No. 1 national ranking going into the Sugar Bowl against No. 2 Penn State.

Coach Vince Dooley got an early indicator that this team might be special. Georgia opened the season on Labor Day night with a game against Clemson, the defending national champions. Walker's play would be limited due to an injured thumb.

Georgia found a way to win, blocking a punt and recovering it in the end zone for its only touchdown. Kevin Butler kicked two field goals, and Georgia won 13–7.

Just five days later, Georgia had to play BYU at home and needed a late field goal from Butler to win 17–14.

And finally, on November 13, Georgia had its biggest gut check of the season. With the SEC championship on the line, the Bulldogs drove 80 yards to take a 19–14 lead. Then Auburn drove to the Georgia 21-yard line in the final moments. With Larry Munson, Georgia's legendary radio voice, imploring the Bulldogs defense to "hunker down one more time," Georgia stopped the Auburn drive on fourth down and had its third straight SEC championship.

Herschel Walker, who had 1,752 yards that season, won the Heisman Trophy, the second player in school history—Frank Sinkwich won it in 1942—to do so.

A win over Penn State in the Sugar Bowl would have given Georgia its second national championship in three years. But Todd Blackledge threw a 47-yard touchdown pass in the fourth quarter to give Penn State a 27–17 lead, and the Nittany Lions held on to win 27–24.

Georgia finished its three-year run with a record of 33–3 with three SEC championships.

Georgia thought it would have another national championship contender in 1983 because Herschel Walker was coming back for his senior season. But on national signing day, it was learned that Walker had signed a pro contract with the new USFL. His college career was over, and Georgia was left to ponder what would happen without him.

1983: TOUCHDOWN LASTINGER!

Suddenly, Herschel Walker was gone, and with that came all kinds of dire predictions for Georgia's fate in 1983.

But Georgia's seniors had other plans. There was a ton of talent on the defensive side of the ball. Defensive end Freddie Gilbert was an All-American. Defensive back Terry Hoage was an All-American in 1982 when he led the nation in interceptions with 12.

After a 16–16 tie with Clemson on September 17, Georgia reeled off seven straight wins. But there were some nail-biters along the way:

• Hoage had to leap to tip away a pass in the end zone to preserve a 20–13 victory at Vanderbilt.

• Trailing 9–3 against Florida in Jacksonville, Georgia drove 99 yards to win 10–9.

• Georgia had a chance to win its fourth straight SEC championship when it faced Auburn in Athens on November 12. Had Herschel Walker stayed, it would have been his last home game as a Bulldog. But Herschel was gone, and Auburn won 13–7.

• Georgia Tech was in position to beat Georgia at Grant Field in the closing moments, but Tony Flack intercepted a John Dewberry pass, and Georgia held on to win 27–24.

So the Bulldogs were 9–1–1 and had their choice of bowl trips. They could go to the desert of Arizona and play in the Fiesta Bowl and have a good time in the warm weather. Or they could go to the chillier climes of Dallas and the Cotton Bowl, where they would play No. 2 Texas. The Georgia seniors picked Dallas.

"Texas had one of the best defenses I have ever seen," said Dooley. "We figured that our best chance was to sort of hang around and keep it close and maybe we'd get a break at the end."

Trailing 9–3, Georgia finally got that break when Texas punt returner Craig Curry fumbled a kick and Georgia recovered on the Longhorns' 23-yard line. On third-and-4 from the 17-yard line, the Bulldogs elected to run instead of pass. Lastinger found an opening and scored the touchdown to give the Bulldogs a 10–9 victory. The win gave Georgia a final record of 10–1–1 and a No. 4 national ranking. Later that night, No. 1 Nebraska lost to Miami in the Orange Bowl, so the loss to Georgia cost Texas the national championship.

Bulldogs in Their Own Words

JOHN LASTINGER

QUARTERBACK, 1979–1983

One of the great things about football is that no matter how bad things get, if you just keep trying and you just keep working, things have a way of turning out okay. That's what happened to me in my five years at Georgia.

At one point in my career it looked like I was going to be a guy who came to college and never did very much. Before it was over I had played in a national championship game and got a chance to score the winning touchdown in the Cotton Bowl. That was almost 30 years ago, and in many ways I still can't believe it happened to me.

I was never really a big Georgia fan growing up. I was a college football fan who liked a lot of teams. I remember Johnny Musso at Alabama and Sullivan and Beasley at Auburn. I loved Archie Manning and went down to the Gator Bowl [on January 1, 1971] and saw him play Auburn with a cast on his arm.

I was an okay high school player. I think people noticed me because they came to Valdosta to recruit Buck Belue, our quarterback, who was a year older than me. I played wide receiver as a junior, and after Buck went to Georgia, I played quarterback as a senior.

I really wasn't crazy about playing quarterback, but I wanted to help the team. And we had a very good team in 1978. We lost to Clarke Central, coached by Billy Henderson, for the state championship. Jim Bob Harris was the quarterback for Clarke Central, and he went on to play at Alabama.

It came down to Auburn, Alabama, and Georgia. The difference was Coach Dooley and Wayne McDuffie, who were recruiting me.

People were telling me not to go to Georgia because I would play behind Buck my whole career. But Coach Dooley assured me I could play another position if I wanted to. Besides, I trusted Buck, and he kept telling me about all the great players Georgia was bringing in. That was good enough for me.

I got to Georgia in the fall of 1979 and was quickly moved to defensive back. I just loved playing for Coach Erk Russell, the most incredible motivator I have ever met. We opened the season with Wake Forest, and we heard that they were terrible. Well, they embarrassed us [22–21]. We couldn't stop them. The next Monday we started two-a-days again, and I was moved to backup quarterback. My days as a defensive back were over.

What was weird about that year was that at the end of the season we were 5–4, but all of our losses were nonconference—they were all to ACC schools! If we beat Auburn, then we would win the SEC championship. I remember the week before the Auburn game, Erk kept saying, "Let's piss 'em off in New Orleans," which was where we would play in the Sugar Bowl if we won. It didn't matter. Auburn beat us good [33–13].

After that season we went through a brutal off-season workout with Coach [John] Kasay. My body had never been through such a shock. My legs were so sore that I had to pick them up to get them over the curb as I was walking to class. But it helped me, because I got bigger and stronger and was able to compete.

That spring I moved solidly into the backup quarterback spot behind Buck. Coach George Haffner came in as offensive coordinator, and I was very excited. I showed up at spring practice ready to go. But during a workout I partially tore my anterior cruciate ligament. I had to redshirt the entire 1980 season when we won the national championship. All I did was hold a clipboard and chart plays.

Before we got to the spring of 1981, I hurt my knee again playing basketball. I had to wear a heavy brace in spring practice. That was the low point for me. I was thinking that I would be another one of those athletes who goes off to college, hurts his knee, and is never heard from again. At that point I was motivated by fear. I did not want to be another statistic.

I got to play pretty often as Buck's backup in 1981, and we had a good year. Then came the spring of 1982, and Buck was leaving. I figured it was my time, but all I read in the newspapers was that we had signed this all-world freshman named Jamie Harris. All the stories said, "Look for Lastinger to play early, but look for Jamie Harris to take over by midseason."

I was thinking, *Damn, boys, I've been through a lot. I'm not going to just give up.* But it was a struggle to stay positive.

We started the 1982 season with a couple of close wins against Clemson [13–7] and BYU [17–14]. The defense scored the only touchdown against Clemson, and Kevin Butler bailed us out with a late field goal against BYU, who was quarterbacked by Steve Young. We were winning, but it was bittersweet because I had definitely hit a slump.

The low point for me was a game against Vanderbilt. Terry Hoage was the star of the Georgia highlight tape for that game. I was the star of the Vanderbilt tape. I was that bad.

That was the point at which Coach Haffner started losing patience with me. They weren't asking me to do a whole lot, but I wasn't even getting that done.

I kind of hung on and played a little bit better against Kentucky [a 27–14 win] the following week. We came back and won, and I started to get back in their good graces.

Two weeks later we went to Jacksonville and kicked Florida pretty good [44–0]. All of a sudden we were undefeated and going to Auburn as the No. 1 team in the nation.

Auburn was ready to play. I thought we might put them out of it early, but then Lionel James ran for a touchdown, and it was like somebody hit a switch. It was going to be a war. But we won there [19–14] and walloped Tech [38–18], and then we were going to the Sugar Bowl to play Penn State for the national championship.

Back then it was pretty unusual to have a No. 1 versus No. 2 matchup in a bowl game, so that was something special. To tell you the truth, the outcome of that game [Penn State won 27–23] still bugs me. Every Christmas somebody calls me and tells me they are watching it on ESPN Classic.

We fell behind early because they were determined that Herschel was not going to beat them. I was pleading with the coaches to start throwing the ball more, because that was our best chance. We finally cut it to 20–17, but we never got the break we wanted. I remember that I missed Clarence Kay wide open in the end zone early in the game, and we had to kick a field goal. Those four points were the difference.

Still, it was a great season [11–1], and we had a bunch of guys coming back, including Herschel. Or so we thought.

I remember coming back from class and going to lunch when one of the guys told me that Herschel was gone, that he had signed a pro contract. Man, everywhere you looked there were reporters. We had a news helicopter land on the practice field. It was unbelievable! A bunch of us tried to get to him to let him know

John Lastinger's up-and-down career ended in glory when he scored the winning touchdown to beat Texas 10–9 in the Cotton Bowl.

we weren't mad. After everything Herschel had done for us, how could we be mad at him?

Not long after that we got together and decided that we were not going to let this hurt our team. As great as Herschel was, we still had a lot of good players. I was excited as spring practice began—and then I promptly blew out my other knee. It was supposed to be a simple arthroscopic surgery, but I woke up with a cast on my leg.

Then I really got down. I just didn't know if I had the motivation to come back again.

I ended up going back to Valdosta for the summer, which was one of the best decisions I ever made. There, I met Jim Madaleno, the trainer at Valdosta State, and he challenged me to get better. He told me he was going to work with me seven days a week, two times a day. He promised that when I went back to Athens in August I would be ready to play.

I was in great physical shape for preseason practice, but I didn't throw a lot during my rehab, and it showed. In our first two games against UCLA and Clemson, I didn't play very well. Todd Williams came in for me against Clemson and played great.

After that game, Coach Dooley brought me into his office to talk. He asked me if I wanted to start the next game against South Carolina. I told him, "Coach, I'd love to start, but I'm going to have to be perfect or these people will want my head on a platter. And Todd played very well in the second half against Clemson."

Coach Dooley went with Todd. I was a senior and had lost my job.

Todd played well against South Carolina, but he hurt his leg. I ended up taking the field, and the crowd booed me. When I took the field for the second half, they booed me again. A year before, something like that might have made me crumble, but this really didn't bother me. I played pretty well that day [a 31–13 win] and basically started from that point on.

There are a lot of great memories from the rest of that season. We drove it 99 yards to beat Florida [10–9]. All we were hoping for when that drive started was just to get the huddle out of our own end zone, but we had a bunch of mature, experienced guys who could handle that situation.

We lost to Auburn [13–7] or we could have won our fourth straight SEC championship. We had a chance to win when we got an onside kick late, but Auburn was very, very good.

Then we had to get a late interception from Tony Flack to beat Georgia Tech [27–24]. John Dewberry was their quarterback, and I couldn't have stood it if they had beaten us.

Not long after that game, Coach Dooley brought some of the seniors in and told us we had a couple of choices for bowl games. We could go to the Fiesta Bowl and basically just have a good time. Or we could go to the Cotton Bowl to play No. 2 Texas and maybe have an impact on the national championship. There was no question in anybody's mind. We were going to Dallas.

The coaches didn't show us a whole lot of film on the Texas defense. When we got there we saw why. Texas had one of the biggest, fastest defenses I had ever seen. I think eight of their 11 guys ended up playing in the NFL. They could put eight guys in the box because their defensive backs were so good they could cover anybody.

We didn't do anything on offense all day, but late in the fourth quarter we were still within striking distance at 9–3.

I remember that we had to give up the ball with about five minutes left because we couldn't get a first down. I was mad because I was afraid that we wouldn't get the ball back. I always had the utmost respect for Coach Dooley and his decisions, but I was mad.

Well, we got the ball back when their guy fumbled the punt and we recovered down deep in their territory. All day long we had been waiting for a break, and it had finally come. Somehow, some way, we knew we had to get that ball into the end zone.

The first play we put a guy in motion and ran a fullback dive, which didn't get much. I carried out the fake and noticed that when I got to the corner, there was really only one support guy, because their cornerback had gone all the way across the field with our guy in motion.

I was thinking that we might have something there.

The second down went to Tron Jackson and left us about four yards short of a first down. I figured that we would have to throw the ball downfield to get the first down.

But Coach [Charlie] Whittemore signaled in the play, and the coaches had obviously seen what I saw on first down. They called an option to the right.

We put a man in motion to the left, and the Texas cornerback went with him. That left one corner on that side with the safety, Jerry Gray, in the middle of the field. My job was to read the corner. If he came to me, I was to pitch the ball. If he leaned to the pitch man, I was to keep it. Gray was supposed to come over and run support if I kept it.

The key to the play was getting a good block on the linebacker, and we did. When I got to the outside, the corner went with our defensive back and, for a split second, I saw an opening to the goal line. I could see Gray coming over.

The first thing I thought about was that I had the first down. Then I realized I might be able to get to the goal. I saw the orange pylon, I saw Jerry Gray, and I thought, *Lord, please let me get there first.*

Jerry got there, but it was a moment too late. We went into a heap in the corner of the end zone, and when I looked up the official had his arms raised in the air. The pylon actually stuck to my pants. My buddy Perry McIntyre took a great picture of it.

I just remember my teammates grabbing me. I was thinking that so many players have had their Georgia moments and maybe now I had mine.

We won the game [10–9], which was a fitting way for that group of seniors to go out. It was just hard to believe that after all the bad stuff that had happened in my career, this was the way it was going to end. This was how I was going to be remembered.

That was almost 30 years ago, and today it is still fun to go back to Athens. When they say my name at the stadium now, people cheer, and I smile. I remember there was a time when they didn't do that.

When it's all said and done, that's what being a Georgia Bulldog is all about. It's about never quitting. It's about a bunch of guys pulling together toward a common goal. During my time at Georgia I formed relationships that will be with me for the rest of my life. Georgia is where I grew up and learned to be a man.

That's why Georgia is such a special place.

John Lastinger had a record of 20–2–1 in games he started during the 1982 and 1983 seasons. Today Lastinger lives in his native Valdosta, Georgia, where he works for an investment company.

2002: Georgia Wins First SEC Championship in 20 Years

Georgia was a charter member of the SEC when it was formed in 1933. The Bulldogs won their first SEC championship in 1942. In one stretch under Wally Butts, Georgia went 11 years, 1948 to 1959, without winning an SEC championship.

Georgia fans thought *that* was as bad as it could ever get. But after Georgia won its third straight SEC championship in 1982, the Bulldogs started a streak of 20 consecutive years without a conference championship.

That is why the 2002 Georgia team is so special.

The Bulldogs had shown glimpses of what they could become the previous season. It was Mark Richt's first season as coach, and he needed his first defining victory. He got it when Georgia won at Tennessee 26–24 on a touchdown with only seconds left.

All-America tackle Jon Stinchcomb called that win a "starting point for building the team that would win the SEC championship in 2002." And the wins started to pile up. Georgia showed again how special it was on October 5 when it went to Alabama and won 27–25 on a late field goal by Billy Bennett.

Georgia lost to Florida in Jacksonville 20–13 when it clearly had the better team, but the Bulldogs still had a chance to win the SEC East when they went to Auburn on November 16.

It will go down as one of the biggest plays in Georgia history. Trailing 21–17, David Greene threw a 19-yard touchdown pass to Michael Johnson with only 1:25 left to give the Bulldogs a 24–21 victory. The name of the play was 70-X-Takeoff.

Georgia dominated Arkansas 30–3 in the SEC championship game and beat Florida State in the Sugar Bowl to become the first team in school history to win 13 games in a season. Had Georgia beaten Florida, the Bulldogs might have gotten a shot at the national championship. They finished No. 3 in the final polls.

Bulldogs in Their Own Words

FRED GIBSON

Flanker, 2001–2004

I have to be honest and say that when I was growing up in south Georgia, I really didn't know anything about Georgia. I watched Florida because they were the hot team. I liked the way they

Fred Gibson was an immediate star as a freshman in 2001 and is considered one of Georgia's greatest receivers.

played and the way they threw the ball all over the place. That just seemed like the place for me.

But when it came down to signing day, I had a difficult decision to make. I had narrowed it down to Georgia and Florida. As I was headed to school that day, I had both scholarships in my hand, and I still didn't know what to do.

The story I like to tell is that I decided to flip a coin: *if it's heads, I'm going to Florida. If it's tails I'm going to Georgia.* Let's just say that it came up for Georgia and that it was the luckiest thing that ever happened to me.

One of the reasons Georgia was a good situation for me was that I knew I would get a chance to play right away. I started out as a freshman behind Reggie Brown, but then Reggie got hurt. I hated that for Reggie, but it was my opportunity to show what I could do. I think I had something like five 100-yard games in a row, and I got the chance to make some plays.

That team had some high moments and some low moments, but I don't think any of us will forget the win at Tennessee [26–24] in 2001. I think that was when we knew that, down the road, we would probably be a good football team.

It was really fun to be a part of that SEC championship team in 2002. When people told me that Georgia had not won an SEC championship in 20 years, it was really hard for me to believe. That was a super night, playing Arkansas in the Georgia Dome. It was something I will never forget.

The 2003 season was the most frustrating thing I've ever been through. I kept getting hurt, and that was really hard for me to accept. The team was out there fighting, but I couldn't get out there and help. Nothing like that had ever happened to me. I just felt like I couldn't do anything right.

But I was excited for my senior season. That's one of the funny things about being in college. When you're a freshman, you look down the road and think you've got plenty of time to do what you want to do. You don't worry a whole lot because if you miss something today, you will always get a chance to do it tomorrow.

But when you're a senior, this is it. It's like, *I can't believe it has gone by so fast.*

Like I said, I didn't understand Georgia football and what it was all about until I got here. People would mention Herschel Walker, and I really didn't know who Herschel Walker was. Everybody would look at me like I was crazy. "How could you not know about Herschel Walker?" they would say.

But in my years at Georgia, I have to say I learned a lot. I know so much more now about the school and its history and what it really means to be a Georgia Bulldog. And to me it is the greatest feeling in the world.

Georgia has the greatest atmosphere for football. The fans are great and they really care. I may have wondered about my decision back when I was a senior in high school, but there is no doubt in my mind now that I made the right decision. You can now say that I'm a Bulldog through and through. I couldn't ask for anything more than being at Georgia.

Fred Gibson left Georgia with 2,884 yards receiving, the second-highest total in school history.

2005: D.J. Shockley Finally Gets His Moment

David Greene, who had set an NCAA record with 42 wins as a starting quarterback, was gone. David Pollack, who had become only the second player in Georgia history to be named All-America three times, was gone. Thomas Davis, an All-America considered to be the best safety to play at Georgia since Terry Hoage, was gone.

Georgia's offense was going to start over under senior quarterback D.J. Shockley, who had been waiting four years behind Greene for his chance to play. All of the signs pointed to 2005 being a building year for Georgia.

But sometimes things just fall into place. Georgia rolled to a 7–0 record, but in that seventh game against Arkansas, Shockley suffered a knee injury that would keep him out of the following week's game with Florida in Jacksonville. Florida got a couple of quick touchdowns in the first quarter; Georgia never recovered and lost 14–10.

Two weeks later, Georgia's hopes of winning the SEC championship seemed to be over when Auburn's John Vaughn kicked a 20-yard field goal with six seconds left to give the Tigers a 31–30 victory over the Bulldogs.

But Georgia was able to clinch the SEC East the following week with a 45–13 win over Kentucky, which put the Bulldogs into the SEC championship game against LSU. The Tigers were 10–1, ranked No. 3, and came into the game believing a win would keep their hopes alive of playing for the national championship.

This, however, was going to be Shockley's night as he threw touchdown passes for 45 and 29 yards to Sean Bailey and scored another touchdown on a seven-yard run. Georgia won easily 34–14 for its second SEC championship since 2002. Shockley was named the Most Valuable Player in the game.

The game earned Shockley, who could have left to be a starting quarterback at a lot of other schools, a special place in the hearts of the Georgia people.

"There were times I could have left but I trusted Coach Richt that Georgia was the best place for me," Shockley said after the game. "He told me that if I stayed, I would leave Georgia with a smile on my face. And he was right."

Shockley finished third in the voting for the Associated Press Player of the Year. He received the Bobby Bowden Award, which is given to a player who excels on the field while showing extraordinary character.

2007: Blackshirts Deliver an Unforgettable Season

Georgia didn't win an SEC championship in 2007, but the team remains a favorite because of how it finished—with an 11–2 record and a No. 2 national ranking.

The Bulldogs looked like a team that was ready to fall apart on October 6 when it went to Tennessee and got embarrassed 35–14 by the Volunteers. After that game, Georgia was 4–2 and facing an uncertain future.

"What bothered me was that we really didn't compete against Tennessee," said Coach Mark Richt. "That should never happen at Georgia."

Richt searched for a way to push this team's emotional buttons and found it in two games.

On October 27 against Florida in Jacksonville, Richt made it clear that he wanted a show of emotion if Georgia scored first against the Gators, who had won eight of their last nine games against the Bulldogs. So when Knowshon Moreno scored at the six-minute mark of the first quarter, the entire Georgia team left the bench and stormed into the end zone. Richt said later that he never intended for that to happen, but the message had been sent. Georgia was not backing down on this day and went on to beat the Gators 42–30.

Quarterback Matthew Stafford (7) shows off his black jersey against Hawaii during the Sugar Bowl, January 2008. *Photo courtesy of AP Images*

On November 10 against Auburn in Athens, Richt dipped into his bag of tricks again. Georgia warmed up for the game in their traditional red jerseys. But when they took the field for the kickoff, they were in black jerseys for the first time in school history. The energy level at Sanford Stadium has never been higher. Auburn never had a chance as Georgia dominated the Tigers 45–20.

Georgia rolled to three more wins against Kentucky, Georgia Tech, and previously undefeated Hawaii in the Sugar Bowl.

The Bulldogs almost made it to the SEC championship game that season, but Tennessee beat Kentucky in four overtimes to win the spot in Atlanta against LSU. Had Kentucky beaten Tennessee, Georgia would have been in the SEC championship game against LSU and could have conceivably played for the national championship with a victory. That's how close the 2007 team from Georgia came to winning it all.

Still, the team finished No. 2 in the final polls, which set the stage for a preseason ranking of No. 1 in 2008.

chapter 10
ALWAYS *a* BULLDOG

TO THOSE OF US WHO WERE FORTUNATE ENOUGH to attend the University of Georgia, regardless of the time or the circumstance, a part of our hearts will forever be in Athens.

Yes, we have moved on to other chapters in our lives and some of us have been removed from the campus for a very long time. Many of us now have children and grandchildren.

But, regardless of our age or our station in life, going back to Georgia, as I did many times in the writing of this book, is to rekindle a spark. It reconnects us with shared experiences that have spanned the generations. I have many friends who graduated from Georgia before me and many who graduated after me. I watched my daughter grow up and become a part of the Georgia family and make friends who will last her a lifetime. It is Georgia that made all those relationships possible.

At the end of the day, this book is a tribute to that Georgia family. From the founding of the university in 1785 until today, Georgia has made it possible for people from all walks of life to come together for a common purpose. If you spend four years on the campus (some of us had to stay longer) and get a degree, you are forevermore changed and changed for the better.

Collectively, we are *Always a Bulldog*, and I think that makes us pretty damned lucky. As we close out this book, here are the players and coaches of Georgia to tell us why, in their hearts, they will always be Bulldogs.

HERB ST. JOHN

GUARD, 1944–1947

The way I got to Georgia was kind of an accident, but I'll tell you what—it was the best accident that ever happened to me.

We moved to Jacksonville, Florida, when I was in the second grade, and I played football at Andrew Jackson Senior High. I was lucky enough to be an all-state player in my junior and senior years.

In 1943, when I was a senior, we invited a team from up North to come down and play us in Jacksonville. Tom Lieb was the coach at Florida back then, and after that game, Coach Lieb came up to me and said he had seven scholarships left. He said one of them was for me if I wanted to come to Florida. I told him that was exactly what I wanted to do, so I figured I was going to Florida. He said, "Fine," and that he would be in touch with me later.

Not too long after that, I got a Christmas card from Coach Lieb, but that was the last time I ever heard from him.

Mike Castronis, who went to the same high school as I, was a player at Georgia at the time, and he was home for Christmas. He came over to the house and told me that the coaches at Georgia really wanted me to come up there. So I told Mike, "Fine. Tell them to send me a bus ticket, and I will come."

So they sent me a ticket, and I went to Athens. I got off the bus at 4:30 in the afternoon and by 5:00 I was registered in school. The next morning I was in class and on my way.

Of course, this whole story has a funny ending, because I eventually found out what happened at Florida.

After I got out of Georgia and played a couple years of pro ball, I went back to Jacksonville and decided to get into teaching and coaching. As it turned out, I needed two more courses to get my teaching certificate. I decided to get those courses at the University of Florida.

While I was there, I ran into a Florida coach that I knew and asked him why they never talked to me again after Coach Lieb offered the scholarship. As it turned out, they had contacted my draft board and learned that I was going to get drafted in the spring of my freshman year. So they decided not to offer me a scholarship.

Well, they were right. I was in the middle of spring practice my first year when I got my invitation to see Uncle Sam. But when I went down to Camp Blanding to get my physical, they declared me 4-F. So I went back to Georgia and played three more years, plus two more in the pros. I understand some of the Florida coaches caught hell after that happened.

Also in that spring of 1945, I made one of the most important decisions of my life. I was missing my high school sweetheart, Barbara, who was back in Jacksonville. I remember my line coach, J.B. Whitworth, telling me to "go home and marry that girl." So that's what I did, and I brought her back to Georgia with me.

We still feel like the years we spent in Athens were the best days of our lives. We had a great time and didn't worry about anything. We would spend our last dime and didn't worry about where the next one was coming from.

I had a chance to play on some good teams and with some very good players at Georgia. Johnny Rauch was our quarterback, and there were other great ones like Dan Edwards and Weyman Sellers.

But for my money, Charley Trippi is the best player I ever saw, played with, or played against. There was nothing on a football

Herb St. John, a three-time All-SEC guard, almost went to the University of Florida.

field that Charley could not do. And for all the talk about his ability on offense, he was one of the best defensive backs who ever played football at any level.

I remember my sophomore year, in 1945, when Charley came back from the service in time for our game with LSU. We were 4–0 at the time and thought we might win them all. But against LSU I think most of us spent too much time looking at Charley and not enough time blocking. LSU killed us [32–0]. We lost the next week against Alabama but then won the rest of them.

My favorite game in my entire time at Georgia is when we played Alabama in Athens in 1946. Alabama had Harry Gilmer at quarterback. He was known for the "jump" pass and was considered one of the best quarterbacks in the country. But that day we did not allow Gilmer to complete a pass, and we won 14–0. I had something to do with Gilmer having a bad day, so I got a lot of joy out of that.

I guess the person who had the most influence on me at Georgia was Coach Wally Butts. On the street, Coach Butts could be the finest man you ever wanted to meet. But once he got on that field, he was deadly serious. If you weren't on that field for business, then, brother, you were in the wrong place.

But I can honestly say that in my four years there I never heard a cross word from him. What he and Coach Whitworth taught me was very important when I decided to become a coach. I would not have had the success I had in life if not for those two men.

Going to Georgia changed my life more than any single thing I can think of. I made a lot of good friends, some in football and some not, who are still my friends today. It was an incredible time in my life, and every year I look forward to getting together with all of the guys who played for Coach Butts.

They still call us "Wally's Boys." I'm very proud of that.

Herb St. John was a three-time All-SEC guard and was named All-America in 1946.

CLAUDE HIPPS

HALFBACK, 1944, 1949–1951

You look back now and you realize that your character and competitive attitude were formed on the football field and in the classroom at Georgia. People will always remember that you played at Georgia, and it means a great deal to you. I was born a Bulldog, and I will always be a Bulldog.

Hipps was the captain of Georgia's 1951 team. That season he was a first-team All-SEC player and led the team in interceptions with six.

JOHN CARSON

END, 1950, 1952–1953

I loved playing football at the University of Georgia, but my first love was always golf. I really didn't have any choice. I grew up in Cabbagetown, a little community in the southeastern part of Atlanta. I lived on a tough little nine-hole course called the James L. Key Golf Course, and I pretty much played every day, so I got to be pretty good at it.

When I wasn't playing golf, I caddied. Mama liked that because I was always able to bring home a few extra dollars.

When the time came to go to college, I got more golf scholarship offers than anything else, because at that time I was winning a lot of tournaments. In fact, I never even thought about football until 1947, when the Atlanta school system changed.

They took the two main schools in town and split them up into a bunch of schools and scattered them all around Atlanta. I ended up at Roosevelt High and played on their first-ever football team. Football was completely different from golf, and I kind of liked it and thought I might be good at it, too.

As a senior, I was just sort of waiting around to see what the best situation would be for me to play golf and football in college. We were playing in the state basketball tournament in 1949 when Coach Wallace Butts and Coach Quinton Lumpkin came to

John Carson was both an All-America football player and an All-America golfer.

see me. My mother was really impressed by Coach Butts, and she didn't want her boy going very far away from home. So the decision was pretty much made for me. I was off to Georgia.

Coach Butts really didn't like the idea of me playing golf. He thought it took too much time away from football in the off-season, and I had to miss some class time in the spring when I was playing in tournaments. But he finally understood how I felt about golf. If I was sick, I could go off and play golf and get well. That's how much I love the game.

I played a little football in 1950, but then in 1951 I tore up my shoulder and couldn't play at all. I dislocated the shoulder so badly that I had to wear a harness to keep it in place.

I guess the funniest thing—maybe that's not the right word—that happened to me, and the one most folks know about, was in 1952 when we played Auburn in Columbus. We were playing in one of those municipal stadiums built by the Civilian Conservation Corps, and it seemed like it only took a couple of years for those things to get old.

Well, I was sitting on the toilet before the game, and when I went to flush, the hot-water valve busted and sent about six inches of scalding hot water up my rear end. It scalded everything—and I do mean everything.

They had to lay me out on a table because the hot water had literally peeled the skin off of me. It really hurt, but you know Coach Butts: there was no such thing as being injured. They put a bunch of Vaseline on me, and off I went.

Despite the pain, I made a long touchdown catch of about 76 or 77 yards from Zeke Bratkowski, and we won the game 13–7. The Auburn guy I beat on the play for the touchdown was Vince Dooley, who would later become a great coach at Georgia.

Later on that day I ended up in the emergency room in a hospital in Newnan. I called Coach Lumpkin and told him I was in pretty bad shape. I finally got well, but nothing ever got to me like that again.

In 1953 Zeke and I had a pretty good year, but we didn't win a lot of games, and that was tough. I felt bad for Coach Butts because he was used to winning and did not handle losing well. But still, that man is tops on my list. Zeke and I had pretty good pro careers and we couldn't have done it without the help of Coach Butts.

There were still a lot of fun times. I remember when Coach Butts and Coach Lumpkin decided they were going to take up golf. Bless their hearts, they just couldn't do it, but it was fun watching them try.

And Dean [William] Tate, God rest his soul, always seemed to be into something. One year he accused me of faking the mumps just to get out of the spring game. I asked Dean Tate, "Have you talked to the doctor? I really have the mumps, and I would like to have children some day, so I'm going to be careful." That Dean Tate was a piece of work.

If you talk to the guys who played in my time, they will tell you they wish we had won more for Coach Butts because he deserved it. But Georgia was a special place then, and it still is today. I'm glad I got a chance to go there and be a part of one of the great traditions in college football.

Carson was both an All-America football player and an All-America golfer for Georgia. He is one of only two Georgia athletes in history (Herschel Walker is the other) to be named All-America in two sports.

EDMUND RAYMOND "ZEKE" BRATKOWSKI

QUARTERBACK, 1951–1953

I played at a small Catholic high school in Illinois, located about 30 miles from the campus of the University of Illinois. But as luck would have it, my high school coach, Paul Shebby, coached Charley Trippi when he was in high school in Pittston, Pennsylvania. That's how I got introduced to Georgia.

Back in those days it was okay to work out for the coaches on recruiting visits. In fact, Charley Trippi was there for my workout. I wasn't really a quarterback in high school because we played the old Notre Dame box offense. But I guess Coach [Wally] Butts saw something he liked, because the next thing I knew I was on my way to Georgia.

I had never been down South before. When those guys started calling me a "Yankee," I kept thinking, *I don't play for the baseball team.* But it was a great experience for me because I hadn't traveled very much at that time.

The transition to college wasn't hard because I didn't have time to think about it. Being a quarterback for Coach Butts back then meant you were about as busy as anyone on campus. Because of everything I had to learn on the football field, I never had a class after 1:00 PM in my entire time at Georgia. My assignment was to be on the field every afternoon and just throw and throw and throw.

It really paid off for me. I have had a lot of important influences on my life, like Coach Shebby, Coach George Halas, and Coach Vince Lombardi. But right up there with them was Coach Butts.

Yes, he was a taskmaster, but if he had not made me do all that throwing, there is no way I could have played in the NFL for 14 seasons. Anybody who played for Coach Butts didn't realize until he left Georgia what Coach Butts did for us in terms of being mentally and physically tough. If you could make it through one of Coach Butts' practices, you could do anything.

I remember a time after one of the G-Day games in either 1951 or 1952. I thought we had had a pretty good day throwing the ball. But when the game was over, Coach Butts cleared the stadium and said, "We're going to score 20 times from the 25-yard line by running." We did it and had to stay out there until it was almost dark.

Zeke Bratkowski took the lessons he learned from Wally Butts and played in the NFL for 14 seasons.

I just wish we could have won more games for him. We were 7–4 in 1952, and today that would get you a decent bowl bid. The 1953 season, my last, was really difficult because we won only three games. That season I really felt sorry for him. I was the captain, and after the last game with Georgia Tech [a 28–12 loss] in Atlanta, I stood up and spoke for the team and told him how we cared about him. I just thought he needed to know that we felt bad about the season, too.

Today's kids don't know how tough it was at Georgia back then. A lot of guys had been in World War II, and they loved to pull pranks. We had what we called "Rat Court" for the freshmen every Wednesday night. Each freshman had to run errands and shine shoes for one of the seniors on the team. Every Wednesday they found out if they were a good rat or a bad rat. The bad rats would get some licks from a belt to keep them alert.

We would make guys sit naked on a block of ice for 10 minutes and then make them pick up a marshmallow with the cheeks of their rear ends. Or we would take them out of town, throw their clothes in the bushes, drive off, and make them find their way back to Athens.

We even had something called "Louise Parties," but I don't think I can talk about that here.

Yeah, we did a lot of crazy things, but the day you got to put on your letter jacket with the G on it for the first time…man, that was a special day. Winning my first varsity letter and becoming a member of the G-Club is something I will never forget.

There were so many people who helped me. As a senior, I led the nation in punting, but the only reason I became a great punter was because Quinton Lumpkin, who was an assistant coach, would play a game called Pushback. We would get on a field about 200 yards long and keep kicking the ball to each other, trying to push the other one back to the end of the field. Quinton was a great athlete. He would kick the ball over the fence onto Milledge and make me jump the fence to get it.

All the football players lived in the dorm, but the guys from Ohio, Pennsylvania, and the other northern states would kind of congregate on the third floor. The southern guys—we called them the blue blazers and khaki pants guys—would be on the lower floors. They wore ties to class. We northern guys would wear sweatshirts and blue jeans. It was just a different way of life for a lot of us.

But when we got on the field together it didn't matter where we were from—we were a team. I wish we could have won a few more games together. And because of pro football—I played 14 years and coached 26—I haven't gotten back to Athens as much as I would have liked.

But there is no question that my years at Georgia set the stage and gave me the tools that I would need to be successful. It is a great town and a great school. I still feel lucky to have been a part of it and am always proud when people call me a Georgia Bulldog.

Bratkowski was a three-time All-SEC quarterback who went on to play 14 seasons in the NFL. He was a part of three NFL championship teams with the Green Bay Packers.

JIMMY ORR

Wide Receiver, 1955–1957

I grew up in Seneca, South Carolina, but I guess you could say I was a Georgia fan pretty early in life.

For my 10th birthday I asked my parents to take me to a game in Athens so that I could see Charley Trippi play. That was in 1946, and they took me to see Georgia play Oklahoma A&M—Georgia won 33–13. I still remember everything about that day.

I was always impressed by Georgia. Trippi had kind of been my hero growing up. Plus, they threw the ball a lot, and that was what I was interested in.

I ended up going to Georgia, but I sure took a roundabout way of getting there.

Growing up, I played all sports, but I grew to like basketball the most. It wasn't very complicated: basketball is a lot easier on your body than football, and it seemed that in football I got hurt all the time. A lot of basketball was being played among all the textile mills at that time, so you could really play all the time. I was an all-state basketball player at Seneca High School, and I just thought I was better at basketball at that particular stage in my life.

So when I got out of high school, I turned down some football scholarships and walked on at Clemson to play basketball. After a semester, I transferred to Wake Forest, still hoping to play basketball. I wasn't up there long before I realized that they had a lot of good players and that I really wasn't going to be able to play at that level.

I went back home and tried to figure out what I was going to do next. A family friend, Neal Alford, had gone to Georgia and played a couple of years before getting hurt. He decided to become a trainer. I talked to him about talking to Coach Butts to see if Georgia had any interest in me as a football player.

I talked to Coach Butts, and he told me to come on, but he couldn't give me a scholarship. So that's how it all began.

I played freshman ball in 1954, but I will never forget our first game against Ole Miss in Atlanta in 1955. I was like the fifth-string running back and never thought I would get into the game.

But back then there were all these substitution rules that said if you came out early in a quarter, you couldn't go back in until the next quarter. Well, we got caught in a substitution crunch and a couple of guys got hurt, so they had to put me in the game. They threw me a pass for about 50 yards right before halftime, and I

Jimmy Orr came to Georgia without a scholarship and went on to lead the SEC in receiving twice in his career.

caught it and scored a touchdown. We got beat 26–13, but that got me a foothold, and I think it also caught Coach Butts' attention.

I'm proud to say that I went on to lead the SEC in receiving that year [with 24 catches] and again in 1957 [with 16 catches]. But what I'm most proud of in those two seasons is that I never dropped a pass.

This is probably a good place to talk about Coach Butts and the passing game. Coach Butts had his critics because he ran very tough practices, but the man was way ahead of his time when it came to the passing game. What I learned from him and Coach Sterling Dupree made me ready to go when I got to the pros.

I remember when I was a freshman in 1954, we would have these "extra" workouts at the stadium. I'm not sure if they were legal or not. But Coach Dupree worked with me and taught me how to run what we called "straight line" patterns and how to break them off at the last second. He and Coach Butts taught me a lot of little tricks of the trade, which put me ahead of the competition when I got to the NFL.

In fact, when I was a rookie at Pittsburgh, Buddy Parker, the coach, brought me into his office one day after watching me work out and run some pass patterns. He said, "How did you learn all this?" He said I was far ahead of the other rookies. I told him that was the way they taught football at Georgia. Our passing game at Georgia was really ahead of a lot of pro teams at the time.

In my three years we only won 10 games. That's not very many, and it's hard to say what the problem was. I've often wondered if it had something to do with the fact that Coach Butts ran such tough practices. In the mid-'50s that might have hurt his recruiting.

But I will always have the memory of the Georgia Tech game in 1957. Man, Tech and Coach Bobby Dodd really had it going back then, and they had some really good players. We were 2–7, so nobody really gave us a chance. They had beaten us eight straight games, and the Georgia people were starting to wonder if we were ever going to beat Tech again.

I remember the wind was blowing really hard in Atlanta. It was not a nice day. But we hung in there and had a chance to score a touchdown. We got the ball back around midfield in the third quarter after a fumble. Everybody in the huddle knew how important the drive could be, because we didn't know how many chances we'd get.

Theron Sapp gets the credit for scoring the touchdown to win the game, but I always tell Sapp that the only reason he got any yardage in that drive is that he had to run right off of my blocks.

I also bailed him out when I caught a 13-yard pass from Charlie Britt on third-and-12. That gave us the first down we had to have.

I'll never forget the touchdown play from the 1-yard line. I was at right end, and the guard and tackle on that side were supposed to block down. I was supposed to kick out the defensive end. The play worked perfectly. Sapp ran right off my tail and scored. We won the game 7–0.

After all that frustration, it was a great way to go out in my final game.

Now a word about Theron Sapp. We give him a hard time because they retired his jersey and named him "the Drought Breaker" because of that one game against Georgia Tech. But let me tell you this: Theron Sapp was one helluva football player. He was second in the SEC in rushing that year to LSU's Jimmy Taylor, even though we had a mediocre football team.

I enjoyed playing pro football because, like I said before, I was ready when I got there. Once you get up there you don't have long to convince them that you can play. I got to play with the greatest quarterback of all time, John Unitas, when I was with the Colts, and I got to be part of a world championship team.

But for me, everything started at Georgia. I not only learned how to play football, I learned how to get along with people. I made friendships that are still with me today. It was one of the most important times of my life. I've had a chance to live all over the country and do a lot of different things, but I will always be a Georgia Bulldog. That never changes.

Jimmy Orr led the SEC in receiving in 1955 and in 1957. In those two seasons Orr never dropped a pass. He went on to have a successful NFL career with the Pittsburgh Steelers and the Baltimore Colts.

PAT DYE

GUARD, 1958–1960

I have to say there ain't a man alive who has more respect for Georgia than I do, and there will always be a place in my heart for Georgia. When you look back on it, you're thankful for the opportunity that was given to you. Georgia gave me the foundation that I would live the rest of my life on. And I really can't put into words how grateful I am for that.

Dye was an All-America guard in 1959 and 1960. His brothers Nat and Wayne also played at Georgia. He won four SEC championships as the head coach at Auburn from 1981 to 1992. He is in the College Football Hall of Fame as a coach.

FRANCIS TARKENTON

QUARTERBACK, 1958–1960

The thing about Georgia is that it never leaves you, no matter where you go in life. Athens..., The Arch..., the history of Georgia—it's just part of the fiber that is me. Growing up in Athens and being a Bulldog is special. It is part of your soul. Being a part of that great university for four years—with all of its traditions—served as the launching pad for everything else I wanted to do.

Tarkenton was an All-SEC quarterback in 1959 and 1960 and led Georgia to the 1959 SEC championship. He played for 18 seasons in the NFL and participated in three Super Bowls. He is a member of the College Football Hall of Fame and the Pro Football Hall of Fame.

LEN HAUSS

Center, 1961–1963

[Hauss remembered his rookie year with the Washington Redskins when he lined up in practice against Sam Huff, the future Hall of Famer.] So we went on the first sound, and I knocked Huff on his rear. Everybody cheered. Huff got up and said "That's the way, Hauss. There's an old Georgia Bulldog. I never knew a Georgia Bulldog in my career who wouldn't knock you on your butt." Then I heard one of the coaches say, "All those guys from Georgia are always tough."

So here is a Hall of Fame player and a legend like Sam Huff thinking I am tough because I'm a Georgia Bulldog. And there are coaches who, because I'm a Georgia Bulldog, think I'm tough. That meant something to me then and it still means something to me today. That's why I will always be a Bulldog.

Hauss played 14 seasons in the NFL and was All-Pro five times.

PRESTON RIDLEHUBER

Quarterback, 1963–1965

I was lucky enough to play pro football and to have some success in business, but something always kept drawing me back to Georgia. I remember what Mr. Bulldog, Herschel Scott, used to say: If you're very good and say your prayers at night, when you die, God will let you go to Athens. That's the way I feel about Georgia. I was blessed the day I became a Bulldog.

Ridlehuber was the MVP of the 1964 Sun Bowl.

BOB TAYLOR

RUNNING BACK, 1963–1965

Being a football player at Georgia helped me in my life and in my career in so many ways. I was shy when I got there in 1962, and the four years I spent there made me a much better person. I was proud to be a Bulldog then and I'm proud to be a Bulldog now. Because once you're a Bulldog, it stays with you the rest of your life.

Bob Taylor was leading the SEC in rushing in 1965 when he suffered a broken leg against Florida State. He is best known for scoring the winning touchdown on the flea-flicker play in Georgia's 18–17 win over Alabama in 1965.

VINCE DOOLEY

HEAD COACH, 1964–1988

At Georgia, we always worked very hard to build a reputation that our players would embrace and that our opponents would have to acknowledge. And that reputation was this:

- When you play Georgia, you better buckle up your chin strap because you're going to be in a battle.
- When you play Georgia, we are going to hit you for 60 minutes and the game is going to go down to the wire.
- We may not win, but if you play for Georgia then you better be laying it on the line every play in every game. If you do that, then we'll win our fair share.

When I think about what it means to be a Bulldog, I always go back to tenacity and loyalty. Georgia people are committed to their state, their university, and their football team. Once you become a part of the Georgia family, you have a support structure that is second to none.

Dooley is Georgia's all-time winner with 201 career victories in 25 seasons as head coach. He also served as athletics director from 1979 to 2004.

BOBBY ETTER

Place-kicker, 1964–1966

I've been lucky my entire life. I was lucky that Dickie Phillips [defensive guard, 1964–1966] was my best friend so that Georgia would take a look at me. I was lucky to be there when one of the greatest coaches in the history of college football [Vince Dooley] took over the program. I was lucky to be a part of a championship team [1966], which is always special. I wanted to be a teacher, and Georgia gave me the education to pursue that dream. I wouldn't trade anything for the years I spent at Georgia.

Etter led the SEC in scoring in 1966. In 1964 he picked up a loose ball on an attempted field goal and scored against Florida to give the Bulldogs a 14–7 victory. He later received his Ph.D. in mathematics from Rice University. Today he is a professor at Sacramento State University. He was inducted into the Georgia-Florida Hall of Fame in 2002.

JOHN KASAY

Offensive Guard, 1964–1966

Bottom line: I never felt I could be as happy somewhere else as I was at Georgia. And if I couldn't be as happy somewhere else, why would I be stupid enough to leave? I would have hated to do that to myself. I wouldn't trade when and what I did [at Georgia] if I knew I could start over right now. The experience that I had with the guys that I coached and the guys I came along with was the best in the world. Shoot, I wouldn't trade the memories I have for all the rice in China.

Kasay, who grew up in Pennsylvania, went to work for the UGA athletics department right after his playing days. He never left Athens. His son, John David, was an All-SEC place-kicker for Georgia and still kicks in the NFL. Kasay recently came out of retirement to help with Georgia's strength and conditioning program.

KIRBY MOORE

QUARTERBACK, 1965–1967

I get asked a lot what playing football at Georgia meant to me. There is really no way you can measure it. As a former player, I've had opportunities to sit with governors and heads of large corporations—they want to talk to you as much as you want to talk to them. There is a bond with my teammates and to the Georgia people that is hard to describe. And there are people who want me to represent them because they remember me as the "old Georgia football player." Becoming a Bulldog was one of the smartest things I ever did in my life.

Moore was captain of Georgia's 1967 team and went on to become a successful attorney in Macon.

STEVE GREER

Defensive Lineman, 1967–1969

I grew up in Greer, South Carolina, which is only 40 miles away from Clemson. [The town was named after Steve Greer's great-great-grandfather.] When I was young, people could sit on the hill at Clemson's stadium and watch the football game for only 50¢. In that area, if you were good enough to play college football, everybody just figured that you were going to Clemson or South Carolina.

It was the fall of my senior year, and Coach Frank Inman came to my practice. My high school coach, Phil Clark, came to me and told me that a guy from Georgia was there to see me. I really didn't know anything about Georgia. I just remembered seeing the road signs to Athens when we would drive down to Atlanta.

Coach Inman invited me and my teammate Steve Woodward to come down for a game. I don't remember what game it was, but I do remember the enthusiasm of the Georgia crowd.

This was the fall of 1964, and that was Coach Dooley's first year at Georgia. They let us sit along the sideline, and I remember that the other team was driving the ball and had to settle for a field goal. When the Georgia defense came off the field, the crowd gave them a standing ovation. I thought, *These people are crazy about football!* It really made an impression on me.

Well, it got down to signing day, and Steve Woodward, myself, and Kent Lawrence, another South Carolina boy from Central, were down at Florida on a recruiting visit. I'm pretty sure it was our last one.

On Friday night Florida was really pushing us. Larry Smith, who had been a great player there, was really on us hard and trying to get us to sign. I remember we got back to the room and decided to go home. We had had enough. On that trip back home all three of us decided to go to Georgia.

That freshman class in 1965—the one I came in with—has to be one of the most talented groups of people to come to Georgia. I'm not just talking about football. We had great players—Jake Scott and Bill Stanfill went on to be All-Pros. We also had six lawyers, two judges, and three doctors in that group. Billy Payne was a great football player but became famous for bringing the Olympics to Atlanta. Kent Lawrence became a judge. Happy Dicks is a doctor. Sonny Purdue was a walk-on in that class and became governor of Georgia.

I played freshman ball in 1965, and in the spring of 1966 I got a pretty good scare. I tore up my knee and had to miss the entire 1966 season. Bruce Kemp, a really good running back, got hurt about three days before I did, and we spent the entire season rehabilitating together. I'm not going to kid you, it was hard. Some folks thought I might never make it back, but those people didn't know that I loved to play football more than anything in the world.

I made it back for the 1967 season, but I wasn't very big. Before I got hurt I think I was up to 220 pounds, but after the injury I just couldn't put on any weight. I might have been 205 pounds.

I remember my second game in 1967. We went up to Clemson, and obviously that was an important game to me. I lined up at nose guard for the first play of the game, and opposite of me was a guard named Harry Olszewski. He looked like he was 30 years old. Right before the ball was snapped, he turned to the Clemson lineman next to him and said, "Hey, look, I've got a dad-gum baby in front of me!"

But we won the game 24–17.

What's funny is that four years later, when I was playing in the Canadian League, I lined up for the first play of the game and there was Olszewski again! He still thought I was a baby!

The 1968 season was really special. We had a couple of ties against Tennessee and Houston, but we won the rest and gave Coach Dooley another championship. There was really only one downer on the year.

We knew going into the game with Auburn that if we won we would get an invitation to the Orange Bowl. All the guys wanted to go to the Orange Bowl.

We beat Auburn [17–3] to clinch the championship, but on Sunday in the team meeting Coach Dooley told us that we were going to the Sugar Bowl. Some of the guys got upset. Jake [Scott] even said something about it in the meeting. But I understand why Coach Dooley made the decision he did. We had a chance to go to the Sugar Bowl, win or lose against Auburn, and you just didn't pass up something like that. When I became a coach I understood it even better.

That didn't have anything to do with us losing to Arkansas [16–2] in the Sugar Bowl. They just beat us.

We thought we were going to be pretty good again in 1969, but Jake left early and played in Canada. Dennis Hughes, our really good tight end, got banged up. And we lost a lot of really good players from the year before. Probably the game that sticks out in my mind most is the one with Ole Miss and Archie Manning in Jackson.

Archie was one of the greatest quarterbacks ever to play college football, and he drove us crazy with his ability to scramble. On this particular play I think I had already missed him a couple of times, and then I got off the ground and saw him coming back to me. So I just reached down and hit him with everything I had, right up under the chin.

Somebody later sent me a magazine article where a reporter asked Archie about the hardest he had ever been hit. He said it was from "this little nose guard at Georgia. He hit me so hard he knocked me out, and my teeth hurt for three weeks after that."

This was in the first half, and they had to help Archie get to the locker room. When the third quarter started, he still was not on the field. I figured we were in good shape. We had the lead, and their star player had been knocked out of the game.

Sometime in the third quarter I remember we made a good defensive play, but I heard the Ole Miss fans erupting. I look over to the tunnel, and there's Archie running back onto the field. I turned to somebody and said, "Oh, hell. We're in trouble."

Archie came back out and beat us [25–17]. He was one helluva football player.

We were 3–0 before we played Ole Miss, but after that things didn't go all that well. We beat Vanderbilt the next week but lost four out of the last five. We went to the Sun Bowl and probably should have stayed at home. Nebraska wore us out [45–6] with a group of guys that would go on to win the national championship in 1971.

But all in all, I was a lucky guy at Georgia. I got to play for a man like Erk Russell who, for my money, is the best defensive coach who has ever lived. He demanded excellence without screaming. There has never been a greater motivator. If you called up one of Russell's players today and asked him to run through a brick wall in a business suit, he'd die trying. That's how much Erk means to us.

Dick Copas took me under his wing as a student. Back then Dick had to do everything for the football players: class scheduling,

For his size, All-American Steve Greer is considered to be the best nose guard ever to play at Georgia.

tutoring, books, study halls. Today they have a building full of people to do that. He made sure I was always doing right. He really took an interest in me. But I remember that if Dick took the palm of his right hand and started rubbing his eye with it, then look out, you were about to be in big trouble.

Coach Dooley gave me the chance to come back and be a part of this great university and this great program. He is a leader of the very best kind.

When I think about what it means to be a Bulldog, I think about the guys I came in with in 1965. All of us who stayed here the whole time still try to keep in touch. If one of those guys calls you in the middle of the night and is in trouble, you are going to be there to help him. You won together and you lost together. You hurt together. You bled together. I know it's a cliché, but it's true. You bond with people when you go through that kind of shared experience.

One of my former players once wrote a poem about what playing at Georgia meant to him. He ended it with the line, "For a Bulldog, by God, I am, and a Bulldog I'll always be."

I think that about sums it up.

Greer was an All-America nose guard and captain of Georgia's 1969 team. He returned to Georgia in 1979 as an assistant coach. In 1996 he was named Georgia's director of football operations. Today he is retired and living in Athens.

CHIP WISDOM

LINEBACKER, 1969–1971

I got to coach in a number of other places, but Georgia will always be where my heart is. That's where I met my wife, Brooke. Georgia always had the prettiest girls—and the smartest. When I was recruiting, I would always tell the guys that the three biggest decisions of your life are who you marry, what you're going to do for a living, and where you are going to college. And where you go to college often has a lot to do with the other two decisions. Georgia set the stage for the rest of my life. And there is not one chapter I would rewrite.

Wisdom was a three-year starter at linebacker and was an assistant coach at Georgia for nine seasons.

RAY GOFF

Quarterback, 1973–1976 & Head Coach, 1989–1995

When kids who played for me call me and ask my advice, I realize I have made a difference in their lives. That's all that matters to me. I wasn't the best coach Georgia ever had, but I wasn't the worst, either. I can look in the mirror and know that I gave that job everything that I had, and I always did what I thought was right for the University of Georgia. I still love Georgia and that will never change.

Goff was the SEC Player of the year in 1976 and was Georgia's head coach from 1989 to 1995.

DICKY CLARK

Defensive End, 1974–1976

The greatest thing that I learned at Georgia was about a group of guys working together to reach a common goal. And we did that with the championship of 1976. A lot of us have gone our own ways, but when I see a teammate I don't think, *Here is a guy I used to know.* It's, *Here is a dear friend.* It may have been 10 years since we talked, but we can pick up right where we left off. Those lessons and those kinds of relationships are what Georgia gave me. And you can't put a value on that.

Clark was defensive captain of Georgia's 1976 SEC championship team.

MATT ROBINSON

QUARTERBACK, 1974–1976

There can never be another relationship like the one you have with the guys you played football with. We experienced things together that other people will never experience. I look back on my life, and I realize that different decisions could have sent me in some different directions. But I do know this: I never once second-guessed my decision to go to Georgia. And I never will.

Robinson led the SEC in passing in 1974 and went on to play 11 seasons in the NFL and USFL.

BILL KRUG

DEFENSIVE BACK, 1974–1977

People still ask me if I have any regrets about leaving home and going to Georgia, and I tell them that going to Georgia was the greatest thing that ever happened to me. I learned so many things there that I used in my future life. You can't put a dollar value on the relationships I developed at Georgia. As you get older that kind of thing means more and more to you. That's why Georgia will always be a special, special place.

Krug, a native of Suitland, Maryland, was an All-SEC defensive back in 1976 and 1977.

FRANK ROS

Linebacker, 1977–1980

It's hard to completely explain what those years [at Georgia] would mean to the rest of my life. Just think about all those traditions of being a football player at Georgia: playing between the hedges, the fans on the track (which I still miss), the overall thrill on game day in Athens. And what it means to be a Bulldog on Saturday night after a win. Knowing that you played for the best, most respected football program and coach in the country. I also had a chance to play with the man who I think was the greatest football player of all time: Herschel Walker.

Ros was the captain of Georgia's 1980 national championship team.

EDDIE WEAVER

Defensive Tackle, 1978–1981

People ask me all the time what I enjoyed most about playing football at Georgia. I always go back to a little phrase that Coach Dooley used. He always said it was the little things that set you apart and make you special. Coach Dooley was talking about football at the time, but I've found that you can apply that to everything in life. At Georgia I learned that there is nothing like being with a group of guys that you trust to hold on to the rope when things get tough. I also learned that no matter how tough things get, you never quit. You just keep playing. You just keep working. Those are the kind of lessons you never forget.

Weaver was an All-SEC player in 1980 and 1981.

KNOX CULPEPPER

LINEBACKER, 1981–1984

I will never forget the immortal words of Lewis Grizzard, one of the greatest Bulldogs of them all: "The game of life is a lot like football. You have to tackle your problems, block your fears, and score your points when you get the opportunity." Georgia gave me that opportunity, and for that I will always be grateful.

Culpepper was a two-time All-SEC linebacker and the captain of Georgia's 1984 team.

TROY SADOWSKI

TIGHT END, 1985–1988

What I am most proud of is that my senior class gave Coach Dooley his 200th win, against Georgia Tech [24–3]. Then, after he announced his retirement, we were able to send him off as a winner by beating Michigan State in the Gator Bowl. I'm just glad I was there when he was carried off the field for the final time down there in Jacksonville. Whenever anybody mentions Georgia, it always puts a smile on my face. There really is no experience to compare to being a Georgia Bulldog.

Sadowski was All-America in 1985 and played 10 seasons in the NFL.

GARRISON HEARST

RUNNING BACK, 1990–1992

There were a number of reasons I chose to go to Georgia. I grew up in Lincolnton, which is only 60 miles away from Athens. When

I was growing up, I used to go to games at Georgia all the time. It was a place where I felt comfortable.

Just looking at the football side of it, I knew there was going to be an early opportunity to play, and that was important to me. Rodney Hampton was leaving at running back, so I knew I'd get an early chance to prove myself, and that's all I wanted.

The running backs coach was Willie McClendon, and I liked him a lot. My relationship with him was one of the big reasons I said to myself, *Forget this other stuff and go to Georgia.* I wanted to play for Coach McClendon.

I looked at some other schools. I had a really good visit to South Carolina. I also went to Florida State and Tennessee. I was scheduled to visit Clemson, but on the day I was supposed to go, Danny Ford resigned as head coach. I canceled that trip.

Besides, Lincolnton was a big Georgia town, and two of my former teammates—Dwayne Simmons and Curt Douglas—were already there, so really there was no way I could go anywhere else. I would never hear the last of it.

I loved being in college and being a part of the atmosphere of the games at Georgia. It was really exciting. What I didn't love was losing, and we lost seven games when I was a freshman. This was something I was not used to. At Lincolnton we only lost two games in my four years of high school football. College life was great, but I wanted to win and win soon.

In 1991 everything changed. Wayne McDuffie came in as offensive coordinator and changed everything we were going to do offensively. He made it clear to me that we were going to throw the ball because we had great receivers and Eric Zeier was coming in at quarterback.

I have to admit that initially I was a little upset with the new offense. I trusted Coach McDuffie because he recruited me for

Florida State. He promised me that even though we were going to throw, it would help the running game. But at first I thought he was stressing the pass so much that he was going to forget about the run.

Well, he was right, because after a while things began to balance out. Because we were throwing the ball so much, teams couldn't put eight or nine men in the box to stop the run.

The perfect example of this was the game we played against Clemson. Man, I had a ball that night. Clemson was ranked pretty high, and people didn't know if we could do anything. We beat them [27–12], and I don't ever think they figured out what we were doing.

But at times we played like we were still trying to learn the offense. Somehow we got beat at Vanderbilt [27–25]. We got up on them early, but we didn't put them away. I still can't believe that happened!

All of us knew that we were going to have a really good team in 1992. It would be the second year for everybody in this new offense, and we wouldn't have to play and learn at the same time. We went into the winter quarter workouts saying that we just needed to get faster and stronger and we'd be ready.

Let me tell you, that team could play with anybody. Offensively, that team could do everything, but we were five points from playing for the national championship.

It's hard to talk about the games we lost to Tennessee and Florida that year. Against Tennessee [a 34–31 loss] we were moving the ball up and down the field on those guys. That game really ate me up when we lost it.

I still haven't gotten over the Florida game [a 26–24] loss. I only had 12 carries in that game, and I was standing over on the sideline begging them to please use me. I hated losing that game because I thought I could have contributed more.

In 1992 Garrison Hearst won the Doak Walker Award, which goes to college football's best running back.

We did finish off that season with a good win over Ohio State [21–14] in the Citrus Bowl. Man, did they talk a lot of junk. They thought they were the team of the century because they were from the Big Ten. They thought they shouldn't have to play a team like Georgia. But we showed them why the SEC is the best conference in the country.

People are going to be surprised to hear me say this, but there are times now that I wished I had stayed for my senior year instead of turning pro. If I had it to do all over again I probably would stay, because I really missed my friends. I know that I missed out on a lot by not being a senior in college.

I loved being a college student, and I loved being at Georgia. Going to Georgia was really the turning point in my life because it taught me so much. It taught me a lot about football, but it also helped me learn about what it is like to be around people from all over the country. Georgia gave me the chance to make some lifelong friends who are still close to me today. It's a special place, and I loved every minute I stayed there.

Garrison Hearst was an All-SEC and All-America running back in 1992 and received the Doak Walker Award, which goes annually to college football's best running back. Hearst played for the Arizona Cardinals, the Cincinnati Bengals, and the San Francisco 49ers before being traded to the Denver Broncos in 2004. He retired after the 2004 season.

ERIC ZEIER

QUARTERBACK, 1991–1994

The bottom line for me has always been this: we didn't win as many football games as we would have liked at Georgia and we didn't reach all of our goals. But even if I had never played football, Georgia is where I would have gone to college. I made friendships there and established relationships that will be with me for the rest of my life. You can't put a price on that.

Zeier left Georgia in 1994 as the SEC's all-time leading passer with 11,153 yards.

MIKE BOBO

Quarterback, 1994–1997

When your dad is also your high school coach, you look at the recruiting process a lot differently. [Bobo's father, George, was a longtime head football coach at Thomasville High School. When Bobo signed with Georgia in 1993, his dad left his head coaching job to become an assistant in the Athens area so that he could see his son play on a regular basis.]

He wanted me to never lead another coach on. So if I wasn't interested in a school, I had to tell that coach up front. It made for a much simpler process for me.

To tell the truth, I was never really a big Georgia fan growing up in Thomasville. Both my parents went to Georgia, but I was a big Auburn fan. Dad never pushed me toward Georgia, even though he went there.

But when it came time to make a decision, I had to look at what was the best situation for me. It was 1993, and I liked what Georgia was doing in their passing game with Eric Zeier. I knew that if I went to Georgia I could learn under Eric for a couple of years and then get my chance to play. I thought it was the perfect fit for me.

The plan in the fall of 1993 was that I would redshirt because Eric was a junior, but I quickly found out that that plan was not

Former Bulldogs quarterback Mike Bobo is now Georgia's offensive coordinator.

set in stone. Just prior to the first game with South Carolina [quarterbacks coach] Steve Ensminger brought me in and said, "We were going to try and redshirt you, but you're the backup quarterback. If Zeier goes down then you're the guy. If it's just mop-up duty, we'll send the other guy in."

Well, there were no problems with that for the first three games, but then we went down to Ole Miss. Those guys just beat poor Eric to death. They hit him something like 38 times in the game. Over on the sideline under my breath I was telling him, "Get up, get up." I was thinking, *Oh my Lord, I'm going to go into this game and get drilled.* I don't know how Eric survived that night, but he did, and I did get to use a redshirt that year.

In 1994 I was the clear backup to Eric. Now, the job of a backup quarterback is to prepare like he is the No. 1 guy, because he's only a snap away from being in there. That is easy to say, but sometimes it is hard to do because Eric would get most of the reps in practice. Here I have to give Eric a lot of credit, because he was competitive in everything he did. In every drill, every day, he competed, because he wanted to be the best, and that made me compete, too. That helped me stay sharp and stay perfect. I was really fortunate to play behind a guy like him, and that really helped me.

My most meaningful playing time that year came in the last regular season game, against Georgia Tech. Eric got hurt in the second quarter, and I had to play the rest of the day. I can't tell you how nervous I was, because the first time that you go out to play some meaningful minutes, you're not completely sure if you belong out there. I remember watching the game on tape, and when I came off the field for the first time the TV camera cut to me. I was trying to drink some Gatorade, but my hand was shaking so badly the drink was splashing out of the cup.

But I did have some success that night. [Bobo came off the bench to complete 13 of 16 passes for 206 yards and a touchdown in a 48–10 win over Georgia Tech. He had a 30-yard touchdown pass and another completion for 50 yards.] From that game on I felt like I could play at Georgia.

Ironically, when I had my first big success at Georgia, my dad wasn't there to see it. We moved the Tech game to the Friday after Thanksgiving for television, and his high school team was in the state playoffs that night.

In 1995 I became the starter, but my season didn't last very long. We went down to Ole Miss, and I got hurt in the first quarter. I checked off to a pass, and we missed a block. I got hammered and suffered a fractured knee that knocked me out for the rest of the season.

That was a tough year all the way for injuries. Robert Edwards got hurt in the game with Tennessee. I got hurt and was out for the year. It also turned out to be Coach [Ray] Goff's last year. In many ways I just didn't think it was fair for that group of coaches to get fired because of all those injuries.

The 1996 season was one of the toughest of my life. Coach Jim Donnan had come in with a brand-new system. I came off the knee injury, but I never really got back into shape. I was catching a lot of heat because I really wasn't playing very well.

The only bright point we had in that entire season was when we came back to tie Auburn and finally beat them in four overtimes [56–49]. The good thing about that game was that we finally started to believe in one another and started playing hard. After that, the players bought in to what Coach Donnan was doing. We knew we had a chance to be good down the road.

In the off-season Coach Donnan brought me in and laid it on the line. He told me I was not going to be guaranteed the starting job for next season. He was going to throw it open for competition in spring practice.

At that point I thought about moving on. I was going to graduate that spring anyway, and I knew I wanted to get into coaching. I thought that maybe I should just get on with my life.

But then I realized how lucky I was to be playing football at Georgia and that when my playing days were over that was going to be it. So I decided I would do everything I could to make my senior year special. I worked my tail off and got in shape, and when the season rolled around I was ready to go.

We knew going into the Florida game that season that we could win. It didn't matter how many times Florida had won in a row [seven]. That game really epitomized what that Georgia team was all about. I threw three picks early, but we never got down. We just kept playing and beat those guys pretty good [37–17].

As great as that win was, there has never been a sweeter win than the one at Georgia Tech in 1997. To drive the ball the length of the field to win [27–24] in the final seconds at their place—man, it doesn't get any better than that. I get chills right now just talking about it.

The seniors on that team made up their minds before the season. We didn't talk SEC championship. We talked about getting Georgia back to being competitive with the best teams around, and I think we did that in 1997. We won 10 games. We beat Florida and we beat Tech. In my mind that's a pretty good year.

As much as I enjoyed my playing days at Georgia, the real honor has been the opportunity to come back as an assistant coach and to work for Coach Mark Richt. Under Coach Richt, Georgia is winning again, and we're competing for championships again. When I was a student at Georgia, I knew it was one of the greatest places in the country to go to school. Now every day I get up in the morning and go to work for a university I love that is located in one of the best college towns in all the world.

It just doesn't get any better than this.

Bobo led Georgia to a 10–2 season in 1997 and a big upset of No. 6 Florida, 37–17, in Jacksonville. Today Bobo is the offensive coordinator for the Bulldogs.

DAVID GREENE

QUARTERBACK, 2001–2004

The great thing about winning the SEC championship was that I was born in 1982, and it was hard for me to believe that Georgia had not won a championship for as long as I was alive. I know we can't wipe out all the suffering the Georgia people had to go through in those 20 years, but I am glad I was part of the team that got us back there.

Greene won 42 games as Georgia's starting quarterback, which was an NCAA record at the time. He was the quarterback on Georgia's 2002 SEC championship team.

DAVID POLLACK

DEFENSIVE END, 2001–2004

When I look back, I realize that the good Lord was looking over me when he sent me to Georgia. I just know there is a reason why I'm here. Knowing what I know now about college and about football, I can't imagine being anywhere but Georgia [for my college experience]. There is just something special about being a Bulldog.

Pollack was a three-time All-American, only the second in Georgia history. Herschel Walker (1980–1982) was the other.

MARK RICHT

Head Coach, 2001–Present

The thing that has struck me the most in my time here is the passion of the Georgia people. Looking at the program from the outside, I always thought that Georgia fans were some of the best in the country. But to see it on a daily basis makes me appreciate how special the Georgia people really are. The love fans have for Georgia is felt very deeply and it is passed on from generation to generation. That love for this program and this university is why Georgia is such a great place.

Richt has won 96 games and two SEC championships in his 10 seasons at Georgia.

AFTERWORD: THE BEST IS YET *to* COME

I HAD BEEN BACK AT GEORGIA for only a couple of weeks when we played our first home football game of the season against Louisiana-Lafayette. When the Redcoat Band played our alma mater, I realized that it had been about 18 years since I had heard it. That's when it hit me. I really had to take a minute and soak it all in. I was finally home.

I had spent the past 18 years at Florida and because the annual football game with Georgia is in Jacksonville, I just never got a chance to hear our alma mater. When I heard it again, that moment confirmed something that I already knew: there is no place quite like the University of Georgia.

Today I can look out of my office and see the red house where I took piano lessons for 10 years. Not far from there is Baxter Street, where I went to elementary school, middle school, and high school. Baxter Street dead-ends into the University of Georgia campus, where I went to college. I was so blessed to grow up in Athens. Then Sheryl and I were blessed with the chance to come back and to again be a part of this special community.

All of us who went to Georgia know that there are very few places that have such a good town-and-gown relationship. Athens is a city that revolves around the university. You can be on campus and on one street you can walk right into the downtown area. There is a family feel to Athens that has a quality of life that is second to none.

In many ways it is hard to put your finger on what makes Georgia and Athens so special. But people tell me that they can feel it when they come back to campus. The falls are so beautiful here. People love to come back not only for the football games but to remember what it was like during that very important part of their lives. Our campus has certainly changed a lot over the years, but a lot of the traditional areas are still there.

We have a great deal of tradition at Georgia, both athletically and academically. That tradition and that history are things that we take pride in and will always enjoy.

But I have told our staff at Georgia that what we can't do is spend a whole lot of time looking back. You can look back for lessons learned and to determine how to make things better in the future. What we can't do is to think that things will just continue on a good path because we want them to and because we take so much pride in what we've accomplished in the past.

That is when you get into trouble. That is when you stop working to get better every single day. That is when you lose your edge.

That is where I want Georgia to be in athletics as we move forward. Not long ago I had a meeting with the entire staff, and the theme of the meeting was "It's not okay just to be okay."

The University of Georgia wants to be the best public institution of higher learning in the country. Will we get there? I don't know, but that is the goal, and as a university we are striving toward that goal every day.

The same thing applies to athletics. We have some sports that have achieved success on a national level for some time now. We have other sports that have not. Why is that? What is keeping us from achieving greatness across the board?

Our goal at Georgia is to consistently be among the top 10 athletics programs in the country. The goal at Florida was to have

Greg McGarity, an Athens native and a University of Georgia graduate, returned as the school's director of athletics in August 2010.

every sport play in the NCAA championships. Did it ever happen? No, but that was the goal, and it is a worthwhile one. We have to come to work every day knowing that mediocrity is not acceptable.

Of course we will always embrace the past and take pride in our great tradition at Georgia. That's the good news. But here is the really good news: at Georgia, the best is still to come. My family and I are just so thrilled to be back in Athens and to be given the opportunity to be a part of it.

It is really good to be home.

Greg McGarity is a 1976 graduate of Georgia's Henry W. Grady School of Journalism. He worked for the Georgia Athletic Association in several capacities before going to the University of Florida in 1992, where he rose to the rank of executive associate athletics director.

On August 13, 2010, McGarity was named athletics director at Georgia. Greg and his wife, Sheryl (also a 1976 Georgia graduate), have a son, Alex, who graduated from the University of Florida.

BIBLIOGRAPHY

Barnhart, Tony. *Southern Fried Football*. Chicago: Triumph Books, 2008.

Barnhart, Tony, Vince Dooley and Mark Richt. *What It Means to Be a Bulldog*. Chicago: Triumph Books, 2004.

Burns, Robbie. *Belue to Scott!* Clearwater, FL: H&H Publishing, 2010.

Cromartie, Bill. *Clean Old-Fashioned Hate*. Atlanta: Gridiron Publishers, 2000.

Dooley, Barbara. *Put Me In, Coach*. Athens, GA: Longstreet Press, 1991.

Dooley, Vince. *Dooley's Playbook*. Athens, GA: Hill Street Press, 2008.

Dooley, Vince, with Blake Giles. *Vince Dooley's Tales from the 1980 Georgia Bulldogs*. Champaign, IL: Sports Publishing LLC, 2005.

Dooley, Vince, with Loran Smith. *Dooley's Dawgs*. Athens, GA: Longstreet Press, 2003.

Dooley, Vince, with Tony Barnhart. *Dooley, My 40 Years at Georgia*. Chicago: Triumph Books, 2005.

Garbin, Patrick. *About Them Dawgs!* Lanham, MD: Scarecrow Press, Inc., 2008.

Magill, Dan. *Dan Magill's Bull-Doggerel*. Athens, GA: Longstreet Press, 1993.

Munson, Larry, with Tony Barnhart. *From Herschel to a Hobnail Boot.* Chicago: Triumph Books, 2009.

Nelson, Jon. *100 Things Bulldogs Fans Should Know and Do Before They Die.* Chicago: Triumph Books, 2010.

Schlabach, Mark. *Georgia Football Yesterday and Today.* Fairlawn, OH: Westside Publishing, 2009.

Scherer, George. *Auburn-Georgia Football.* Jefferson, NC: McFarland & Company, Inc., 1992.

Seiler, Sonny, and Kent Hannon. *Damn Good Dogs!* Athens, GA: Hill Street Press, 2002.

Smith, Derek. *Glory Yards.* Nashville: Rutledge Hill Press, 1993.

Smith, Loran. *Beloved Dawgs.* Athens, GA: Longstreet Press, 2005.

Smith, Loran. *Wally's Boys.* Athens, GA: Longstreet Press, 2005.

Smith, Loran. *Between the Hedges: 100 years of Georgia Football.* Athens, GA: Longstreet Press, 1992.

Smith, Loran, with Lewis Grizzard. *Glory! Glory!* Atlanta: Peachtree Publishers Limited, 1981.

Thilenius, Ed, and Jim Koger. *No Ifs, No Ands, a Lot of Butts.* Atlanta: Foot & Davies, 1960.